# English
# Roots

For
Sam and Thomas

# English Roots

# Roots

## A Family History

NIC MADGE

ALAN SUTTON PUBLISHING LIMITED

First published in the United Kingdom in 1995 by
Alan Sutton Publishing Limited
Phoenix Mill · Far Thrupp · Stroud · Gloucestershire

British Library Cataloguing in Publication Data

A catalogue record for this book is available from the British Library.

ISBN 0 7509 1139 5

Typeset in 10/12pt Times.
Typesetting and origination by
Alan Sutton Publishing Limited.
Printed in Great Britain by
Ebenezer Baylis, Worcester.

# Contents

**List of Illustrations** vii

**Family tree** viii

**Preface** xi
by David Hey, Professor of Local and Family History, University of Sheffield, author of *Family History and Local History in England* and editor of the *History of Myddle*.

**Introduction** xiii

1. **Thomas (*c.*1610–*c.*1644) and Joane (*c.*1610–*c.*1660)** 1
Arrival in Rowland. Details of cottage and land farmed. Payment of poll tax. Involvement in Civil War – Battle of Marston Moor. Nocturnal burial of Joane.

2. **John (1638–1690) and Mary (*c.*1640–1702)** 16
Payment of hearth tax. Plague. Appearances before Manorial Courts. Lead mining and appearance before Barmoot Court. Catholicism and prosecution for not attending church. Death of Samuel Ashton. Contents of cottage. Description of farming. Payment of land tax. Mary's will.

3. **Robert (*c.*1670–??)** 35
Appearances before Manorial Courts. Lead mining and appearances before Barmoot Courts. Poor rate assessment.

4. **Henry (1702–1765) and Hannah (1700–1784)** 46
Shortage of land and the need to move. Gorsebank Farm, Baslow. Bonnie Prince Charlie. Education of children. Payments by the chapelwardens to Henry for odd jobs.

5. **Thomas (1731–1788) and Sarah (1737–1812)** 54
Coming of the Industrial Revolution. Northwood. Acquisition of freehold land. Improvements in farming. Enclosure Award. Land tax payments. Furniture. Thomas's will. The exhumation of Benjamin Ashton's body.

6. **Henry (1761–1850) and Mary (1784–1859)** 69
Marriage six months before birth of eldest child. Education of children. Effect

of agricultural depression. Examination of pauper relative by Justices of the
Peace. Growing industrialisation and effect on Darley Dale. Tithe Commutation
Act. Land farmed by Ashtons. The 1832 Reform Act and elections. Railway
passing through Ashton farmland. Sale of farm.

7. **Robert (1807–1886) and Ellen (1817–1894)** 84
Robert's move to Manchester. Manchester in the 1830s and 1840s. Working as a
servant. Marriage five days before birth of eldest son. Shop in Dickinson Street.
Driven out of business by recession. Working as a hackney cab driver for
brother Valentine. House on banks of River Irwell. Description of neighbours.

8. **John (1841–1916) and Sarah Ellen (1855–1932)** 98
Manchester in the 1850s and 1860s. Robert's children. John working as a
blacksmith and then cab driver. Death of John's first wife in childbirth.
Provision dealer and licensee of The Vine Tavern, beer-house. Marriage of John
and Sarah Ellen. Deaths of five of their children. Prosecution for selling beer
out of hours. Jewish immigration and move to Great Clowes Street. Neighbours.
Investments. Death of brother from untreated syphilis. Funeral of John. Payment
of rates. Sarah Ellen's move to Urmston and in later years.

9. **Jack (1885–1975) and Lucy Jane (1882–1965)** 114
Schooling. Brother Val's work in South America. Lucy Jane, dressmaker and
courtship. Description of houses they lived in. First World War – particularly
accounts taken from Jack's diary. Wounded and convalescence. Move from
Manchester to suburbs. Description of house and family life. Second World War.

10. **Epilogue** 140
Personal recollections of Jack and Lucy. Accounts of lives of Jack's brothers
Tom and Val – particularly Val in South America. Brief updating of what has
become of Jack, Tom and Val's children.

**Appendix: How to Find Out About Your Family History** 145
A brief introduction to the steps which can be taken by anyone whose family
comes from England or Wales.

**Glossary** 151

**Bibliography** 153

**Index** 159

# List of Illustrations

## FIGURES

| | | |
|---|---|--:|
| 1. | Extract of Militia Muster Roll (1638/9) for Rowland | 7 |
| 2. | Portrait of Rowland Eyre of Hassop | 9 |
| 3. | Extract of hearth tax return (1664) for Rowland | 17 |
| 4. | St Giles's Church, Great Longstone | 28 |
| 5. | Extract of Mary Ashton's will (1703) | 30 |
| 6. | Gorsebank Farm, Baslow | 49 |
| 7. | Extract of Baslow parish register showing marriage of Thomas Ashton and Sarah Taylor (1761) | 57 |
| 8. | Extract of will of Thomas Ashton (1788) | 65 |
| 9. | Cottage in Northwood bequeathed by Thomas Ashton | 66 |
| 10. | Family tree showing the relationship between William Grafton and the Ashtons | 75 |
| 11. | Photograph of John Ashton (c.1887) | 103 |
| 12. | 192, Great Clowes Street (c.1910) | 105 |
| 13. | George and Violetta Hale with Eric, Winifred and Phyllis (c.1908) | 107 |
| 14. | Sarah Ellen Ashton with granddaughters Winifred and Phyllis Hale (c.1910) | 108 |
| 15. | Lucy Jane Lowe's immediate relatives | 116 |
| 16. | Jack Ashton – self portrait (1904) | 118 |
| 17. | Valentine from Jack Ashton to Lucy (1907) | 119 |
| 18. | Postcard from Val Ashton in Guayaquil, Ecuador (1914) | 120 |
| 19. | Val Ashton | 121 |
| 20. | George Ashton | 122 |
| 21. | Jack Ashton | 125 |
| 22. | Builders' description of houses on Grange Estate, Cheadle Hulme | 135 |
| 23. | Tom and Gertie Ashton's wedding (1924) | 143 |

## MAPS

| | | |
|---|---|--:|
| 1. | The Eastern Peak District | 3 |
| 2. | Rowland, Hassop and Longstone | 4 |
| 3. | Thomas Ashton and the Civil War | 11 |
| 4. | Gorsebank Farm, Baslow | 49 |
| 5. | Northwood and Darley Hillside (1760–1850) | 62 |
| 6. | Broughton and Cheetham Hill (1850) | 92 |
| 7. | Lower Broughton (1892) | 93 |
| 8. | The Somme Battlefields | 123 |

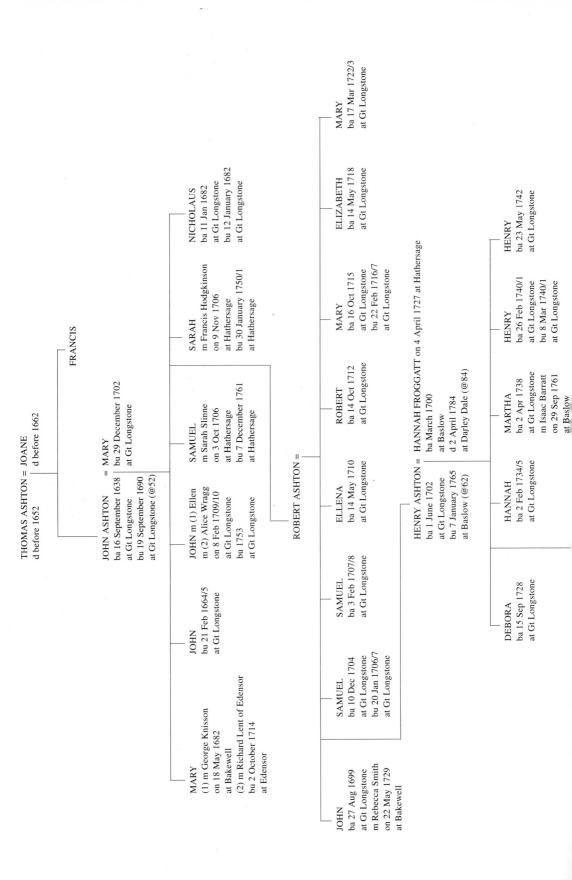

THOMAS ASHTON = JOANE
d before 1652    d before 1662

FRANCIS

JOHN ASHTON = MARY
ba 16 September 1638    bu 29 December 1702
at Gt Longstone    at Gt Longstone
bu 19 September 1690
at Gt Longstone (@52)

MARY
(1) m George Knisson
on 18 May 1682
at Bakewell
(2) m Richard Lent of Edensor
bu 2 October 1714
at Edensor

JOHN
bu 21 Feb 1664/5
at Gt Longstone

JOHN m (1) Ellen
m (2) Alice Wragg
on 8 Feb 1709/10
at Gt Longstone
bu 1753
at Gt Longstone

SAMUEL
m Sarah Slinne
on 3 Oct 1706
at Hathersage
bu 7 December 1761
at Hathersage

SARAH
m Francis Hodgkinson
on 9 Nov 1706
at Hathersage
bu 30 January 1750/1
at Hathersage

NICHOLAUS
ba 11 Jan 1682
at Gt Longstone
bu 12 January 1682
at Gt Longstone

ROBERT ASHTON =

SAMUEL
ba 10 Dec 1704
at Gt Longstone
bu 20 Jan 1706/7
at Gt Longstone

SAMUEL
ba 3 Feb 1707/8
at Gt Longstone

ELLENA
ba 14 May 1710
at Gt Longstone

ROBERT
ba 14 Oct 1712
at Gt Longstone

MARY
ba 16 Oct 1715
at Gt Longstone
bu 22 Feb 1716/7
at Gt Longstone

ELIZABETH
ba 14 May 1718
at Gt Longstone

MARY
ba 17 Mar 1722/3
at Gt Longstone

HENRY ASHTON = HANNAH FROGGATT on 4 April 1727 at Hathersage
ba 1 June 1702
at Gt Longstone
bu 7 January 1765
at Baslow (@62)

ba March 1700
at Baslow
d 2 April 1784
at Darley Dale (@84)

JOHN
ba 27 Aug 1699
at Gt Longstone
m Rebecca Smith
on 22 May 1729
at Bakewell

DEBORA
ba 15 Sep 1728
at Gt Longstone

HANNAH
ba 2 Feb 1734/5
at Gt Longstone

MARTHA
ba 2 Apr 1738
at Gt Longstone
m Isaac Barratt
on 29 Sep 1761
at Baslow

HENRY
ba 26 Feb 1740/1
at Gt Longstone
bu 8 Mar 1740/1
at Gt Longstone

HENRY
ba 23 May 1742
at Gt Longstone

THOMAS ASHTON = SARAH TAYLOR on 5 January 1761 at Baslow
ba 8 June 1731          ba 13 February 1736/7
at Gt Longstone         at Darley Dale
bu 21 April 1788 (@56)  bu 11 June 1812
                        at Darley Dale (@75)

THOMAS                      CHARLES                     ANN
ba 1 Jan 1764               ba 28 Aug 1768              ba 5 Apr 1772
at Pentrich                 at Darley Dale              at Darley Dale
m Mary Barker               m Elizabeth Gibbon          m John Wildgoose
on 24 Oct 1792              on 1 Nov 1790               on 11 May 1791
at Darley Dale              at Bakewell                 at Darley Dale
d 16 Sep 1845                                           bu 18 Oct 1800
at Darley Dale                                          at Darley Dale

HENRY ASHTON = MARY MARPLE on 20 December 1802 at Darley Dale
b 15 November 1761    ba 18 April 1784
at Darley Dale        at Baslow
d 9 March 1850        d 2 June 1859
at Darley Dale (@88)  at Wichnor (@75)

ELIZABETH        HARRIOT            CHARLES         ELLEN           HANNAH          SARAH
ba 8 Apr 1813    bas 25 Jun 1815    bo 21 Apr 1818  ba 8 Aug 1820   bo 26 Feb 1824  bo 25 Mar 1827
at Darley Dale   at Darley Dale     at Darley Dale  at Darley Dale  at Darley Dale  at Darley Dale
                 m Jonathon Fogg                                                    bu 11 Sep 1845
                                                                                    at Darley Dale

VALENTINE                VALENTINE
ba 31 Dec 1809           ba 14 Jan 1811
at Darley Dale           at Darley Dale
bu 21 Jan 1810           m Ann Clare
at Darley Dale           on 22 Dec 1829
                         at Manchester Cath.
                         d 9 Sep 1898
                         Winton

JANE
bo 21 Sep 1808
at Darley Dale

ROBERT ASHTON = ELLEN STEEL on 20 March 1837 at St Mary's Manchester
bo 30 July 1807      b c 1817
at Darley Dale       in Scotland
d 26 May 1886        d 25 June 1894
at 28, Elton Street, at 4, Alma Street,
Broughton (@79)      Eccles (@77)

ANN
bo 25 Oct 1804
at Darley Dale
m John Shepheard
on 29 April 1823
at Manchester
Emigrated to USA

HENRY
bo 4 Jun 1803
at Darley Dale
d 27 Jan 1860
at Wichnor
m Ann

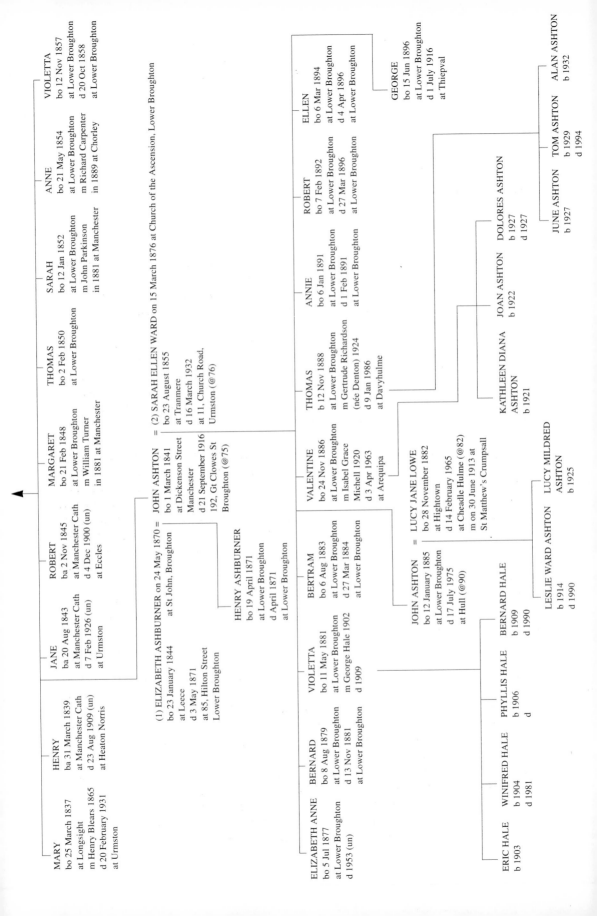

MARY
bo 25 March 1837
at Longsight
m Henry Blears 1865
d 20 February 1931
at Urmston

HENRY
ba 31 March 1839
at Manchester Cath
d 23 Aug 1909 (un)
at Heaton Norris

JANE
ba 20 Aug 1843
at Manchester Cath
d 7 Feb 1926 (un)
at Urmston

ROBERT
ba 2 Nov 1845
at Manchester Cath
d 4 Dec 1900 (un)
at Eccles

MARGARET
bo 21 Feb 1848
at Lower Broughton
m William Turner
in 1881 at Manchester

THOMAS
bo 2 Feb 1850
at Lower Broughton

SARAH
bo 12 Jan 1852
at Lower Broughton
m John Parkinson
in 1881 at Manchester

ANNE
bo 21 May 1854
at Lower Broughton
m Richard Carpenter
in 1889 at Chorley

VIOLETTA
bo 12 Nov 1857
at Lower Broughton
d 20 Oct 1858
at Lower Broughton

JOHN ASHTON
bo 1 March 1841
at Dickenson Street
Manchester
d 21 September 1916
192, Gt Clowes St
Broughton (@75)

= (2) SARAH ELLEN WARD on 15 March 1876 at Church of the Ascension, Lower Broughton
bo 23 August 1855
at Tranmere
d 16 March 1932
at 11, Church Road,
Urmston (@76)

(1) ELIZABETH ASHBURNER on 24 May 1870 =    at St John, Broughton
bo 23 January 1844
at Leece
d 3 May 1871
at 85, Hilton Street
Lower Broughton

HENRY ASHBURNER
bo 19 April 1871
at Lower Broughton
d April 1871
at Lower Broughton

ELLEN
bo 6 Mar 1894
at Lower Broughton
d 4 Apr 1896
at Lower Broughton

GEORGE
bo 15 Jun 1896
at Lower Broughton
d 1 July 1916
at Thiepval

ROBERT
bo 7 Feb 1892
at Lower Broughton
d 27 Mar 1896
at Lower Broughton

ANNIE
bo 6 Jan 1891
at Lower Broughton
d 1 Feb 1891
at Lower Broughton

THOMAS
b 12 Nov 1888
at Lower Broughton
m Gertrude Richardson
(née Denton) 1924
d 9 Jan 1986
at Davyhulme

VALENTINE
bo 24 Nov 1886
at Lower Broughton
m Isabel Grace
Michell 1920
d 3 Apr 1963
at Arequipa

JOHN ASHTON
bo 12 January 1885
at Lower Broughton
d 17 July 1975
at Hull (@90)

= LUCY JANE LOWE
bo 28 November 1882
at Hightown
d 14 February 1965
at Cheadle Hulme (@82)
m on 30 June 1913 at
St Matthew's Crumpsall

BERTRAM
bo 6 Aug 1883
at Lower Broughton
d 27 Mar 1884
at Lower Broughton

VIOLETTA
bo 11 May 1881
at Lower Broughton
m George Hale 1902
d 1909

BERNARD
bo 8 Aug 1879
at Lower Broughton
d 13 Nov 1881
at Lower Broughton

ELIZABETH ANNE
bo 5 Jul 1877
at Lower Broughton
d 1953 (un)

KATHLEEN DIANA
ASHTON
b 1921

JOAN ASHTON
b 1922

DOLORES ASHTON
b 1927
d 1927

LUCY MILDRED
ASHTON
b 1925

LESLIE WARD ASHTON
b 1914
d 1990

JUNE ASHTON
b 1927

TOM ASHTON
b 1929
d 1994

ALAN ASHTON
b 1932

BERNARD HALE
b 1909
d 1990

PHYLLIS HALE
b 1906
d

WINIFRED HALE
b 1904
d 1981

ERIC HALE
b 1903

# Preface

An interest in one's ancestors is a natural human concern, shared by people all over the world and throughout time. Until recently, however, only the pedigrees of the great and the mighty appeared in print. The family histories of ordinary people were passed down orally, and like the published histories of noble and gentry families these accounts were often romanticised without strict regard to the truth.

A great change has occured during the last quarter of the twentieth century. The establishment of record offices throughout the country, the availability of printed records or transcripts on microfiche or microfilm, the foundation of numerous family history societies, and the chance to join taught courses on how to trace a family tree have made it possible for everyone who is interested to do his or her own research. The romantic myths are soon stripped away as the enquiry proceeds. Instead, a much more satisfying and accurate picture emerges.

Another welcome change is that family historians are no longer content with constructing a family tree. That is merely the starting point of an enquiry into how the various members of one's family lived: what their homes were like, how they earned their living, what their spiritual concerns were, and so on. Such questions naturally lead on to an interest in the local history of the places where they settled. The family historian then wants to know how the story that has been unravelled fits into the general patterns of British social and economic history. How typical, or how unusual, was the family's experience? Such a progression of interest is not simply a one-way process, however, for the findings of family historians, when placed together, are beginning to add a great deal to our knowledge of the past and are influencing the ways that professional historians pursue their research. Family history is part of a movement that approaches history from the viewpoint of ordinary people, rather than from that of those in power.

A few years ago, I expressed the hope that, "One day we shall have a number of substantial family histories on our shelves, not just the histories of aristocratic and gentry families but of the ordinary men and women who were far more numerous and whose stories are often just as interesting as anyone else's. When that day arrives we shall have a much better understanding of the social and economic history of England." (*Family History and Local History in England*, p 1). Nic Madge's book is an important step in that direction. It is concerned with the Ashton family who in the seventeenth century were small farmers in the Peak District of Derbyshire. They first appear in local records at the time of the Civil War, when they were tenants of the Eyres, an ancient and prolific gentry family who were much involved in the lead trade. The family were living in a simple, one-hearth cottage when the hearth tax was levied after the Restoration. One can hardly get more "ordinary" than that!

Nic Madge makes good use of the sources that are available to family and local historians in the early modern period – parish registers, probate records, tax returns, accounts of the overseers of the poor, etc. He uses these not only to trace his own family, but to place them firmly in an historical context, both locally and nationally. For a few generations the Ashtons moved from one farmhouse or cottage to another within a few miles' radius of the place where they were first recorded. In this, they were entirely typical of countryfolk in the Tudor, Stuart and Hanoverian periods.

The decision made by a member of the family to move to a large industrial town in the first half of the nineteenth century was one taken by many other people at that time. Sometime during the 1820s or 30s Robert Ashton left for Manchester, where he found employment as a house servant. His children were to do better as Manchester's economy flourished. By this time, the records are fuller and photography had been invented, so much more information can be found about working-class families. Nic Madge uses a wide range of sources to good effect. He carries his story into the twentieth century, up to the time of his own memories of his grandparents and their children. He ends with a brief account of the records he has used, with the aim of persuading others to trace the histories of their own "ordinary families" in this way, against the background of national social history.

The story of the Ashtons is therefore of wider interest than might be supposed, for it demonstrates how a family that for generations had lived in the countryside became urbanised. Life in Victorian Manchester was very different indeed from that in a seventeenth-century hamlet, remotely sited in the Peak District.

David Hey
Professor of Local and Family History
University of Sheffield

# Introduction

The quest which led to the writing of this book originally started on a Welsh beach, when, as a boy, I asked my parents how I was related to some distant cousins. My parents drew a rough family tree in the sand. My subsequent visits to local record offices initially concentrated on solving the genealogical puzzle of who begat whom and when each person died. As the many, many thousands of people, who have researched their own families can testify, this was an intriguing, not to say obsessive, exercise in detective work. It was however a personal and relatively (in two senses of the word) limited activity.

It proved though to be only the starting point in discovering far more about the way in which ordinary people lived their lives. As I traced back the families of several grandparents and great-grandparents, I found masses of fascinating information, particularly about the Ashtons, my mother's family. English record offices are full of literally tons of documents which, when put together, portray the day-to-day life of the average English man and woman during the last few centuries. Some of it is very personal information, like the list of cooking implements in the inventory prepared in 1703 and attached to Mary Ashton's will or the threat of a manorial court to fine Robert Ashton in 1706 if he did not remove the midden or dung-hill which he had heaped against the wall of a neighbour's cottage. Other documents, like the Militia Muster Roll prepared in 1639 listing "all the able men for warre" in Derbyshire, or the taxation returns from the middle of the seventeenth century onwards, showed more obviously how the family fitted into society as a whole.

For me the most interesting aspects of history are the way in which ordinary people went about their day-to-day lives, and the way in which the lot of the common people has changed as the years have gone by. Despite the increase of interest in social history, these are subjects about which only a small proportion of authors have written. Historical biographers have understandably written about the famous. Most of the family histories which have been published have described the landed gentry or nobility. There are accounts of poverty and the operation of the Poor Laws, particularly in the nineteenth century, but the mass of the population, who were neither rich nor poor, have largely slipped through the net.

The aim which I set myself in writing *English Roots* was to recount the social and economic history of the last three hundred and fifty years, as seen through the eyes of one family, who could be taken as being representative of the population as a whole. I wanted to describe the changes in their lives, and the reasons for them, against the background of the transformation which society in general was undergoing. The Ashtons happen to have been my mother's family, but they were typical of the vast majority of English people. In the 1640s the way of life in the English countryside was in many ways far closer to that of medieval times than to that of the modern day. Four-fifths of the English population were tilling the land. The Ashtons were no exception. In the seventeenth and eighteenth centuries they were "husbandmen", farming a few acres of land which they rented from the lord of the manor, making their own bread and brewing their own beer and living as a largely self-sufficient family unit. In the early nineteenth century, as the Industrial Revolution gathered pace, there was widespread migration from the countryside to the new industrial cities. The Ashtons followed the national trend, moving to Manchester in the late 1820s or early 1830s, and then to the suburbs in the 1920s. Their story is not just a journey though time. It is a journey from a rural hamlet to a vast industrial city. It is also an account of the transformation from a simple self-sufficient way of life to a complex urban economy.

Throughout the book, when I have referred to money, I have simply given amounts in pounds, shillings and pence. There were twenty shillings or two hundred and forty old pence (240d) in a pound. One shilling was the equivalent to 5p. One penny now is the equivalent to 2.4d or old pence. Given the length of the period covered, I have not sought to express any direct comparisons with the modern day value of money.

So far as dates are concerned, it is important to remember that until 1752 the calendar year began on 25th March. I have followed the standard practice of giving two years for all dates before 1752 falling between 1st January and 24th March. Accordingly 1st March 1680/1 was, at the time, thought of as being in the last month of 1680, whereas now it would be thought of as being in the third month of 1681.

I would not have been able to write this book without the help of many people. Firstly my parents, Mildred and Ken, have spent many hours answering questions and discussing drafts of my manuscript. Other relatives have passed on invaluable information. In particular I am very grateful to my uncle Leslie, who carried out some research of his own, and to my mother's cousins Bernard, Joan, June and Kathleen. Many other people have helped by talking to me and, in the case of Bill and Elaine Scott, showing me round their home in Rowland. Staff in many record offices have assisted by finding documents and answering questions. I am particularly indebted to the staff of the Derbyshire Record Office at Matlock, the Lichfield Joint Record Office, the Sheffield Record Office, the Salford Local History Library, the Manchester Local History Library and Archives Department, the Public Record Office (both in Chancery Lane and at Kew), the House of Lords Record Office, the British Library and the Church of England Record Centre. Finally I wish to thank all the people who read some or all of my draft manuscript, particularly David Adams, Tim Ashworth, Claire Fazan, Rob Harding, David Hey, Sue Lawrence, Robin Lewis, Margaret O'Sullivan, Bob Rowthorne, Lyn Willies and, above all, Nicola Wyld. Their helpful comments have been very much appreciated, although any errors (I hope there aren't any!) are of course mine.

I am grateful to the following for permission to reproduce illustrations:

(4 and 7) Lichfield Joint Record Office for LJRO/B/C/11 Mary Ashton (1703) and Thomas Ashton (1788);
(6) Derbyshire Record Office;
(1 and 3) Crown Copyright, reproduced by permission of the Controller of Her Majesty's Stationery Office (SP 16/405 and E179/245/7);
(2) Huddleston Collection: photograph Courtauld Institute of Art;
(Map 6) Manchester Central Library: Local Studies Unit;
(Map 7) 1892 Lancashire Ordnance Survey, 25 inch, Sheet CIV 6: by permission of the British Library.

Publication has been assisted by a loan from the Marc Fitch Foundation.

# 1

One day during the middle of the 1630s Thomas and Joane Ashton arrived in the hamlet of Rowland in the Derbyshire Peak District. Their origins are now lost in the mists of time and no record of their marriage or of Thomas's baptism survives. However it is likely that they came from the lead mining village of Stony Middleton which lay a couple of miles to the north-east. Thomas was probably one of the younger sons of another Thomas Ashton, a husbandman who lived there.

Thomas and Joane travelled to Rowland with a horse and cart[1] containing what household possessions they owned along one of the old pack horse trails or drovers' roads which crossed Longstone Edge, the limestone ridge just to the north of Rowland. They encountered herds of sheep and no doubt heard the shouts and whistles of the shepherd boys looking after them. They passed lead miners digging into the limestone and the white hummocks of rock which were the results of their excavations. A few years before, when the philosopher Thomas Hobbes was a tutor at the Earl of Devonshire's home at Chatsworth, he had climbed Longstone Edge on the way to Castleton. While crossing the Edge, he witnessed the aftermath of an accident in which two lead miners were buried and killed by a fall of rock and earth.

The view which Thomas and Joane saw as they approached Rowland must have been similar to that which Hobbes described in his poem, De Mirabilis Pecci:

> From thence our horse with weary feet and slow
> Towards a steep Hill's High top, do climbing go;
> And after many a tug and weary Strain,
> Half breathless, they the Summity do gain,
> Turning about with wonder we espy
> The birds now lazily to creep not fly.
> And that the Pico of the Mountains brow
> Had pierc'd the body of the Clouds quite through
> Derwin appears but as a crooked line,
> And Chatworth as a point it doth entwine.[2]

From the summit of Longstone Edge it was possible to see the dozen or so cottages which made up the hamlet of Rowland, or Rulland as it was pronounced by the locals.[3] The houses were scattered on both sides of "The Street", a twisting lane which led on through fields and then woodland towards the Wye Valley. Nowadays all the cottages in Rowland are built of the local grey limestone, but in the 1630s some of them may still have been built of wattle and daub.[4] Perhaps Thomas and Joane could see a couple of women washing clothes in the Washbrook, the small stream which ran through Rowland, while another woman drew water from one of the hamlet's wells. Beyond the hamlet they could see Beggarsway Lane, a track which joined the villages of Hassop and Longstone.

Further away there was a wide expanse of countryside with hills and valleys, woods and fields. Within living memory the area of the patches of farmland had grown, as large areas of the forest which had covered much of this part of England had been cut down.[5] The small town of Bakewell built in the Wye valley was largely hidden from view, although the top of the church spire was just visible. The village of Ashford, also in the river valley, was a little to the right. Far away in the distance there was a line of hills including Aldwark and Minninglow, where, before the Romans came, local inhabitants had buried their dead beneath barrows.

Over to the left, a mile or so away, smoke rose from Hassop Hall, although the building itself and the neighbouring village were largely hidden by trees. The hall was the home of Thomas Eyre, Lord of the Manor of Hassop and Rowland. Beyond were the lands of the Earl of Devonshire, including Chatsworth and the villages of Pilsley and Edensor. Further round to the left was the village of Baslow where the road to Chesterfield started its climb over the dark millstone grit hills which formed the eastern boundary of the Peak District.

To the right, about a mile and a half away, nestling into the gentle slopes beneath the Edge, was the slightly larger village of Great Longstone, with its squat church tower. Beyond Longstone, the rolling countryside was interrupted by the deep valley of Monsal Dale.

The hamlet of Rowland had been settled by Norsemen in the ninth or tenth century. Its name, derived from the old Norse, "ra" and "lundr" meant "grove where roe deer are found"[6] and it is easy to imagine descendants of the Vikings living in wattle and daub huts in a clearing in the woods by the small stream running down from the Edge. Rowland was mentioned in the Domesday Book as Ralunt, a berewick of Ashford. By the fifteenth century, the manor of Rowland was owned by the Stafford family of Eyam, but when Gertrude Stafford, daughter and heiress of Humphrey Stafford, married Rowland Eyre she brought Rowland and the neighbouring manor of Calver into the ownership of the Eyre family.[7] Rowland Eyre had died in 1624 and his son Thomas Eyre had become Lord of the Manor.

Before setting out for Rowland, Thomas Ashton had persuaded Thomas Eyre's steward to rent him one of the cottages, with a croft, a barn and about eleven acres of land in Rowland when they became vacant. The steward had already known of Thomas. Like Mr Eyre and his household, the Ashtons were recusants who refused to take the Anglican Communion. They were adherents to the "old religion" of Catholicism. Thomas Eyre also had dealings with Robert Ashton of Stony Middleton, who may have been Thomas's brother. He, like the Eyres, had made substantial sums of money from lead mining. Robert Ashton already rented land from the Eyres and was later to lend money to Thomas Eyre's son, Rowland.

Although Thomas was to rent the house and land as a "tenant at will", with no formal lease, he knew that if he paid the rent, maintained the buildings and repaired the fences and ditches in the fields, he and his children could probably stay in the hamlet as long as they wished. Some of the other families who rented cottages and land had lived in Rowland for generations. Ancestors of the Lowes, who lived towards the top end of the hamlet, had been mentioned in Court Rolls during the reigns of Henry VI and Edward IV in the fifteenth century.[8] Since the Eyres had acquired the hamlet, they had gained a reputation as benevolent landlords.[9]

The cottage, the croft and the barn were a little way down a muddy track leading off The Street towards the stream. The cottage was on the right hand side. The wall adjoining the track, which faced north, did not have any windows. The cottages in Rowland had been built before glass was used in ordinary buildings[10] and so, although Rowland was situated on a sheltered south facing slope, all the houses had been built with the aim, so far as was possible, of keeping out the cold north winds of winter. The roofs were thatched.[11] When Thomas and Joane moved in, their cottage had two rooms. The inside of the walls probably

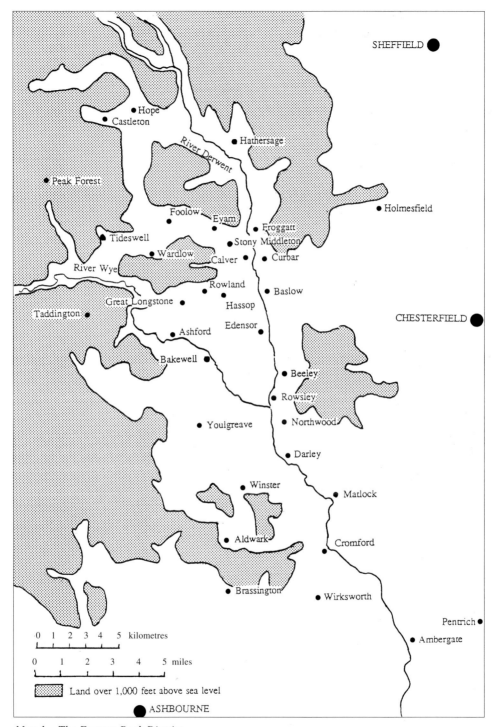

*Map 1 – The Eastern Peak District.*

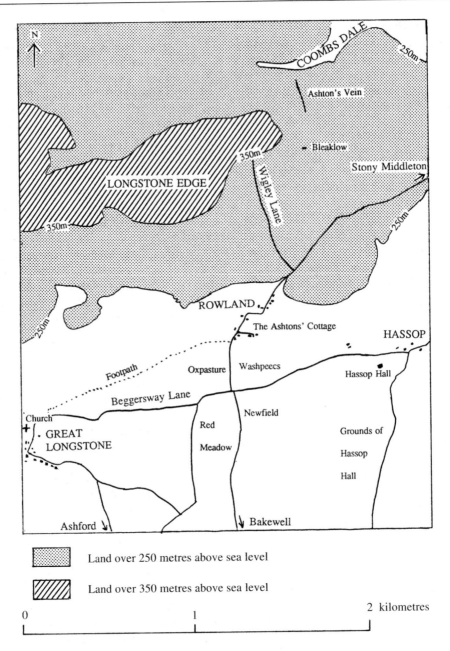

*Map 2 – Rowland, Hassop and Longstone.*

consisted of bare stone. The floor may have been laid with flagstones, but it is more likely that it was earthen, made of a mixture of beaten earth, lime, ashes and even horse dung.[12] The barn was also built of limestone and had three bays. The croft or "home close" was a small area of arable land measuring less than three-quarters of an acre. There was a well in the yard.

The land which Thomas and Joane were to farm was scattered among the hamlet's three fields, the Washpeecs, the Red Meadow and the Newfield. Just below the village between The Street and the stream, there were two acres of pasture in the Washpeecs. On the southern side of Beggarsway Lane, or "The Highway", as it was sometimes called by the villagers, were four and a quarter acres of pasture in the Little Newfield. Further away from the village in the direction of Bakewell, there were one and a half acres in the Greate Newfield which were used for growing corn, normally oats, in the spring and summer. After harvest time, cattle, which were confined in pens which the villagers made out of branches and brushwood, grazed on the stubble in the Newfield. During the winter the sheep on the Edge were moved down to the lower fields around the hamlet. To the west of the Newfield, next to the lane leading to Ashford, in the Red Meadow, there were two separate areas of pasture, each of about an acre and a half. All the villagers also had the right to graze cattle and sheep on the hamlet's common land.[13]

The yearly rent for the land and buildings was £4, although Thomas probably also had to pay a fine or premium at the beginning of the tenancy. It would be some time before Thomas and Joane would be able to harvest any oats, or any of the livestock would be ready to be eaten, but it is likely that Thomas's father gave them some hens, a few sheep and a cow. He probably also provided some money for the rent and to buy hay for the winter and lambs in the spring. Other family gifts may have included bed-linen and household goods, possibly as part of Joane's dowry.[14] Thomas and Joane knew that these gifts were to count as their share of the inheritance when his father died and that he would leave them nothing in his will.[15]

In June 1637 Thomas Eyre, who was about 85 years old, died. He was succeeded as lord of the manor by his son Rowland. One provision in Thomas Eyre's will stated:

> Also my minde and will is that my sonne shall suffer all my tennants who have noe leases to enjoye their farmes after the same rent which they then pay for the terme of one and twentie years after my death paying the same rent yearly and keeping their houses in good repair and using themselves dutifully towards him.[16]

This twenty-one year rent freeze was not legally enforceable, but Rowland followed his father's wishes. It was of considerable benefit to the Ashtons. In a survey carried out in 1652 prior to the sale of Rowland Eyre's lands which had been sequestrated during the Commonwealth, the rent for the Ashton farm and land was still £4 per annum, whereas the estimate of the true rental value was £7 2s 8d.[17] Prices undoubtedly rose over this period, as a result of a number of factors including the war, bad harvests and the increased production of silver in South America.[18] Rents also rose, but it may be that the surveyors over-estimated the rents which could be charged to Eyre's tenants to increase the sale price of the land.

By the autumn of 1638 the peace which had existed throughout the north of England for almost seventy years since the rebellion of the northern earls in Queen Elizabeth's time appeared to be breaking down. The attempts by the King, Charles I, and his Archbishop of Canterbury, Laud, to impose the English Prayer Book on the Presbyterian Church of Scotland had provoked widespread opposition and, indeed, rioting, north of the border. Earlier in the year a National Covenant pledging opposition to church reform had been circulated throughout Scotland. Both Charles and the Scots mobilised for war. In December 1638 Charles issued a declaration stating:

> The defence and welfare of our people and kingdom being our principal care, we are now called upon, by an extraordinary and unexpected occasion to prepare the forces and places of strength in this our kingdom in a more than usual manner to prevent such mischiefs as may otherwise fall upon the same if we should be taken unprovided.[19]

The Privy Council sent out directions to Lord Lieutenants in the northern half of England to muster the trained bands (the local part time militia) and to report how many able-bodied men there were in each county who could be called upon to fight in an emergency. On 1st January 1638/9[20] William, Earl of Devonshire, Lord Lieutenant of Derbyshire, wrote to the Privy Council with "a list of all the able men for warre in the County of Derby from 16 to 60 yeares of age". The list had been prepared, village by village, by local constables. In Derbyshire as a whole the names of 17,308 men were recorded. In Rowland there were fourteen men, including Thomas Ashton.[21] The other men listed were Francis Bagshawe, James Legge, Rowland Blande, John Hardie, Robert Ashburie, Richard Blande, Richard Jepson, Rowland Clarke, William Gryme, William Lowe, Thomas Bowe, Thomas Smith and Bryan Cleyton. Two and a half centuries later, when information was collected for the 1881 census, representatives of only two of these families remained in Rowland – a Thomas Ashton and a James Bland. Now there is no one living in the hamlet with any of these surnames.[22]

In the light of the number of men recorded in the Muster Roll and the number of cottages, the population of Rowland in 1638 must have been in the region of fifty to seventy people, including children.[23] It was considerably smaller than the surrounding villages. In comparison with Rowland's fourteen able-bodied men, Hassop had thirty-five men, and the neighbouring manor of Calver had forty-seven men, although both these figures would have included men who were solely engaged in lead mining. Great Longstone had 106 men, Ashford 144 men and Bakewell 200 men. The largest village in the immediate vicinity of Rowland was Hathersage with 237 men, while Youlgreave to the south had 358 men. Derby, the county town, is recorded as having 657 able-bodied men.

Another consequence of the unsettled times was an increase in taxation to pay for Charles's armies. In July 1641 Parliament approved a poll tax to raise the money which was needed to pay off the soldiers in the northern army before it was disbanded. The tax had nothing to do with peoples' ability to vote, but was levied by "poll" or, in other words, by head. The king's poor financial position led him to issue a proclamation urging his subjects to pay the new tax speedily. It was levied at different rates, depending on rank and income. Dukes were to pay £100 whereas viscounts and barons paid £40. Persons having an annual income of £50 were to pay forty shillings, those with an income of £20 five shillings, those with an income of £10 two shillings and those with an income of £5 one shilling. All other people, including women, servants and children aged over sixteen, but with the exception of those receiving alms, were to pay six pence. Catholics were made to pay double these sums, the Act stating that:

> every person who is a Popish Recusant . . . convict or which is or shall be indicted for Popish Recusance . . . or shall not have received the Holy Communion according to the Rites of the Church of England within the whole year next before the passing of this Bill, every such person shall pay double the rate and proportion . . . imposed on him.

The tax was collected by petty constables who handed the money which they received over to commissioners nominated by Parliament. In 1642 Thomas and Joane paid a total of eight shillings. Perhaps they both had annual incomes in excess of £10. On the other hand their joint total income may have been £10 or more and the balance was made up by four people, sons, daughters or servants, living with them.[24]

By 1642 England was drifting into civil war. After an unsuccessful attempt to arrest leading MPs Pym and Hampden in Parliament, King Charles left London and travelled northwards. Parliament ordered the local militia to assume a state of readiness, while Charles

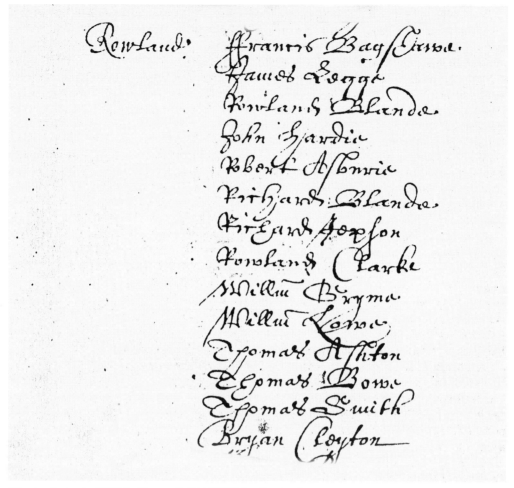

*Fig. 1 – Extract of Militia Muster Roll (1638/9) for Rowland.*

attempted to raise forces in York. In June the King refused to accept Parliament's Nineteen Propositions which would have involved him giving up control of the militia and the right to appoint ministers. As a result, Parliament issued a proclamation claiming to exercise sovereign power in place of the King. In July war was declared and in August Charles raised his standard at Nottingham. The first major battle was fought at Edgehill in Warwickshire in October.

The Civil Wars of 1642 to 1649 were to lead to social chaos throughout the country and to have more effect upon the ordinary population than any other conflict until the World Wars of 1914–1918 and 1939–1945. It has been estimated that at times as many as one in ten of the male population was in arms and that approximately 100,000 men died as a result of the fighting.[25] Besides the major campaigns when armies marched across the countryside, no doubt trampling crops and seizing livestock, there were localised minor scuffles and skirmishes throughout the land, as the gentry fought out their quarrels and grievances. The wars were frequently an excuse for lawlessness and looting.

An example of this kind of activity, which probably involved Thomas Ashton, was a raid mounted in 1643 by Rowland Eyre against John Jackson, an attorney, who lived in nearby Bubnell. Eyre aided by "a rude and debauched company" of men burst into Jackson's home and carried off "a greate stocke of corne and of householld stuffe consisting of Bedding Drapery Pewter Brasse and other utensills and householld furniture to a greate value besides a good quantity of wool and other goods and provision for keeping and mainteyning of his family [including] Beefe bacon butter cheese corne and grayne of all sorts." They also broke into the false roof of the premises and seized papers including "Bonds Bills Leases deeds of assignment and other deeds and writings". Some belonged to Jackson. Others were "committed unto his trust and care by severall men his clients". Jackson's wife was forced to escape in "a disguised habit." Jackson subsequently took court proceedings against Eyre and some of the more prominent men who accompanied him. They were jointly fined £400.[26] Thomas Ashton was probably too insignificant to be known to Jackson and was not mentioned by name in the court proceedings.

As 1642 and 1643 passed by, the local gentry in Derbyshire played their part in the war by raising bands of men and fortifying their houses. The Earl of Devonshire, a Royalist, garrisoned Chatsworth, three miles to the south-east of Rowland. On the Parliamentary side, by the end of October 1642 Sir John Gell of Hopton already had a company of men numbering two hundred.[27] He had become sheriff of Derby in 1635 and aroused animosity by attempting to levy £3,500 from the county for ship money.

Rowland Eyre, the lord of the manor of Hassop, Calver and Rowland, because of his Catholic beliefs, was naturally drawn towards the Royalist side. He fortified Hassop Hall, probably with earth works. The Earl of Newcastle commissioned him as a colonel in the Royalist army and he began to raise and drill men.

The natural inclination of many husbandmen must have been to stay at home with their families and to look after their crops and livestock. Many men in Thomas's position had never travelled far from home and their ties to the land must have been strong. However there can be no doubt where Thomas's sympathies lay and it can be assumed that he answered Rowland Eyre's call and was recruited into the regiment which Eyre formed. Although the feudal duty to provide service to the lord of the manor had by this time been superseded by rent payments, Eyre's tenants would have felt a strong obligation to follow his summons to arms, particularly in view of the freeze in rents provided for by Thomas Eyre's will. The ninety-six "able men for warre" from the three manors of Hassop, Calver and Rowland recorded in the 1638 muster must have formed the core of the regiment which Eyre recruited.

Moreover Thomas's religious beliefs meant that he was even more likely to have followed Rowland Eyre than many of the other tenants. Their shared religion and the regular attendances by Thomas and his family at Hassop Hall to receive the sacraments must have enhanced Thomas's loyalty and sense of obligation towards the lord of the manor. Also, as a Catholic, he is likely to have thought that he had much to gain from a Royalist victory and much to fear from Parliamentary success. The Catholics hoped that if King Charles, who after all had a French Catholic wife, won with help from them, his indebtedness would lead to a measure of toleration. On the other hand greater persecution was feared if Puritans, who were already destroying church stained glass, paintings, carvings and other images, which they considered to be popish idolatry, came to power. Indeed an account by one of Sir John Gell's supporters describes six Royalist colonels in Derbyshire, including Rowland Eyre, as having "such regiments as theire owne interest, backed with the commission of array and the popish party could raise for them."[28]

Initially Eyre's regiment stayed close to home and played little active part in the war.

*Fig. 2 – Portrait of Rowland Eyre of Hassop.*

Much of the south of the county was held by Gell for Parliament and Eyre kept his troops in the relative security of the Peak, either at Chatsworth or at Hassop. Thomas Ashton was no doubt in Rowland to bring in the harvest in 1642 and 1643. Early in 1644 Eyre was in the Ashbourne area with a band of men, trying to capture supplies and hinder Parliamentary communications between Derbyshire and Lancashire.[29] Bands of his men, probably on horseback, seized and plundered carts and pack-horses, terrorised locals with parliamentary sympathies, and generally made a nuisance of themselves.

In May 1644 however, Eyre and his men were captured. The Parliamentary forces under Sir John Gell learnt that about two hundred of Eyre's men were spending the night in the church at Boylestone, between Derby and Uttoxeter. (It was not just Parliamentary soldiers who abused church buildings.) Thomas Ashton was probably among them. Under instructions from Gell, a Major Saunders approached Boylestone with 500 horse and dragoons early in the morning. He

ordered his dragoons to dismount and then they noiselessly surrounded the building, which appears to have been carelessly left without watch or sentry, so as to make escape impossible. The moment daybreak came, and before the troops inside the church had begun to bestir themselves, the Major and his officers shouted simultaneously at the different doors and windows for their surrender, threatening to fire in upon them in the event of refusal. The Royalists, finding themselves caught in a trap of their own devising, surrendered at discretion. The small south door of the chancel was opened, and they were ordered to come forth one by one. As each man stepped forth into the dim light, he was seized, stripped of his arms and carefully guarded.[30]

The men, who had been captured without any casualties on either side, were held prisoner for a while in the church and then marched under guard to Derby. However, one of the problems faced by both sides in the Civil War was the impossibility of keeping large numbers of prisoners for any length of time. Eyre's men must have been released almost at once. Thomas Ashton soon found his way back to Rowland.

His stay there was almost certainly brief. Eyre's regiment was among the Royalist forces which fought at the Battle of Marston Moor on 2nd July 1644, and it seems that almost immediately after their release they marched north westwards out of Derbyshire, to join up with Prince Rupert's army near Bolton.[31] Prince Rupert of Bavaria was King Charles's nephew. He was a young professional soldier who was both daring and courageous. He inspired respect among his men, but was a proponent of the ruthless continental style of warfare and during the Civil Wars acquired a reputation for cruelty. With an army of two thousand horse and six thousand foot, he had marched northwards through Cheshire, captured and plundered Stockport ("the towne was the souldiers rewarde") and moved onto Bolton which on 28th May, after a fierce battle, was also captured. More than one thousand men defending Bolton were massacred before the soldiers sacked and plundered the town.

On 1st June, near Bolton, Prince Rupert was joined by the Royalist Northern Army under General Goring and the Derbyshire regiments, led by John Frescheville of Staveley, John Millward of Snitterton and Rowland Eyre. Thomas Ashton was probably among those soldiers.[32] The Derbyshire regiments mainly consisted of foot soldiers, but Eyre had "some horse as well". The Northern Army and Derbyshire regiments added another five thousand horse and eight hundred foot, but they were "not soe well appointed as was expected" – not particularly surprising in the case of Eyre's men, since they had been captured and disarmed by Major Saunders less than a month before. It seems though that what they lacked in weapons they tried to make up for in ferocity. Sir John Gell, who was now well out of the way of the action, observed that the Derbyshire regiments were "extremely barbarous and plunder all but Papists", although he too had acquired a reputation for causing "the greate suffering of many, and . . . the terror and affrightment of others" in Derbyshire.[33] Gell's own men were described as "the most licentious, ungovernable wretches that belonged to the parliament."[34]

Supplying the Royalist army with provisions does not seem to have been too much of a problem. The new forces which joined Prince Rupert arrived "with a great drove of cattle out of the Enemyes quarters as they march." The war was an excuse for the soldiers to loot, pillage and plunder as they progressed through the countryside. Even in the more disciplined and ordered society of the seventeenth century, when there was far less serious crime, lawlessness was often only just below the surface.

The Royalist army moved on to Wigan. Given the fate which had befallen Stockport and Bolton, it is perhaps not surprising that its citizens chose to receive "the Prince and his army with great tokens of joy, the streetes being stowed with rushes, flowers, and boughes of trees." Between 7th and 10th June Rupert besieged Liverpool and then crossed the Pennines via Clitheroe (24th June), Skipton (26th June) and Denton, near Ilkley, (29th June) to try to relieve the Parliamentary forces' siege of York. Since 22nd April the Royalist forces in the

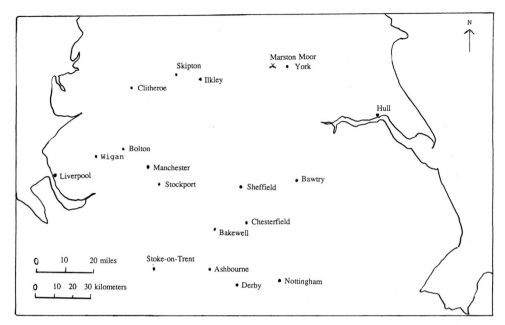

*Map 3 – Thomas Ashton and the Civil War.*

city had been cooped up by the Scots army, the Parliamentary forces from Yorkshire and Lancashire under Sir Thomas Fairfax, and the Eastern Association Army under the Earl of Manchester.

Rupert's army reached York and raised the siege on 1st July.[35] His troops, together with the garrison which came out of the city, now amounted to between 18,000 and 21,000 men. They were outnumbered by the three Parliamentarian armies which consisted of about 28,000 men. Rupert drew his army up on boggy moorland at Marston Moor on the 2nd, but, because his infantry was late in coming out of York, decided to delay attacking the enemy until the next day. The Parliamentary commanders however saw that the Royalist forces were not fully prepared and attacked straightaway.

From about two o'clock in the afternoon Rupert's forces faced a bombardment from the allied armies. Their main artillery weapons were Sakers, firing three and a half inch calibre cannon balls weighing five to six pounds for distances of over 2,000 yards. They also faced barrages of case shot, wooden boxes stuffed with scrap iron, which when fired produced a shrapnel-like effect. At about five o'clock, during gaps in the bombardment, the Royalists could hear the Parliamentary soldiers singing psalms. Shortly afterwards the allied forces charged forward from the higher arable ground on which they had been positioned towards the Royalist lines.

Eyre's regiment was drawn up in the front line on the Royalist left wing, under the command of General Goring, who, despite having a reputation for being a flamboyant drunkard, was a good military tactician. The soldiers under his command numbered 2,500 and were numerically inferior to Sir Thomas Fairfax's cavalry and the three regiments of Scottish horse which they faced. However they had the advantage of the terrain. In order to attack, Fairfax had to lead his men along a narrow lane between a hedge and a ditch. Many fell to Royalist musketeers. Goring's horse then counter-attacked riding up towards the higher ground. Fairfax fled and many of Goring's cavalry chased them, in an ill-disciplined manner, leaving the battlefield to plunder the Allied baggage-train. However the remnants of Goring's men who stayed on the battlefield were soon confronted by the Eastern Association Army now under the command of Oliver Cromwell. They had already routed the Royalist right wing and in a disciplined manner were coming round the rear of the rest of the Parliamentary forces. By this time Goring's cavalry was fragmented and he was left with only about a thousand men. They were heavily outnumbered by the 4,000 men under Cromwell who faced them. They stood their ground and large numbers of Goring's men were slaughtered.

Goring and the other commanders fled to York. Throughout the battlefield, the Royalists had been comprehensively beaten. Marston Moor was a decisive battle and resulted in the loss of much of the north of England to Parliament.

The battle must have been a terrifying experience for the many ordinary men like Thomas Ashton who were not professional soldiers. Amid the smoke from 10,000 muskets and the spasmodic rain storms confusion reigned. Many men did not wear any uniform and in the mêlée it was often hard to tell friend from foe. Cavalry charges were made against opposing cavalry and against infantry men standing behind pikes. In other parts of the battlefield hand-to-hand fighting took place using swords. The battle continued past dusk. Men became separated from their regiments and communication between commanders and troops frequently broke down. Besides the sound of gun and cannon fire, there were the screams of dying men and horses.

It is not clear whether Thomas fell at Marston Moor, or, if he did not, where, or when, he did die. There is no record of his burial in the Great Longstone parish registers, but that is not surprising in view of his Catholicism. He certainly died before 1652 when his wife Joane was described as "Widdowe Ashton".[36] During the couple of days following the Battle of Marston Moor approximately 4,150 men were buried, one in ten of those who took part. Hundreds, possibly thousands, died later from wounds. Although many soldiers survived sword wounds, and lived to petition quarter sessions for relief for much of the rest of the century, gun shot wounds were more likely to turn septic and to lead to blood poisoning. Thomas's chances of survival were better if he was on horse and if he pursued Fairfax's routed men in the hope of plundering the baggage wagons. In those circumstances he probably stood a reasonable chance of making his way back to Rowland. If he was on foot, or if he remained on the battlefield and faced the attack from Cromwell's men, he would have been in the part of the battlefield where the Royalists suffered their greatest casualties and may well have been one of those who was buried at Marston Moor. Eyre did survive and was captured again in 1646 at the siege of Lichfield.

Back in Rowland, the Ashtons continued to farm their land, sowing oats in the spring[37] and harvesting it in the autumn. They used Eyre's mill to grind their oats and baked their own bread and brewed their own beer. They tended their sheep and cattle, moving them according to the season – up onto the Edge in the summer and down to the fields around the hamlet in the winter. Rowland remained something of a backwater, and whilst the villagers no doubt heard rumours of the execution of Charles I in 1649, it may be that their day to day lives were affected very little by the changes brought about by the Commonwealth. There is no evidence that the Ashtons suffered any further for their Catholicism during this period. The Peak District was still relatively remote from central government.

The Eyre family did however suffer for their support of the King. Their lands were sequestrated and as early as 1643 the members of the Derbyshire Sequestration Committee were calling upon Eyre's tenants to pay their rents to them. These calls do not seem to have been effective until 1647 or 1648 and the Ashtons probably continued to pay their rent to Rowland Eyre's steward until then. In 1651 Parliament passed an "Act of Sale for the several lands and estates forfeited to the Commonwealth for Treason". Rowland Eyre was one of the seventy-one people named in the Act. In 1652 Eyre's lands were surveyed and on 6th October 1652 the Commissioners for Forfeited Estates contracted to sell them, including the hamlet of Rowland, to a Major John Wildman. Wildman paid the first half of the purchase price on 1st November and on 3rd November the Commissioners ordered the local Sequestration Committee to "forbeare to levy . . . any of ye rents or profits" due from Eyre's premises.[38] In fact Wildman was acting as an agent for Eyre who succeeded in regaining control of his estates, albeit at a price.

Joane Ashton, Thomas's widow, died sometime between 1652 and 1662. Her burial is not recorded in the parish registers for Great Longstone. It is possible that she died during one of the periods when the registers are illegible, but more likely that, as a Catholic, she was buried secretly at night. This was common practice among Catholics in the Peak District during the seventeenth century. They wanted to be buried in consecrated ground, but Anglican parsons took the view that people who were recusants died excommunicated and so tried to prevent their burial in church graveyards. Often secret Catholic burials took place and the parish registers for nearby Hathersage, where there was a large Catholic community, record many burials "at night". The mourners wearing hoods and carrying lighted tapers and candles before the corpse must have been an eerie sight as they made their way through the dark across the fields between Rowland and Longstone.[39]

## Notes

1. The inventory of possessions prepared after the death of Thomas's son John in 1690 refers to an old cart.
2. Thomas Hobbes, *De Mirabilis Pecci*, 1636, translated from the Latin by Cotton. Derwin is a reference to the River Derwent.
3. This is the spelling most commonly used in the Great Longstone parish registers for this period.
4. R J Brown, in *The English Country Cottage*, refers to the period 1550–1660 as being "the golden age" of English cottage building (pp 28–9). See too W G Hoskins, *The Midland Peasant*, p 194.
5. Lambeth Palace Library, Shrewsbury Papers, COMM xii a 2 p 2 (survey of October 1649).
6. Although Cameron in *The Place Names of Derbyshire* at p 162 gives the alternative meaning of "boundary grove", in his later book, *English Place Names*, he gives only this meaning (p 187).
7. Yeatman, *A Feudal History of Derbyshire*, vol 1, p 498, vol 3, p 368; Wright, *Longstone Records*, p 128; Peter Furness, The Family of Eyre of Hassop, 1870, Vol 10, *The Reliquary*, pp 232–6. Tilley in *Old Halls, Manors and Families of Derbyshire* states that the Manor of Rowland was owned by the Staffords during the reign of King John. The Eyres had owned the neighbouring manor of Hassop since 1498 – Lyson, *Magna Britannia*, p 30.
8. Quoted in Yeatman, vol 3, pp 343, 348, 352, 359, 362, 368 and 389.
9. Furness, p 232. See too J D Chambers and G E Mingay, *The Agricultural Revolution 1750–1850*, pp 20, 46.
10. See Mildred Campbell, *The English Yeoman Under Elizabeth and the Early Stuarts* p 232, where she suggests that glass became common in the homes of ordinary people in the middle of the seventeenth century, W G Hoskins, *The Midland Peasant* pp 285–93 and R J Brown, pp 253–4. Unglazed windows were often covered with oiled cloth.
11. White's *Gazetteer of Derbyshire*, 1857, p 15, refers to the roofs of "those farm houses previously thatched" as having recently been replaced with slates.
12. *Dictionarium Rusticum* (1704) and J Lawrence in *The Modern Land Steward* (1806) quoted in R J Brown, *The English Country Cottage*.
13. This description is taken from the survey of Rowland carried out prior to the sequestration of the Eyre estates in 1652 – Sheffield Library, Bagshaw Collection, 359(7). A well is referred to in the manorial court records for 1702 (see page 42) and is shown on the First Edition Ordnance Survey

Map (25"), 1879, Sheet XXIII.3. There are references to common land in the manorial court records of the seventeenth century.

14. Ralph Houlbrooke, *The English Family 1450–1700*, pp 84–5, Stone, *The Family, Sex and Marriage in England 1500–1800*, p 50, and 72–3.

15. Thomas Ashton is not mentioned as a beneficiary in any Derbyshire Ashton will during this period.

16. PRO, PROB 11, 201. Fines 199, Fo 448.

17. Bagshaw Collection 359(7). For table showing inflation see Briggs, *A Social History of England*, p 135. Cf also land tax assessments in chapter 2.

18. See eg James E Thorold Rogers, *A History of Agriculture and Prices in England*, vol 5, pp 794–7 and 808–10 and G M Trevelyan, *English Social History*, p 119.

19. PRO, SP16, cccciv.

20. Until the modern calendar was adopted in 1752, the year ran from 26th March. "1638/9" is the period between 1st January and 25th March which was then known as 1638, but which would now be known as 1639.

21. PRO SP16, ccccv.

22. Bagshaw Collection 357(7). It seems strange that, with the exception of the two Blandes, there is only one representative from each family. It is unlikely that there were no sons over 16, or indeed brothers, of the men listed, and this may mean that there is under-recording. (A comparison with the number of men listed in "The Humble Petition of Twentie Thousand Myners" (see Chapter 2) provides a further indication that there was under-recording.) The Muster Roll lists no representatives of the Legge, Clarke, Gryme, Clayton or Wilson families in the list of tenants prepared in 1653 (see footnote 13). Some of these men may have been farm hands, or these families may have moved or died out by 1653. PRO, RG11 3447 and Electoral Register for West Derbyshire Constituency, Ashford and Longstone Ward, 1990–1991.

23. E E Rich suggests in *The Population of Elizabethan England* Ec H R 2nd ser., ii (1950) a multiplier of 4 to give the total population. Professor Hoskins in *Local History in England*, p 203, suggests a multiplier of 6 to 7 (cf also Houlbrooke p 24, quoting King). See too Peter Laslett and Richard Wall, *Household and Family in Past Time*, pp 46–8, 76, 83 and 125–203 (mean household size of 100 English communities was 4.75, although none of these communities was in Derbyshire and few were upland settlements in the seventeenth century). The average size of the 25 miners' families in Hassop and Rowland listed in "The Humble Petition of Twentie Thousand Myners" in 1642 (PRO E101/280/18) was 4.88. In 1652 there were a dozen cottages in Rowland. The population of Rowland was 101 in 1801 and rose to 117 in 1811, before declining to 80 in 1851.

24. PRO E179/94/373 and 16 Car. I, c.9. Stephen Dowell, *A History of Taxation and Taxes in England*, p 226, and H Best, *Rural Economy in Yorkshire, being the farming and account books of Henry Best* (1641), Surtees Society, 33, 1857, p 91. Apart from the reference to the additional poll tax paid, it has not been possible to find any other reference to Thomas and Joane being penalised for their Catholicism. There does not appear to be any reference to them in the records of the diocesan courts at Lichfield JRO and their names do not appear in the Recusant Rolls for the years 1634–5, 1636–7, 1639–40, 1641–2, 1643–4, 1645–6, 1646–7, 1647–8, 1648–9 or 1649. (PRO E377/42, 44, 47, 49, 51, 53, 54, 55, 56 and 58.

25. Kenneth Morgan, *Oxford History of England*, p 364, Briggs, p 141.

26. PRO C5/7/67, C6/157/46. MAE Green, *Calendar of the Committee for Compounding*, pp 2319–20 A number of the other named Defendants were also descried as "recusants".

27. A true relation of what Service hath beene done by Colonel Sir John Gell, quoted in Glover, *History of Derbyshire*, Vol 1, Appendix p 57.

28. Sir George Gresley, A true account of the raising and employing of one regiment of foot under Sir John Gell, quoted in Glover, *History of Derbyshire*, Appendix to Vol 1, p 72. The Parliamentarians were however prone to exaggerate the role of Catholics in the King's forces.

29. See Meredith, "A Derbyshire Family in the Seventeenth Century: The Eyres of Hassop and Their Forfeited Estates", *Recusant History* (1965) Vol 8, p 12.

30. J C Cox, *Churches of Derbyshire*, Vol 3, p 21. See too Glover Vol 1, Appendix p 64.

31. Account of Prince Rupert's March into Lancashire, Carte MSS x 664, transcribed in *Transactions of the Royal Historical Society*, Vol XII, New Series, 1898, p 69. Perhaps Eyre had given an undertaking to Gell not to take part in further action in Derbyshire and so chose to join Rupert's forces, rather than disband his regiment. Rosamond Meredith's article "A Derbyshire Family in the Seventeenth Century: The Eyres of Hassop and their Forfeited Estates" (*Recusant History* Vol

8, no 1) provides much valuable information about the Eyres, but her suggestion that the Derbyshire regiments were not at Marston Moor cannot be correct – see eg Gresley, the "Account of Prince Rupert's March supra and De Gomme's battle plan", *Transactions of the Royal Historical Society*, Vol XII, frontispiece. Her dating of the capture of Eyre's men in Boylestone Church also seems to be wrong.

32. Although I have found no documentary proof, I have assumed that Thomas Ashton was in Rowland Eyre's company until the Battle of Marston Moor. For the reasons set out on page 8, it is hard to imagine that Thomas Ashton did not take to arms.
33. Calendar of State Papers, 1644, pp 190/1. Glover, Vol 1, Appendix p 74.
34. *Memoirs of Colonel Hutchinson*, vol i, p 180, quoted in *Dictionary of National Biography*, vol 7, p 993. See too S R Gardiner, *History of the Civil War*, vol 1, p 159.
35. The account of Marston Moor is drawn principally from Peter Newman, *The Battle of Marston Moor*.
36. Bagshaw Collection, 359(7).
37. Probably in March. See J Fitzherbert, *The Book of Husbandry* (1534).
38. PRO, SP23/18, p 780.
39. See eg D J Steel, "Sources of Roman Catholic and Jewish Genealogy and Family History" (Vol 3 of *National Index of Parish Registers*) pp 875–78 and Bossy, *The English Catholic Community 1570–1850*, ch 6 for descriptions of clandestine night-time burials. In the parish registers for Hathersage – eg after reference to the burial of Maria Ashton on 14th February 1637 – "recusans noctu" is written.

# 2

Very little information about Thomas and Joane's children survives. According to the parish registers, only one of their children was baptised in the church in Great Longstone. Almost certainly, because they were recusants, their children were baptised secretly by a Catholic priest, probably a Jesuit, at Hassop Hall. Similarly, there are no records of any marriages of Ashtons who are likely to have been their children.[1]

The son who was the exception, and who was baptised on 16th September 1638 at Great Longstone, was called John. The parish registers refer to him by the Latin version of his name, Johannes. Probably he was born early in September, or possibly during the second half of August.[2] It is not clear why he was the only one of Thomas and Joane's children to be baptised at Great Longstone. It may be that he was a weak baby who was not expected to survive and that no Catholic priest was available to baptise him in time. Another possibility is that he was born during a period when there was particularly strong pressure on Catholics to conform.

The only other Ashton who could have been one of Thomas and Joane's children was Francis Ashton. He was living in Rowland in the second half of the seventeenth century and was probably John's younger brother. After their mother's death, John continued living in the cottage and succeeded to most, if not all, of the land which Thomas and Joane had farmed. It is likely that John was forced to give the lord of the manor a heriot, normally the tenant's best beast, when he succeeded to the land which his father had rented.[3] It seems that Francis either built a small cottage nearby or moved into one which had become vacant.

John and Francis no doubt welcomed the return of Charles II to the throne in 1660. Catholics hoped for greater religious toleration in the light of the declaration made by Charles in exile in Breda when he promised that "no man shall be disquieted or called in question for differences of opinion in matter of religion . . . and that we shall be ready to consent to such an act of parliament . . . for the full granting [of] that indulgence."[4] However the most immediate impact of the Restoration for John was the Stuart kings' perennial need to raise revenue. In the autumn of 1661 commissioners appointed by Charles to collect "a free and voluntary present to his majesty" came to Derbyshire. On 21st October, at Bakewell, they prepared a long list of "subscribers" from neighbouring towns and villages who were prepared to "donate" money to the King. The list which they prepared named six men from Rowland. John, who was described as a husbandman, agreed to pay one shilling. Nicholas Sheldon who was also a husbandman, Rowland Blande, the blacksmith, Thomas Hudson, a cook and Thomas Waddinton, a gardener, also agreed to pay one shilling each. (Hudson and Waddinton presumably worked for the Eyres at Hassop Hall.) Francis Bagshaw, another husbandman, was to pay two shillings. Rowland Eyre of Hassop agreed to pay £40.[5]

It is not possible to ascertain whether these were genuinely voluntary payments, or what, if any, pressure to pay was imposed on the inhabitants of the Peak District. Clearly though no government could rely on raising money in this way, and, before long, the King had persuaded Parliament to introduce a new form of taxation. Hearth tax, more commonly known at the time as "chimney tax", was introduced in 1662 to provide an "ordinary" source of revenue for Charles II – something his father had lacked and which had caused him to resort to methods of taxation not approved by Parliament, such as the collection of ship money. Hearth tax was payable at the rate of two shillings per annum for every hearth or stove. The tax was collected in half yearly instalments of one shilling on Lady Day (25th March) and Michaelmas (29th September). Exemptions were allowed for the poor and for those people who lived in premises worth less than twenty shillings per annum. This meant that Francis Ashton, living in the small cottage adjoining John's home, did not pay any hearth tax.[6]

Assessments of the amount of hearth tax payable in Rowland, made by the constable with jurisdiction over the constablewick of Ashford, only survive for some years. In both 1662 and 1664 John's cottage had one hearth and he was accordingly liable to pay two instalments of one shilling.[7] Other people living in Rowland whose cottages also had one hearth were Francis Bagshawe, Rowland Bland, Nicholas Sheldon, Thomas Lowe, Francis Brightmore, Widow Bland and Richard Jepson. Four cottages, including that occupied by the Hardie family recorded in the 1652 survey were worth less than twenty shillings per annum and so their occupants were not assessed as being liable for any hearth tax. No cottage in Rowland had more than one hearth, although Hassop Hall had twenty hearths.

The hearth tax assessments for Michaelmas 1662 to Lady Day 1664 indicate that over that two year period the collectors for Derbyshire should have recovered £4,064 3s. In fact they collected £3,914 17s 3d, or over 96% of the total due.[8] Nearly everyone listed paid. It was however an unpopular tax and there was one case in Derbyshire where there was a "grievous assault" upon a collector.[9] John Ashton and his neighbours in Rowland may well have been pleased that the monarchy had been restored, but it cannot have been long before they were complaining about paying the new tax to the constable.

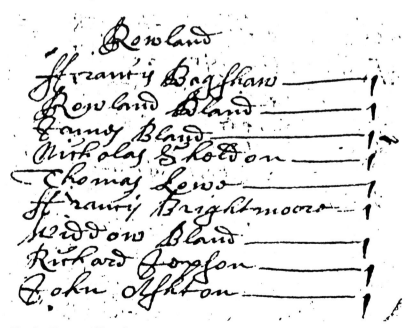

*Fig. 3 – Extract of hearth tax return (1664) for Rowland.*

Sometime early in the 1660s John married. He was in his early to mid-twenties, slightly younger than the average age of men entering into first marriages, which was in the region of 27 to 29. Women tended to marry slightly earlier.[10] John's wife was called Mary, but since there is no record of their marriage, it is impossible to find out where she came from, or even her maiden name. It is likely that if she did not actually grow up in Rowland, she came from one of the neighbouring villages. This was a time when many marriages took place secretly, away from parish churches. John and Mary's marriage may have been solemnised by a Jesuit priest at Hassop Hall, or may even have taken place in John's cottage in Rowland or at Mary's parents' home. Although canons introduced in 1604 stipulated that weddings should take place in church between the hours of eight o'clock in the morning and noon, it was not uncommon, until the passing of Lord Hardwicke's Marriage Act in 1753, for marriages to be performed at night, or in secular places such as inns or private houses or even under trees.[11] These clandestine marriages were obviously the norm for Catholics such as John and Mary, but were also widespread among people who otherwise followed the orthodoxy of the Church of England. Their marriage was probably followed by a wedding feast.[12]

John and Mary's first son, John, died young. He was buried at Longstone parish church on 21st February 1664/5.[13] They had five children who did reach adulthood. Their next son was another John. (It was common for parents to use a name again if the first child who was given the name died. Some parents did this to preserve the memory of the child who had died, but it is more likely that this was an indication of John's desire to have a surviving son named after him.) Their other children who survived infancy were Mary, Samuel, Robert and Sarah.[14] It is possible that Samuel and Robert were named after John's relatives, Samuel and Robert Ashton, who were living in Stony Middleton, and even that they were godparents. None of these children was baptised in the church at Longstone. As with Thomas and Joane's children, it is likely that they were baptised by one of the Jesuit priests who lived with the Eyres at Hassop Hall.

1665 was a year when bubonic plague was causing death in London. Generally it did not spread to the north and west of the country, but there was a serious outbreak in the nearby village of Eyam. The steps taken by the villagers there to avoid spreading the plague are well known. They stayed in their village and arranged for food to be left just outside. During the thirteen months between September 1665 and October 1666, 260 villagers died from the plague in Eyam. They were however successful in preventing further contagion. Despite its proximity to Eyam, there is no evidence that the plague struck in the hamlet of Rowland. Between 1664 and 1667, there was no obvious increase in the number of burials recorded in the parish registers for Great Longstone, which included the inhabitants of Rowland. Throughout this period the number of baptisms exceeded the number of burials.

Between 1664 and 1670 John and Mary substantially rebuilt the cottage in which they lived. Until this time it had consisted of just two rooms with only one hearth and chimney. However by the time of the 1670 assessment for hearth tax[15] there were two hearths – one in the "house" and one in the "parlour" which had been built onto the original structure. There was also a "buttery". Upstairs, probably for the first time, there were "chambers", or bedrooms, above the "house" and the "parlour". The new house was built of rough stone with walls which were almost two feet thick and a thatched roof. The floor of the chamber above the house was supported by one timber beam. The door ways now seem low – between five feet six inches and five feet nine inches above the floor. This may either reflect the fact that our ancestors were generally shorter, or may be because the floors have since been raised.

It is unlikely that the building works included the provision of a privy. Even in 1781, John Wood, the architect who designed many of the terraces in Bath, wrote that in many "villages and towns there is scarcely such a convenience in the whole place for want of which the streets are perfect jakes . . ."[16]

One relic of feudal times which still survived in Rowland during this period was the system of manorial courts. In medieval times there were, in theory, two separate manorial courts for each manor.[17] The Court Baron dealt with transactions relating to land transfers and inheritances, made and enforced regulations which were the equivalent of modern by-laws, and heard small personal actions for debt, trespass etc. The Court Leet, with the "View of Frankpledge", dealt with minor infractions of the criminal law. Bacon described its jurisdiction as being to "inquire of all offences against the peace" and "to punish and remove all public nuisances and grievances concerning infection of the air, corruption of victuals . . . and all other things which may hurt or grieve the people in general, in their health, quiet and welfare." The Webbs stated that it was "difficult to find any kind of personal conduct, whether intrinsically innocent or plainly criminal . . . which might not at one period or another, have found its way as a common nuisance into the presentments of a Court Leet jury."[18]

By the second half of the seventeenth century the functions of the manorial courts in Rowland Eyre's manors had been amalgamated. This was typical of what had happened in many other manors. Although court hearings may originally have been held every three weeks, the records indicate that by the 1660s Eyre's courts sat twice a year. One court hearing was held for all three manors, with the jurors meeting in turn in Hassop, Calver and Rowland.[19]

In practice the court hearings fulfilled several functions. They were used by Rowland Eyre's steward to order tenants to carry out works to repair fences, hedges and ditches. The way in which landlords enforced tenants' obligations through the manorial courts, rather than by means of covenants in leases, was evidence of the way in which the transition from feudal tenure to the modern system of leases had only been partially completed. In addition the court enforced rules and customs about farming which had evolved over the centuries and modified them, as circumstances changed, by issuing new edicts. The laws enforced by manorial courts were often a definition of actual agrarian practice, as it had been pursued "time out of mind".[20] In theory it was possible for the villagers to vote against the wishes of the steward, but the power of the lord of the manor was such that this would only have happened rarely. In any event, since most of the villagers were merely tenants at will, Rowland Eyre always had the ultimate sanction of terminating their tenancies and evicting them if they did anything to displease him.

The court hearings were also a forum in which tenants could resolve minor quarrels and "neighbour disputes" between themselves. They probably performed the valuable function of allowing the tenants to air their grievances and "let off steam" in a safe and controlled environment.

The courts were presided over by Rowland Eyre's steward who, in the late 1660s, was William Nicholson. At the beginning of each hearing he swore in a jury, normally of thirteen tenants. All tenants in the three manors were obliged to attend the court, and the court ritually "amercied", or fined, all those who did not attend, ordering them to pay six pence each. The court also chose one person from each village to serve as "thirdborow" or constable for the next year and one person to be "pinder", in charge of the pinfold in which animals which escaped on to other people's land were impounded until their owners paid a fine for them to be released.

A fairly complete set of minutes of the court proceedings in Hassop, Calver and Rowland exists for most of the eighteenth century, giving a clear view of the way in which the courts worked. Unfortunately, apart from minutes of hearings held on 9th April 1667 and 1st October 1667,[21] there are no court records before 1700.

On 9th April 1667 John Ashton was fined twice by the court sitting in Calver. He was "amercied" one shilling and six pence "for breaking ye office of pinder". John's offence was a "pound breach", involving the removal of one of his animals from the pinfold without paying a fine. He was not alone in doing this. Anthony Gregory, Alles (Alice) Bower, William Froggott, William Cocks, Edward Vallance, William Greene, William Wilson and Nicholas Sheldon were all fined one shilling and six pence for similar offences. (In 1700 the court increased the penalty for pound breaches to five shillings.) John Ashton was also "amercied" three shillings and four pence "for his man makinge a Rescue of Edward Vallance". His farmhand must have seen that one of John's beasts had strayed onto Edward Vallance's land and then been spotted himself going onto the land to bring back the animal, rather than allowing Edward Vallance to take it to the pinfold. Francis Hodgkinson's children were fined twice at the same sitting for "making rescues", once for recovering sheep from Anthony Mosley's land and once for taking them from the Breach Close, an area of land just to the south of the lane from Longstone to Hassop. Other tenants were fined for allowing their horses to roam loose and because there were gaps in their hedges or fences. The fines, which went into Rowland Eyre's pocket, came to slightly over thirty shillings.

At the court sitting on 1st October John was sworn in as a juror. He was also chosen as "thirdborow" for Rowland and sworn into that office. His duties included preserving the King's peace, summoning jurors to court, arresting "vagabonds and night walkers", distraining the goods of defaulters and generally keeping order in the village.[22] John was illiterate and, like the other jurors, he placed his mark at the bottom of the minutes. John's mark was an "A". Mary's mark, which she later made at the end of her will, was an "m". Francis Ashton's mark was a scratchy cross. The only person in the hamlet able to write his own name seems to have been John Bland. He was later to write out Mary's will.

Another aspect of life which was regulated by customary courts was the lead mining for which the Peak District had long been famous. The barmoot courts for each liberty controlled lead mining in much the same way as the manorial courts regulated farming and other aspects of village life. They sat with a jury of miners which not only prescribed rules governing mining, but also punished miners who transgressed them.

The deposits of lead on Longstone Edge above Rowland had been mined since Roman times. It has been claimed that Roman coins have been found in lead workings near Rowland and there are references to lead mining in the manors of Bakewell and Ashford, both in Edward the Confessor's time and in the Domesday Book.[23] The importance of lead to the local economy in the seventeenth century is shown by "The Humble Petition of Twentie Thousand Myners" which was presented to Parliament in 1642 by Derbyshire miners complaining about taxes which the King had imposed on lead. The petition referred to forty-five miners in Hassop and Rowland by name, but when their families and unnamed miners were added the total number of people who were in some way dependent on lead mining in the two villages was 170. In nearby Ashford 123 men were named and the total number dependent on lead mining was 560. In the villages of Great and Little Longstone the equivalent numbers were 146 and 746.[24] By 1649 the tithe of lead ore within the parochial jurisdiction of Bakewell was worth over £1,000 per annum.[25] The mining area of Longstone Edge was controlled by two families. The "lord of the field" for the liberty of Ashford North Side, which included the parishes of Ashford, Wardlow and Great and Little Longstone, was the Earl of Devonshire. The Eyre family controlled the combined liberty of Hassop, Rowland and Calver.

There is no evidence that John's father Thomas ever took any part in lead mining. His was not one of the names listed in the 1642 petition. However John was involved in lead mining. He is referred to in a list of sixty-seven lead miners taken at Hassop on 2nd October 1667.[26]

On 1st April 1668 he was one of twenty-four jurors at the barmoot court for Hassop, Rowland and Calver which approved amendments to Articles governing the conduct of lead miners which had originally been made in 1664. The fact that he was one of the twenty-four clearly meant that he had some status as a lead miner. The inventory of his belongings prepared after he died mentioned "lead ware" worth four shillings and six pence. It did not refer to any lead mining tools, but that omission was probably not significant. It was rare for lead mining tools to be mentioned in Peak District inventories, probably because they were of little value and may well have been left down mines. In any event, by the time of his death, John would have "retired" from active mining, though his experience would still have been valued by the barmoot court.

Throughout this period John and Mary remained Catholics, following customs and rituals which had been outlawed since the English Reformation, a century and a quarter before. Despite the pressure to conform, there was still a small but significant number of Catholics in the north and west of the country, in what have been described as "the dark corners of the land".[27] In 1676, in the diocese of Coventry and Lichfield, which included Derbyshire, there were 1,949 Papists over the age of sixteen, in comparison with 155,720 Conformists and 5,042 Protestant Non-Conformists. There were 65 Catholics in the parish of Bakewell (which included Rowland), 140 in nearby Hathersage and significant numbers in Tideswell and Hope. The diocese of Coventry and Lichfield had a higher proportion of Catholics than any other part of the country.[28] It has been suggested[29] that there were more Catholics in the "dark corners of the land" because the tight parochial machinery of the lowland areas did not operate in the more isolated upland country. An innate unwillingness to change among a conservative population with close ties to the land, and a deep attachment to the customs and rituals with which they were familiar, must also have played their part.

The Ashtons were typical among Catholics of their time, in that they rented land from a well established Catholic landlord, who, it was hoped, would provide an element of protection. In Rowland, members of the Sheldon and Hardie families were Catholics. The Brightmores were also notable in failing to attend church at Longstone.[30] Otherwise the Ashtons were isolated and possibly ostracised from the local community, since most of the Eyres' tenants did conform.

Differences in religious beliefs were extremely significant in an age when the Church played a far greater role in everyday life than it does today. Its influence was second only to that of the state and affected most aspects of life. Its importance was not limited to parishioners' attendance at services on Sundays. Through the parishes, the Church was responsible for many aspects of local government. It provided what little education existed and in an age when few people could read, sermons were one of the main sources of information and influence on the way people lived their day to day lives.

The Ashton's non-conformity involved more than merely going to Hassop Hall for Mass on Sundays instead of the services held at the church in Great Longstone. Catholics fasted on Fridays throughout the year (except at Christmas and on Good Friday) and on all weekdays in Lent. Such fasting did not involve total abstinence, but they could only eat a single daily meal, which could not be taken before midday and which could not include meat. There were other meat-free days, particularly Saturdays throughout the year (except at Easter) and Sundays in Lent. In theory fasting would have marked the Ashtons out from the other villagers, but in practice, it may have made little difference because ordinary people ate very little meat during the winter months.[31]

Attendance at services in the church in Great Longstone would have been contrary to John and Mary's beliefs, but they risked being fined if they did not go to Anglican services. Elizabeth's Act of Uniformity of 1559 provided that a fine of twelve pence could be levied for each occasion that a person failed to resort to his or her parish church or chapel or usual place of common prayer on Sundays or Holy Days. Originally fines were collected by the church wardens and used for poor relief, but an Act of 1581 raised maximum penalties to £20 per month and the offence became indictable.[32] Notwithstanding this, in some places, Mass was said and sermons were preached in barns and farmyards. The Ashtons, and other Catholics in the immediate vicinity of Hassop, almost certainly took Mass in a private room or chapel at Hassop Hall. The Eyres had close connections with the Jesuits, with Fathers Ignatius Cuffaud, John Weedon and Henry Heaton successively living at Hassop.[33] Mass was said by one of these priests.

Although the Ashtons must have been familiar with the ritual of the Mass, they can only have had the vaguest idea of what was actually going on, or of the significance of the various parts of the service. Nowadays there seems to be a considerable irony in people who had no education or schooling, and who could not read or even write their own names, attending services conducted solely in Latin. It is unlikely that they could understand a single word of the service. To the Ashtons however, this would not have seemed the least bit strange. They were merely taking part in a form of worship which had been unchanged for centuries and which they believed to be based upon God's will. Their lack of understanding of the actual words used would have been compensated for by the simple belief that they were doing what was right and that the new forms of service practised by the Church of England were heresy.

Attendance at Mass was also a social and domestic occasion. The Ashtons would have mingled with the Eyres' servants and eaten breakfast at Hassop Hall among the lesser members of the household.[34] At other times the Eyres dined in hall, with tenants who were present on business, seated at lower tables.[35]

There is no evidence that the Ashtons in Rowland were prosecuted for their Catholicism until 1682. Perhaps they were protected to some extent by Robert Ashton, who was related to them and who, after being sheriff, was a Justice of the Peace.[36] He probably played some role in deciding who should be presented before the Grand Jury at the Assizes to face prosecution. It is though, more likely that they received a dispensation allowing them to attend services at the parish church in Longstone sufficiently frequently to avoid prosecution.[37]

However on 1st August 1682 there was "A great presentment of recusants by the grand jury at the Assizes" who were charged with "absentinge from the Church for the space of one and twenty Sundays". Those indicted included Jane Ashton the wife of Francis Ashton, who was described as being of Longstone. Four hundred and fifty "Roman Recusants" were fined at a single session, at the rate of twelve pence for every Sunday they were absent from Church.[38]

The threat of prosecution may have driven the Ashton family into the fold of the Church of England, and from this time it seems that they started to join the majority of the villagers in Rowland on Sundays in walking along the footpath westwards across the fields to Longstone, rather than walking in the opposite direction towards Hassop Hall.

The first indications of their return to conformity are the baptism and burial of John and Mary's son Nicholas. He was born during the bitterly cold winter of 1682/1683 when there was a severe frost in September which did not thaw until 5th February 1682/3.[39] He was baptised at Longstone on 11th January 1682/3, but died almost immediately and was buried the next day. Apart from the fact that there is no record of the marriage of their son Robert (and that in itself was not necessarily a sign of Catholicism), there is every indication that from this time onwards the family conformed. The Eyres on the other hand retained their adherence to the Catholic faith.

It is easy to imagine Rowland as an isolated hamlet completely cut off from the rest of the country. Seventeenth-century roads were certainly very poor, and travel was difficult. There were highwaymen on the roads and, in Derbyshire, it was often necessary for travellers to hire guides to help them find their way. In 1697 it took the adventurous Celia Fiennes, who was travelling on horseback, six hours to ride the nine miles from Bakewell to Buxton. She found that in the Peak District "the common people know not two or three mile from their home."[40] A quarter of a century later, Daniel Defoe described the Peak as being "so inhospitable, so rugged and so wild a place."[41]

However Rowland's inhabitants did have some contact with the outside world. A few people did travel and some news must have filtered through to the villagers by word of mouth. Pedlars wandered from village to village selling their wares. Rowland Eyre visited London from time to time, even though the journey took at least three days.[42] Although nowadays the only road to Rowland is a cul de sac, in the seventeenth century The Street continued on over the Edge towards Stony Middleton and strangers must have wandered through the hamlet from time to time. Drovers' roads crossed the hills to the north and there were tracks for the pack horses which carried lead to the Trent and thence to Hull for shipment to London. Like most other local inhabitants the Ashtons must have walked or ridden to Bakewell for the market which was held on Mondays, where lead and other commodities were sold, and for the annual fair there.[43]

The hamlet itself was a far busier place than it is nowadays, with more people to be seen going about their daily life. The population of Rowland then was larger than today.[44] Also seventeenth-century farming was more labour-intensive and there would have been both adults and children out in the fields, ploughing, sowing, harvesting or mending hedges and fences or looking after livestock and trying to prevent them from straying on to other peoples' land, to say nothing of the activities of the lead miners.

It seems that John and Mary were visited from time to time by Samuel Ashton of Stony Middleton. He was a relative, probably a cousin, but was clearly of a different social standing to them. He described himself as "gent"[45] and was one of the sons of Robert Ashton, who had been sheriff of Derbyshire in 1665 and had been a Justice of the Peace until his death in 1687. On 5th February 1688/9, a Tuesday,[46] Samuel Ashton was in Rowland, almost certainly at John and Mary's cottage, when he was "taken sick suddenly". He may have suffered a heart attack, but whatever the cause, Samuel realised that he was about to die and remembered that he had not made a will. He declared that "he could make a will without writing which would stand good in law." He called upon John and Mary, another relative of his called Thomas White and a woman called Ellen Daud, who were all present, to act as witnesses.[47] Then he solemnly said:

> To my sister Sarah £1,000 to be paid out of my personal estate. To Rachel Ashton of Bradway £10. To Dorothy Ashton £10. To all the rest of my brother Ashton's children £5 a peece. To them at Whiteley Wood £5 a piece. All the rest of my estate to my brother Benjamin Ashton.

Then he died.

The bequest of £1,000 was a considerable amount, but was the kind of sum which could be made in the seventeenth century from lead mining. It may be that it was intended by Samuel to be equivalent to a dowry to enable his sister to marry. Rachel and Dorothy Ashton were Samuel's nieces, daughters of his half brother Robert Ashton of Bradway. By "them at Whiteley Wood", the witnesses believed that Samuel intended to benefit "his nephew Robert Ashton and his nieces, Elizabeth wife of John Bright, Rebecca Ashton and Alice Ashton who were the children of Alex Ashton late of Whiteley Wood deceased, [his] brother by the half blood."

Thomas White wrote out what Samuel had said and the witnesses signed it, although John and Mary who were both illiterate, scribbled their marks at the bottom – an "A" for John and an "m" for Mary.[48] As a result letters of administration were granted to Samuel's brother Benjamin Ashton some two months later, on 11th April.

Some impression of the way in which the Rowland Ashtons lived during the second half of the seventeenth century can be gained from the inventories listing John and Mary's belongings which were prepared after their deaths in 1690 and 1702/3.[49] In the main room of the house, which was lit by candles, there was a large open fire place, with a "landiron" or fire grate. A "payre of gobards" (cobbards) rested on top of this. They were two iron bars with knobs at their upper ends which met at the centre of the hearth and formed a cradle for fuel. In some parts of the country, particularly those away from the coast, people like John and Mary would still have been relying entirely upon logs for heating and cooking, but by 1610 coal was being mined near Chesterfield and Cromford,[50] and John and Mary were definitely burning coal in their fireplace. The inventory prepared after John's death refers to "coales" valued at three shillings and six pence. They were probably brought by pack horse for the journey of approximately twelve miles from the coal pits. The inventories also refer to a "chafening dish" – a metal dish into which hot coals were inserted to heat food. Over the fire there was a spit and "one payre of ratten hookes" – a large iron crook for suspending kettles or pots over the fire. Together with other "old iron in the house" the metal ware in and around the fire place was worth five shillings.

It is tempting to imagine the family using the spit to roast whole sheep or succulent pigs. Such feasts are likely however to have been rare and reserved for special occasions. The spit may have been used to roast joints of mutton, beef or pork which were preserved in brine through the winter after animals had been slaughtered in the autumn when grass or other animal feedstuffs were starting to be in short supply, but the Ashton's diet probably consisted predominantly of cereals.[51] The sheep on Longstone Edge were kept more for their wool than for their meat.

The inventories do not describe the walls or floors of the house. Probably the walls were unplastered, although they may have been white-washed.[52]

The most important wooden items of furniture in the main livingroom which the Ashtons called "the house" were a cupboard, a seat, a table, a form or bench and four stools, which were valued at £1. On the table there were two pewter candlesticks. The only eating or drinking utensils recorded are twelve pewter dishes, two salts (salt containers) and five flagons. Like the dishes, the salts and flagons were probably made of pewter, a mixture of tin and lead, which had become a common material used in the making of household table-ware during Elizabethan times. Pewter ware was manufactured in Chesterfield.[53] The pewter, a warming pan and the chafening dish were together valued at sixteen shillings. There is no reference in the inventories to knives, spoons or drinking vessels although there must have been some.

The cooking utensils recorded were an "iron pott", a "little brass pott", one "scellit" (skillet) and "one little kettle" with a total value of six shillings and six pence.

In the parlour there was an old grate. There was another table with a form (bench), three chairs, a stool and a wooden chest. Both the inventories prepared after John and Mary's deaths refer to a bed in the parlour. John's inventory describes it as a "featherbed with bedstocks (ie bedstead) and furniture belonging to it" worth fourteen shillings. Although it is possible that John and Mary only took to sleeping in the parlour when they became older, it is far more likely that the parlour had always been a bedroom. When cottages consisted of only one storey, there was no alternative, and even after upper storeys were built, parlours often remained the preferred places for heads of families to sleep.[54] John and Mary's parlour must have been warmer than the rooms upstairs, and, in an age when people removed their clothes far less frequently than today and when many beds were surrounded with bed hangings, privacy was unlikely to have been a problem, if indeed it was a concept which existed.

The two upstairs rooms, called chambers, were probably reached by a ladder, rather than by means of a fixed staircase. In the chamber over the parlour, there was a "payre of bedstocks" with two blankets and one bedhilling (a bed cover) with hangings belonging to it. There were also five linen sheets, two pillow beers (pillow covers) and a feather bolster. Six table napkins (one had been lost by 1703) and a "board cloath" (a table cloth) were presumably kept in the "little Coffer" in the room. There was also another "little table" and another form. The contents of the room were valued at thirty-one shillings.

The chamber over the house seems to have been used as much as a store room as a bedroom. Although there were "two beds with furniture belonging to them" (valued at twelve shillings), there were also three different saddles – a side saddle, a hackney saddle and a pillion, together valued at two shillings. There was a trunk, which in 1703 was described as an "old trunk", some planks and "shelfe boards" and a "rugg" which was valued at four shillings.

The family's farming, or husbandry as John and Mary are more likely to have called it, was a mixture of growing crops and raising livestock. Much of the corn which they grew on their strips of land in the Newfield was oats, although they also grew some wheat.[55] The inventory which was prepared after John's death was actually taken on 17th October 1690. This cannot have been more than a month or two after the harvest had been gathered in. The barn contained forty thrave,[56] or 960 sheaves, of corn worth two pounds fifteen shillings and oatmeal worth six shillings. Tenants were obliged to have their corn ground in the Eyres' mill at Calver,[57] a privilege for which they no doubt paid handsomely, probably by having to give a proportion of the corn to the lord of the manor. There was also hay worth £3. In contrast the inventory prepared after Mary's death was taken on 6th January 1702/3 in the middle of winter. Not surprisingly there was far less hay and corn in the barn. Much of it had already been used up and its value had diminished to £2. Although neither inventory makes any reference to vegetables, it is likely that Mary grew vegetables, such as cabbages or carrots for the family's own consumption in the garden adjoining the cottage. It is also possible that the family grew a patch of flax to be spun and woven into linen.[58]

During the 1660s John employed at least one farm labourer to help with husbandry. He is referred to in the manorial court records as retrieving one of John's beasts from Edward Vallance's land. On average there were something in the order of one and three quarter farm labourers for every occupier,[59] but it may be that by the 1680s, when John and Mary had three grown-up sons and one daughter living with them, there was no need for them to employ anyone from outside the family to help with farm work. Indeed some of John and Mary's children may well have worked on other farms, either as labourers or in service. There is no other indication that the family employed any more servants, apart from the possibility that Ellen Daud, who was present at Samuel Ashton's death, was "in service". There was certainly no family by that name in Rowland, although it may be that she was a sister of Mary.

Neither of the inventories refers specifically to a plough, although there is a general reference to "husbandry ware and old iron belonging to a cart" worth ten shillings. There must have been a wooden plough, almost certainly with an iron tip,[60] which would have been drawn by a horse and guided by a man walking behind. The days when English ploughs were drawn by oxen had passed,[61] although the field to the right of "The Street", where it joined the lane from Hassop to Longstone, was still called the "Oxpasture".

The inventory prepared in 1690 does not refer to any livestock at all. In 1703 the inventory takers found two calves, a horse and a pig, which, given the time of the year, were probably in the yard near the house or even sheltered in the barn. The calves were worth £1, while the value put on the pig was four shillings. The horse was worth £1 6s 8d. It is likely that there were other animals, probably some sheep and a few cows, grazing in the fields which John and Mary rented, but that the inventory takers ignored anything which was not in or near the house. Most husbandmen's wives also kept a few chickens.[62]

The contents of the buttery give more clues about the kind of farming in which the family engaged and their other activities. Cows were probably milked in the fields around Rowland, but John and Mary's buttery contained various implements connected with dairying and butter making, including a churn, a milking "kitt" (a small wooden tub), three milking "piggens" (pails), two cream stains (earthenware containers)[63] and six barrels. There were also a water "kitt", six wooden "basons", a "dashen" (a vessel used for preparing oatmeal), a washing "kimnell" (a wooden trough), half a dozen "meat piggens" and six "trenchers" (large wooden plates).

The family almost certainly baked their own bread, with flour made from oats, as was the custom in the Peak District.[64] There was probably an oven for baking bread on one side of the fire place. They definitely brewed their own ale in the buttery. The inventory prepared in 1690 refers to "one brewing fatt" (vat). This would have been a flat-bottomed wooden vessel, possibly lined with lead, in which boiled grain (perhaps oats) was left to ferment.[65]

Although no sheep are specifically mentioned in the inventories, the family definitely spun wool and wove their own coarse cloth, perhaps during the long winter evenings. It was normal for women and children to spin and for most weaving to be carried out by men. The inventory prepared in 1690 refers to two spinning wheels ("one wooll wheele, one little wheele") worth two shillings. The larger wheel was almost certainly a "great wheel", with a spindle set in a wooden frame. The spinner turned the wheel with her right hand and, stepping backwards and forwards, drew out the fleece with her left hand. (It has been estimated that in this way, during a week's spinning, a woman could walk the equivalent of thirty-three miles.) The smaller wheel may have been used for spinning flax into linen.[66]

Inside the house, in the parlour, there were "eight cushions with wool and woollen yarne worth four shillings". Both inventories mention looms – "two lombs" in 1690 and four looms in 1703. Mary must have made most of the family's clothes from the yarn which she spun and cloth which the family wove, but the Ashtons would also have sold surplus cloth. This was the usual way in which cloth was made in cottages throughout the English countryside before factory manufacture began to develop a century later. Despite the small scale of spinning and weaving, cloth was still England's most valuable export to the continent.[67] Spinning and weaving may have been less important to John and Mary than husbandry, but their sons John and Samuel Ashton both described themselves as weavers.[68]

Overall this seems typical of the way in which families of this kind survived in the late seventeenth century.[69] Although John described himself as "a husbandman", the family as a unit was pursuing several activities – growing crops, raising livestock, making butter, spinning and weaving and lead mining. They operated as a largely self-sufficient economic unit in which John, Mary and the children, even before adolescence, would all have had their roles. Although heavier farmwork was the responsibility of John and their sons when they grew up, wives of husbandmen normally played an active part in farmwork. Mary probably also grew vegetables in the garden, milked the cows, made butter and fed the poultry.[70] From the age of eight or so onwards, the children would have watched the sheep, gathered wood, weeded crops, scared birds and looked after younger siblings. At harvest time the whole family worked long hours gathering in the crops.[71] As John and Mary ceased to be able to contribute to the income of the family, they were supported by those children who remained in Rowland and who took over their roles.

The family produced almost all the food which they required, and, in good years, were probably able to sell some surplus crops, although, in view of the relatively small acreage which they farmed, they cannot have had much produce to spare. They spun, wove and sewed to make most of their own clothes and linen. Iron ware would have been bought from the village blacksmith who was a member of the Bland family.[72] The family's pewter ware was made no farther away than Chesterfield and may even have been exchanged for ore which they had mined. The wooden utensils in the buttery and furniture in the "house" may have been made by the Ashtons, but it is more likely that there was a village carpenter. They probably bought leatherware such as saddles and shoes from a local cordwainer, perhaps in Bakewell. Coal would also have been bought locally.

The climate in the hills of the Peak District meant that life could be hard, particularly during the long winters, and the family presumably worried from time to time about the effect that serious illness would have, but the risk of having to rely on parish relief or even of starvation was never too close. It is impossible to say whether or not life was easier or more agreeable than that of later generations during and after the Industrial Revolution, with widespread migration to towns and the introduction of factories. It is also hard to know whether or not the Ashtons considered that their economic position and social standing improved during John and Mary's generation. Although they enlarged and rebuilt their cottage, John continued to describe himself as a "husbandman", a term which not only depicted the way in which he made his living, but which was also used to describe the rank of small to middling farmers. He did not aspire to call himself a "yeoman", the next rung up the social ladder.

John and Mary, who had lived through the Civil Wars, the Commonwealth and the Restoration, were to survive one more dramatic change of ruler – the invasion of William of Orange and the establishment of William and Mary, James's eldest daughter, as King and Queen. At the same time the passing of the Bill of Rights ensured that extra-Parliamentary taxation became illegal; parliaments had to be called every three years and the power to keep an army in peace time had to be approved annually. William and Mary's supporters, and history, referred to this as the "Glorious Revolution" of 1688, but it is likely that John and Mary's sympathies, if they had any, lay with the outgoing Stuarts, and in particular with the deposed James II whose open adherence to the Catholic faith had been the basic cause which had provoked the rebellion. John, whose father had fought for Charles II and who had only recently renounced Catholicism in the face of the threat of prosecution, is hardly likely to have welcomed the accession of the strongly protestant Dutchman.

John died in September 1690 at the age of 52 and was buried on 19th September at the parish church in Great Longstone, the first adult in his immediate family to have been buried with an authorised funeral service since the Reformation. He did not leave a will, but his widow Mary and John Sellars, a husbandman who lived in Great Longstone, took out letters of administration in Bakewell on 17th October 1690. When the inventory of his worldly possessions was prepared after his death, they were valued at fifteen pounds ten shillings.

The basis for the distribution of John's property after his death is not entirely clear. As he died intestate, the 1670 Statute of Distributions ought to have meant that one third of his estate went to his widow Mary and that the remaining two thirds went to his eldest son John.[73] However a comparison between the inventories prepared following John and Mary's deaths, suggests that Mary inherited about two-thirds of John's property. Most of the items listed in the inventory of John's belongings appear in the inventory of Mary's belongings, apart from some of the implements in the buttery, some kitchen ware, the saddles, some linen and two beds.

*Fig. 4 – St Giles's Church, Great Longstone.*

Mary and four of her children, John, Robert, Samuel and Sarah continued to run the farm. Her elder daughter, Mary, had married and moved away. Her first husband was George Knisson who had grown up in Longstone. They were married on 18th May 1682 at Bakewell when he was 33. They had at least one child called Ellen. After his death, she married Richard Lent of Edensor on the Earl of Devonshire's estate. She had at least two further children, John and Elizabeth who were born in 1697 and 1700.

One of the first measures introduced by William and Mary had been the abolition of hearth tax. This was principally an attempt to gain popularity. However they still needed to raise revenue, particularly in view of the large military expenditure incurred in the Nine Years War (1688–97) against France. In 1693 Parliament approved a tax of four shillings in the pound on all incomes for one year.[74] The most significant element of the new tax was the taxation of rents received by landowners, which came to be known as land tax. 20 per cent of rents was to be deducted by tenants before payment to their landlord, and paid instead, via parish collectors, to local commissioners. The assessments made for payment were to form the basis on which land tax was to be levied until its final abolition in the twentieth century.

Although high constables were legally responsible for assessments of liability to pay the new tax, in practice they delegated their obligations. In Rowland, the assessment was carried out on 12th March 1693/4 by Francis Brightmore and Adam Jepson.[75] They both lived in Rowland and rented land from Rowland Eyre. They described the tax as "a grant to their majesties . . . for carrying on the vigorous warr agst ffrance." Each tenant was to pay the tax by equal quarterly instalments. Mary Ashton was assessed as being liable to pay four instalments of four shillings, implying that her annual rent was £4. Her brother-in-law Francis Ashton was assessed to pay quarterly instalments of one shilling and nine pence, implying that his annual rent was thirty-five shillings.

The total annual amount of tax which was to be levied in Rowland according to the 1693 Act, excluding taxation of tithes and the mineral duties known as lot and cope, was slightly less than twelve pounds. This would seem to imply that the total annual rents paid to Rowland Eyre by tenants in the hamlet were slightly less than sixty pounds, a considerable increase on the sum of £26 10s which the tenants claimed to pay to his grandfather when the Commissioners to the Sequestration Committee surveyed the hamlet in 1652.[76] However direct comparisons between rent paid by individual tenants in 1652 and 1693 are difficult because nine new tenants had replaced five of the 1652 tenants and the land tax assessments do not give details of the number of acres rented by each tenant. It seems that most of the increases in rent were borne by the new tenants, while old established tenants, like the Ashtons, were paying little, if anything, more. (It is impossible to ascertain whether the thirty-five shillings paid by Francis Ashton was for land which originally formed part of Thomas and Joane Ashton's holding, and was accordingly the amount of the increase in rent paid by the Ashtons, or whether it was additional land which he was farming, in which case, there had been no increase in Mary's rent compared with that paid by Thomas and Joane.)

The rent which Mary Ashton paid in 1693 was slightly more than the average paid by the villagers, although, in view of the apparent differentials in rent, this is probably not a true indication of the relative size of the land which she rented. James Gooddey (£14), Thomas Hudson (£8) and John Street (£5 10s) paid more. Anthony Mosley and James Bagshaw also paid four pounds. Ten other tenants (including Francis Ashton) paid less.

An indication that Mary became infirm in her later years is given by her will, which not only uses the standard description of the testator as "being weak in body but of sound and perfect memory" but adds that she was "infirm". It is perhaps also significant that in the manorial court records which survive for the years 1700 to 1702, there is no reference to Mary taking an active part in running the farm. The only references are to her sons.[77]

Mary died on 28th December 1702 and was buried the next day at the church in Longstone, probably alongside John, although there are now no signs of the graves of either of them. Mary's will, which she had made in September 1702 was written out by John Bland, and witnessed by him, Mary's brother-in-law Francis Ashton and John Sellers. Using words which were common to most wills of the time, she stated:

First I commit my soul into the hands of Almighty God my Creator, assuredly believing that I shall receive full pardon and free remission of my sins and to be saved by the precious death and meritts of my blessed Saviour and Redeemer Christ Jesus: next my body to be buried in the earth in such Christian and Decent manner as my Executors hereafter named shall think Convenient: And touching such Worldly Estate as the Lord in mercy hath lent mee in this Life, my will and meaning is [it] shall be imployed and bestowed as hereafter by this my last will and testament is expressed.

She then went on to make specific bequests. She left "one ffeather bed, one chest and two pewter dishes" to her son Samuel with instructions to her executors that they were to be delivered to him within a year after her death. She left five shillings to her son Robert. She left her "gown and petticoate" to her daughter Mary. There is no reference to any other personal clothing in her will. She left to her daughter Sarah "one feather bed with bed stockes and cloaths belonging to it now standing in the Chamber and one cheast standing in the parlour and two pewter dishes", together with "one cow called the young black cow". The household goods were to be delivered to Sarah within a year, but her executors were given two years during which they could keep the "young black cow" before handing it over to Sarah. The delay would enable the cow to be served, so that it would not only be

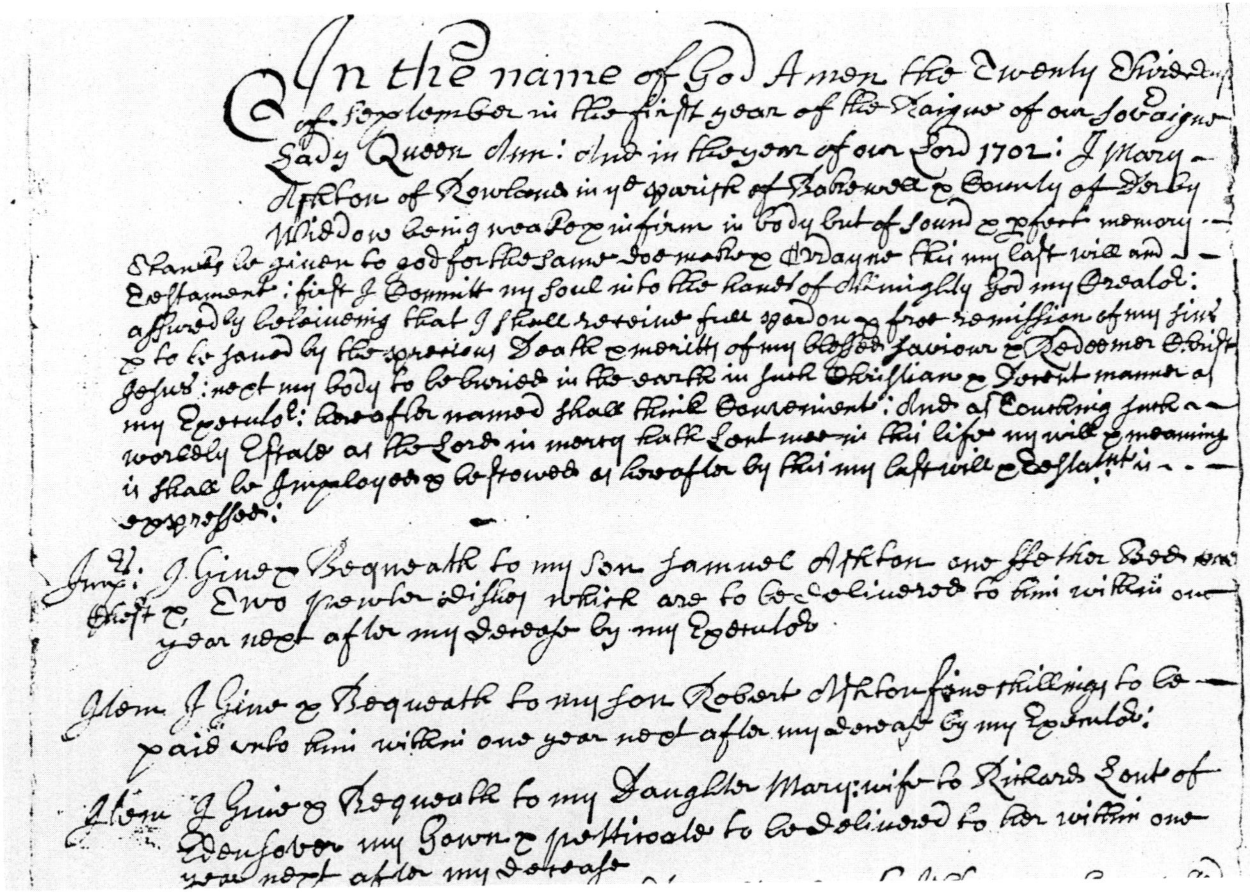

*Fig. 5 – Extract of Mary Ashton's will (1703).*

producing milk by the time that it was delivered, but also that Sarah's brother John would be able to keep the calf which it was hoped would be born. However, if the executors failed to hand over the cow, they were to pay Sarah £5, a sum well in excess of its value. The residue of Mary's estate was left to her eldest son, John, who was made executor.

The bequests were typical of the division of property provided for in contemporary wills made by people of Mary's social standing in the Peak District. The norm was male primogeniture. This applied not only to personal property but also to tenancies.[78] The aim was that neither land nor belongings should be split up to such an extent that holdings became too small to support families satisfactorily. This left a greater onus on younger sons to make their own way in life and upon daughters to marry. The bequests to Robert and Samuel were relatively insignificant. They would however continue within the family economic unit until they married and so would benefit indirectly from the bequest to John.

The bequest to Sarah, who would have been in her early twenties, was designed to help her to marry. It was still normal, even among small farmers, for parents to give dowries or "portions" on their daughters' marriage. During times when the mercenary element involved in choosing spouses was often significant, the size of a daughter's dowry could determine how attractive she was to potential suitors.[79] In fact Sarah married Francis Hodgkinson in November 1706 at Hathersage. He was a younger son of Francis Hodgkinson senior and the brother of the children who were fined by the manorial court in 1667 for "making a rescue". The Ashton and Hodgkinson families had already been close before the marriage – Francis Hodgkinson was one of the men who witnessed the inventory prepared after John Ashton's death.

Her other daughter Mary had probably been given a dowry when she first married in 1682 and so Mary felt no need to leave her anything more than her gown and petticoat. The gift of a shilling to her granddaughter Ellen shows that even after marrying and moving to Edensor, Mary probably continued to visit the family in Rowland.

An inventory was prepared on 6th January, a week after Mary's death, by John Bland and Francis Ashton. Her "goods, cattle and chattels" were valued at ten pounds eight shillings and eight pence.

## Notes

1. Not surprisingly there are no relevant Jesuit records. See Historical Manuscript Commission, Appendix to Second Report (pp 143–8) and Appendix to Third Report (pp 334–41). (Records at Stonyhurst.)
2. See Herlan, McCallum, Doolittle and Cook on the age of children at baptism in *Population Studies from Parish Registers*, edited by Michael Drake.
3. In the eighteenth century those of Eyre's tenants who held twenty-one year leases were obliged to give heriots, whereas those who were tenants at will do not seem to have been obliged to do so – Derbyshire RO (Matlock), Registration and Enrolment of Papists' Estates, eg Rowland Eyre, 1749. For details of heriots received by Henry Aldrich, rector of Darley Dale in 1706 in respect of church lands, see J C Cox, *Derbyshire Churches*, Vol 2, p 174.
4. Richard Lodge, *Political History of England*, Vol 3, p 15.
5. Nottinghamshire Archive Office, DD 3P 2/2.
6. For information about collection of hearth tax in Derbyshire, see David G Edwards, *Derbyshire Hearth Tax Assessments 1662–70*.
7. PRO E179/94/378 and E179/245/7.
8. Edwards, *Derbyshire Hearth Tax Assessments*, p xvii.
9. Cox Vol 2, p 124.
10. Stone, pp 42–44, Houlbrook p 63.
11. Lawrence Stone, *The Family, Sex and Marriage in England 1500–1800* (Abridged Edition) p 31; Ralph Houlbrooke, *The English Family 1450–1700*, p 86; Bossy, *The English Catholic Community*, p 137.

12. See eg Mildred Campbell, *The English Yeoman*, pp 303–4 and Henry Best's *Farming and Account Books*, pp 116–7.
13. Although the Parish Registers seem to indicate that the surname was Aston, the Bishop's Transcripts clearly show the surname as Ashton.
14. John, Samuel, Robert, Mary and Sarah were all beneficiaries under Mary's will.
15. DC 9955. The earlier description is taken from the 1652 survey. Details of the rooms are taken from the inventories prepared after John and Mary's deaths – see below. The current owners of the house believe that it was built in 1667.
16. Quoted in R J Brown, *The English Country Cottage*, p 49.
17. See generally Sidney and Beatrice Webb, *English Local Government from the Revolution to the Corporation Act*, Part I, pp 1–126.
18. *English Local Government*, Part 1, p 27.
19. William Blackstone, *Commentaries on the Laws of England*, 1st edition, 1765, vol I p 356, vol III p 33; Francis Bacon, *The Answers to Questions Touching the Office of Constable (1608)* in Spedding, Bacon's Works, Vol VII, p 749 and p 750; Hone, *The Manor and Manorial Records*, pp 21–2, 72 and 140; and, Levett, *Studies in Manorial History*, p 134.
20. cf EP Thompson, *Whigs and Hunters* p 262.
21. Derbyshire RO (Matlock), D 598M/M1.
22. Hone, *The Manor and Manorial Records*, p 72.
23. Pilkington, *View of the Present State of Derbyshire*, 1789, Vol 1. See too T D Ford and J H Rieuwerts, *Lead Mining in the Peak District*, p 15, and Nellie Kirkham, "Longstone Edge Mines and Soughs", (1966) Vol 5 *Cave Science* 354–68 and 440–69.
24. PRO E101/280/18. In view of the large number of unnamed miners the total of 20,000 may well be an exaggeration, but the names of miners and the numbers in their families give the impression of being accurately recorded.
25. Lambeth Palace Library, Shrewsbury Papers, COMM xii a 2 2. The jurisdiction of Bakewell seems to have been the area of the old parish of Bakewell, probably including the liberties of Ashford and Hassop, Rowland and Calver.
26. Derbyshire RO (Matlock) 598M/M4 and Wager Holmes, Sheffield RO. Although John Ashton attended the barmoot court held on 2nd October 1667 at Hassop, he is not mentioned in the minutes of that hearing. Nor is he recorded in a list of miners taken at the barmoot court hearing of 10th April 1667 held at Calver, or its minutes (598 M/M2 and M3).
27. Bossy, *The English Catholic Community*, p 84.
28. The "Compton Census" of 1676, quoted in J C Cox, *Three Centuries of Derbyshire Annals*, pp 291–5.
29. Bossy, p 84.
30. See the presentment of Catholics in 1682. Although the Longstone registers are hard to decipher during some of this period there do not appear to be any baptism, marriage or burial entries for the Brightmore family.
31. Bossy p 110.
32. An Act "to retain her Majesty's subjects in their true obedience". A G Dickens, *The English Reformation*, pp 414–6; S T Bindoff, *Tudor England*, pp 238–9.
33. Meredith, *A Derbyshire Family in the Seventeenth Century*, pp 52, 55 and 64.
34. Bossy p 128.
35. Meredith, *A Derbyshire Family in the Seventeenth Century*, p 64.
36. He died in 1687 aged 79.
37. See eg ASSI 80/13. Cox, *Three Centuries of Derbyshire Records*, p 285.
38. Derbyshire RO (Matlock), Q/Dissent 3. Although the list of recusants is quoted in Cox, *Three Centuries of Derbyshire Annals*, p 302, his transcript is inaccurate in that it states that Francis Ashton was among those presented, when, in fact, the original refers to "Jana Ashton ux Fransisci Ashton". There are no references to Ashtons in the Papists Returns of 1680, 1705/6 or 1767 (House of Lords Record Office) but these returns only list very small numbers of Catholics.
39. Glover, *History of the County of Derby*, 1829, Vol 2, p 608.
40. *The Journeys of Celia Fiennes*, 1947 edition, p 101.
41. *A Tour Through the Whole Island of Great Britain* (Penguin Classics) p 457.
42. Meredith, *The Eyres of Hassop*, p 13.
43. Moll, *New Description of England 1724*, p 202.
44. The population of Rowland in 1981 was 45.
45. A "gentleman" was someone above the rank of yeoman who did not engage in manual work.

46. Bond, *A Handy Book for Verifying Dates*, p 567; Cheney, *Handbook of Dates*, p 102.

47. Quotations from Sheffield Library, Bagshaw Collection, 3363/10. See too Add Ms 24477 π64 and PRO PROB 11.396. Wills could be made orally until the passing of the Wills Act 1837, although the Statute of Frauds 1677 provided that three witnesses were needed. IGI checks of the names Daud, Dawd, Dowd and similar variations have revealed no entries in Derbyshire. Similarly there is no Derbyshire reference to an Ellen Dodd. Who she was remains a mystery.

48. The paper does not survive, but John's mark appears in manorial court records and Mary's on her own will.

49. Lichfield JRO – John Ashton 1690, Mary Ashton 1703. In general details are taken from the inventory attached to John Ashton's letters of administration which are fuller.

50. See J V Nef, "The Rise of the British Coal Industry", p 56, *Victoria County History of Derbyshire*, vol 2, p 352. See too reference in Wright, Longstone Records, p 323 quoting from the Longstone Overseers' accounts. cf Hoskins, *The Midland Peasant*, p 206 (coal stock in Wigston, Leics started in 1595).

51. cf Cole and Postgate, *The Common People 1746–1946*, p 78, but also see the Accounts of the Master of the Workhouse at Great Longstone for 1 May 1739 to 9 August 1741 quoted in R Thornhill, Further Longstone Records, pp 4–10 which show the purchase of relatively large quantities of meat – eg 30 lbs of beef at 1¾d per lb and a shoulder of mutton and calf's pluck at 1s 8d.

52. cf John Farey, *A General View of the Agriculture of Derbyshire*, 1815, Vol 2, pp 15, 20.

53. David Kiernan, *The Derbyshire Lead Industry in the Sixteenth Century*, pp 90–91.

54. Peter Laslett, *The Times We Have Lost*, p 132. Hoskins, in *The Midland Peasant*, refers to parlours invariably being used as sleeping accommodation and to the transition to sleeping upstairs not taking place until the mid-18th century (pp 285–7 and 309).

55. See reference in manorial court records, 1702, Sheffield City Library, Bagshaw Collection, 344. cf *Victoria County History*, vol 2, p 181.

56. A thrave was twenty-four sheaves of corn. Best (pp 51–2) referred to oats being harvested in late August/early September.

57. Bagshaw Collection 344 (reference in manorial court records for May 1736 to obligation to grind corn in Eyre's mill) and 359(7). See too Sheffield Library, Wager-Holmes 39 (lease in 1815, Francis Eyre to William Kitchen of a parcel of land in Calver whereon a water corn mill was lately standing with sluice and dams). Water driven mills were still used to grind corn until the early twentieth century – see Fred Kitchen, *Brother to the Ox*, p 69.

58. See Reay Tannahill, *Food in History*, p 246; Hone, pp 85–6; Ivy Pinchbeck, *Women Workers and the Industrial Revolution*, p 134; Alice Clark, *Women in the Seventeenth Century*, p 57.

59. Laslett, pp 12–14, 64–5 and Chambers and Mingay, p 18, apparently based on Gregory King's figures in the early eighteenth century. Later Arthur Young calculated that there was on average one hired hand for every forty acres. In 1676, in Goodnestone-Next-Wingham, Kent, twenty-three out of twenty-six yeomen and husbandmen had servants.

60. Hone p 81.

61. cf Best, "we yoked fower oxen in a waine" (p 69), "oxe plough" (p 133) and "a payre of oxen" (p 137).

62. See reference in 1705 manorial court records to Francis Ashton's sheep. From the number of pound breaches recorded in the manorial court records it seems that most tenants had a number of animals. The four looms referred to in the inventory also suggest that the Ashtons may have kept sheep themselves. See too reference to dairying equipment below. As to pigs, see Chambers and Mingay, p 16.

63. Jean Radford of the Local Studies Library, Matlock, says that the term "stain" was in use in the county until the early 1950s in relation to bread. A "bread stain" was an earthenware container for bread with a lid.

64. H Moll, *A New Description of England*, 1724, p 200. T S Ashton suggests that Dr Johnson's celebrated designation of oats as "a grain which in England is generally given to horses, but in Scotland supports the people" was only partially true, for the dietetic boundary was the Trent, not the Tweed. (Economic History of England, *The Eighteenth Century*, p 30.)

65. Kiernan, p 89. For the making of beer with oats, see Moll, p 200.

66. Patricia Baines, *Spinning Wheels, Spinners and Spinning*, pp 42–4 and 56–65; Pinchbeck, pp 121, 129–30; and Clark pp 93–137 and 145–49.

67. See B R Mitchell, *British Historical Statistics*, 1988, pp 325–31.

68. See will of John Ashton (1753) and Samuel Ashton's settlement certificate.

69. cf Hoskins, *The Midland Peasant*, pp 185–94, 200; and David Levine, *Reproducing Families*, especially p 19.

70. cf a North Country farmer writing in *Farmer's Magazine* in 1801 quoted in Pinchbeck referring to small occupiers' "necessity of turning out his wife or daughter to drive the plough in the depth of winter". (p 9), Clark pp 43–64.

71. See eg Houlbrooke, pp 106–7, 153.

72. See references to "a Smithie . . . adjoyning" Rowland Bland's cottage (Bagshaw Collection 359(7) – 1652) and to "a Smithy in possession of Rowland Bland tenant at will at the yearly rent of 2s 6d." (Registration and Enrolment of Papists' Estates, 1717 (Rowland Eyre)).

73. 22 and 23 Charles II c10.

74. See generally W R Ward, *The English Land Tax in the Eighteenth Century*.

75. Sheffield, Bagshaw Collection 353.

76. See page 13.

77. See Chapter 3, pages 40–43.

78. Peter Furness, The Family of Eyre of Hassop, *The Reliquary*, 1870, vol 10, pp 232–6.

79. Houlbrooke pp 84–5.

# 3

At the time of her death, four of Mary's children, John, Robert, Samuel and Sarah were still living in Rowland. For a couple of years all four of them continued to share the farmwork and to weave and spin in much the same way as they had done before their mother's death. However the land which the Ashtons rented was too small to support all of them once they married and had children of their own and in 1705 Samuel decided to move to nearby Hathersage.

This was not however a simple matter because of the reluctance of overseers of the poor to allow strangers from other places to become settled in their villages. Queen Elizabeth's last Poor Law of 1598 provided that overseers in each village should raise a poor rate from occupiers of all land so that they could provide poor relief for those in need.[1] This responsibility only arose if poor people were "settled" in the village in question. "Settlement" could only be acquired in a limited number of ways, for example, by renting land or by being formally apprenticed. An Act of 1662 provided that justices of the peace could remove any stranger trying to settle in a village unless he rented a tenement with a yearly value of £10 or provided a security to discharge any expenses which the parish might incur in supporting him. Throughout the second half of the seventeenth century and during the eighteenth century overseers were concerned to ensure that people from other places did not become settled in their villages. Whenever possible they tried to shift responsibility to the overseers in other parishes. This meant that it was almost impossible to move from village to village and so an Act of 1696/7 empowered poor people to enter any village if they brought with them from their parish of settlement a certificate guaranteeing that they would be received back in their old village if they proved to be a charge on the resources of their new parish.

Before setting out to travel the five miles to Hathersage, Samuel obtained a certificate confirming his settlement from Anthony Barton, the overseer of the poor in Rowland. It was addressed to the Overseers of the Poor and Churchwardens in Hathersage and stated:

Whereas Samuel Ashton of Rowland in the parish of Bakewell & County of Derby, Weaver, is Desirous for a Better way of Liveing to remove himself from Rowland aforesaid to ye Towne of Hathersedge with an intent there to inhabitt but haveing not Qualified himselfe as the Law requires: I doe therefore being the present Overseer of the Poor of Rowland aforesaid hereby Certefie you the said Churchwardens and Overseers of the poor of Hathersedge that we do owne & acknowledge the said Samuel Ashton to be an Inhabitant lawfully settled in our said Towne of Rowland & that I and my successors will at any time when he shall become Chargeable to ye said Towne of Hathersedge Remove him back into our Town of Rowland unless in the meanetyme hee hath acquired some other place of settlement. In witness whereof I have hereunto put my hand & seale this 25th day of June Anno Dom 1705.[2]

The certificate bore Anthony Barton's mark, a "B", and was witnessed by Samuel's brother John Ashton and John Sellers who were both able to write their own names. The certificate was approved by two justices of the peace.

There are no indications as to why Samuel decided to move to Hathersage, or how he intended to better himself. It may be that he wanted to move to Hathersage because he intended to marry a woman called Sarah Slinne. On the other hand there may have been better prospects of work in Hathersage and he and Sarah Slinne may only have become acquainted after he had started living there. In any event Samuel Ashton married her on 3rd October 1706. They had nine daughters and three sons who were all baptised in Hathersage. Samuel was buried on 7th December 1761 when he must have been well into his seventies, if not older.

His sister, Sarah, was married in Hathersage on 9th November 1706. She did not obtain a settlement certificate, almost certainly because she would automatically acquire the settlement of her husband, Francis Hodgkinson.[3] Sarah was buried in Hathersage on 30th January 1750/1.

John and Robert, Mary's other two sons, stayed in Rowland. They had both married before her death, although since no references to their marriages appear in any local parish registers[4] it is impossible to ascertain either the dates of their marriages or the full names of their wives. The parish registers which record the baptisms of Robert's children do not even provide any clues as to his wife's Christian name, because they merely refer to their children as the sons or daughters of Robert Ashton, without mentioning the existence of his wife – confirmation of the way in which contemporary society viewed the relative importance of men and women. He had married in 1697 or 1698. His wife bore nine children between the years of 1699 and 1723. Taking into account the number of children that she bore and the dates of their baptisms, Robert's wife must have been relatively young when she married, probably just under twenty. The children were called John, Henry, Samuel, Samuel, Ellena, Robert, Mary, Elizabeth and Mary. The elder Samuel died in 1706/7 aged just over two. The elder Mary died in 1716/7 aged about sixteen months.

John had married sometime around 1700. His wife was called Ellen and she had one daughter, Elizabeth, who was baptised on 10th March 1701/2, but who died in 1708 when she was six. Ellen died in June 1705 and John remarried on 8th February 1709/10. His second wife was Alice Wragg who came from the nearby village of Ashford. She had seven children, John, Samuel, Robert, Sarah, Anne, Alice and Charity.

The norm among the Eyres' tenants was for eldest sons to inherit tenancies[5] and, after his mother's death, John took over the cottage where his parents had lived. More importantly, he also took over the tenancy of all of the land which his parents had farmed. A survey of Rowland Eyre's estate made in 1717 referred to John Ashton having a twenty-one year lease. His annual rent for the farm was £5 2s 6d.[6] It is very likely that, in order to acquire the tenancy, he was obliged to give the lord of the manor a heriot, in the form of the best beast which he possessed. (Some of the Eyre tenants, as a term of their leases, were also bound to keep spaniels or other "hounds", presumably for use when the lord of the manor went hunting, but none of the Ashtons' leases seems to have included that kind of obligation.)

By 1717 Robert was renting a cottage from Rowland Eyre at an annual rent of one shilling. Later he also acquired a lease of a small amount of land, either by agreement with John, or, by taking over land vacated by another tenant. There are references in the manorial court records for 1720 and 1737 to Robert renting a field in the Rowland Newfield on the south side of the lane from Hassop to Great Longstone. The manorial court records for 1740 and 1741 also refer to "Robert Ashton's croft" and to it being next to John's croft. A survey of Rowland Eyre's land in 1749 referred to Robert renting a small "farm or tenement" for which he paid £1 10s per annum as a tenant at will.[7]

Robert found himself facing the problems which befell most younger sons as a result of the prevailing practice of male primogeniture – the need to find a way of supporting themselves and their immediate families without being able to rent sufficient land. Although Robert's uncle Francis Ashton died sometime after 1705,[8] this did not help because his own son, also called Francis, continued living in his father's cottage and farming the land which his father had rented. By 1717 his cousin Francis Ashton was paying slightly over £5 a year for the "messuage and lands" in his possession.[9]

Even taking into account the fact that Robert probably helped his brother on his farm, particularly during harvest time, and the small amount of land which he later rented himself, it was clear that he would not be able to support his family by farming alone. Perhaps because of this Robert became more actively involved in lead mining than other members of the family. Although his father had been listed as a miner in 1667 and as a juror at the barmoot court in 1668, his participation in lead mining seems to have been subsidiary to husbandry. The same was almost certainly true of Robert's brother John, even though the manorial court records for 12th October 1736 state:

> "We lay a paine that John Ashton remove his Dirt Leade in Rowland Towne Gate betwixt now and ye 20th of this instant or forfitt" three shillings and four pence.

Robert probably started off as a working miner with little capital, looking for veins containing galena or lead sulphide. When a suitable vein was found he entered into partnership with one or two other miners or paid one or two men to help dig pits and shafts to extract the ore. Most of the digging was done with shovels and picks, although in the seventeenth century, miners sometimes lit fires underground so that the heat would crack the veins and loosen them from the surrounding limestone. This practice of fire-setting was potentially dangerous since smoke could suffocate men working in neighbouring mines, and so the barmoot courts which regulated lead mining generally prohibited the lighting of fires underground before four o'clock in the afternoon and even then required "lawful warning" to be given to "adjoining neighbours".[10] Towards the end of the seventeenth century Derbyshire miners started to use gun powder, but during the first half of the eighteenth century it was still used only rarely.

The ore which was extracted was processed in dressing areas, often by women and children, who broke and crushed the rock using hammers and then sieved and washed (or buddled) it to remove the ore. The ore was then smelted in a stone hearth with bellows driven by a water-wheel. These smelting mills looked like blacksmiths' hearths, with hoods and chimneys to draw off the poisonous fumes. Molten lead flowed down a narrow channel from the hearth into a basin or "sumpter pot". Mining technology developed during the eighteenth century, with the use of steam engines and more sophisticated furnaces, such as the Low Arched Reverbatory Furnace or Cupola in which flames from burning coal were drawn over the ore by a draught induced by a tall chimney. The introduction of the cupola into the Peak District in 1735 meant that it was possible to exploit lower grade ore, and it may be that as a result the Ashtons also collected waste from earlier workings to buddle – that would explain why John Ashton had a pile of "Dirt Leade in Rowland Towne Gate" in 1736.

There are no records which state specifically which veins or "rakes" Robert Ashton mined. However it is very likely that he was involved in mining lead from Ashton's Vein,[11] one of several deposits high up on Longstone Edge to the north of Rowland. The old workings along this vein are now marked by an irregular line of mounds and depressions heading in a north north-westerly direction down the shoulder of land between the summit of Longstone Edge and the southern side of the deep valley of Coombs Dale. There are fourteen mounds, most with hollows in the middle where the shafts which have now collapsed would have been. In the eighteenth century many shafts descended to a depth of thirty to fifty feet, although some were two hundred feet deep.

Years later, in 1765, Robert's son Robert "and his grove partners" were working a mine called "Cuckold's Venture" on the Oxpasture, to the south west of Rowland near to the Hassop to Longstone lane. It is possible that this area was also mined by the older Robert.[12]

Miners were free to prospect for lead on land which they did not own or rent and, if lead was found, landowners were unable to prevent its extraction. The only exceptions were churchyards, orchards, gardens and highways where miners were not allowed to dig. The miners' interests were protected by clearly defined procedures administered by the barmaster, who was appointed by the lord of the liberty, and by the barmoot courts which he summoned. The courts were presided over by the lord's steward. The barmaster was responsible for "freeing" all newly discovered veins. This process involved the miner registering the vein with the barmaster who received a "freeing dish" of about sixty pounds of the first ore mined.[13] The miner who had discovered the vein was entitled to work it over a length of two meers, a measurement which varied from place to place. In the Hassop, Rowland and Calver liberties a meer was twenty-seven yards.[14] In other places it was generally in the region of twenty-eight to thirty-two yards in length. After the first two meers, the next meer belonged to the lord of the field. Miners could either purchase the third meer, or work through it, in which case they could not sell any ore mined, since it belonged to the lord. The remaining meers in the vein could be taken up by them or any other miners and were known as "taker meers". If miners stopped working a mine for three weeks it could be "nicked" and freed again by other miners wishing to work it.

Even after veins were freed, the barmaster retained a supervisory role. For example the Hassop, Rowland and Calver articles required him to "go every week once or twice overe the Lord's field, thro' the Rakes or Mynes in his whole lordship & when he finds any of these articles broken & not kept he shall endeavour himself to inquire thereof & present the offenders at the next Court Barmoot from time to time."[15]

Barmasters also collected the mineral duties known as "lot" and "cope". Lot was a fixed proportion of all the ore mined which the miners paid to the barmaster on behalf of the lord of the field, or, in the King's field, on behalf of the Crown. In the liberties of Ashford and Hassop, Rowland and Calver, lot was originally every tenth dish. In other places it was usually the thirteenth, although the whole duty was not always taken. In return the miners claimed that they were entitled to take "grove timber" from the lord's wastes for use in smelting. Cope was a duty paid by ore buyers on every load of ore sold. The amount paid varied, depending on the liberty. Notionally it was paid for the right not to have to have ore smelted at the lord's own smelting mill. In the liberties of Ashford and Hassop, Rowland and Calver it was calculated at the rate of six pence on every load of ore sold.[16]

The barmoot courts controlled by the lord through his steward and the barmaster performed very similar functions to the manorial courts. They prescribed and modified the laws and customs which governed the lead miners and ore purchasers and settled disputes between miners themselves and miners and others. Daniel Defoe after travelling through the Peak District, which he described as "this wonderful place", wrote in the 1720s that the barmoot courts might "be called the greatest of all the wonders of the Peak." He thought it "very remarkable" that the courts managed to keep the peace amongst the miners, who were "of a strange, turbulent, quarrelsome temper, and very hard to be reconciled to one another in their subterraneous affairs." He described them as "subterranean wretches" and the inhabitants of nearby Wirksworth as "a rude boorish kind of people".[17]

In the Hassop, Rowland and Calver liberty, the barmaster was to hold "two Great Courts or Barmoots every year on or about the Feasts of Easter & Saint Michael the Archangel [and] every three weeks a small court if need require".[18] The Great Court sat with twenty-four miners as jurors, while the small court seems to have been made up of twelve "special" jurors. The extent of their control over mining and mineral rights is demonstrated by paragraph 16 of the Hassop, Rowland and Calver Articles made in 1664 which stated:

> If it happen that any myner be damped, murthered [ie murdered] or slain in any Grove [ie mine], neither Escheator, Coroner nor any other Officer shall meddle with, but only the Barmaster or his Deputy.[19]

Other paragraphs in the articles dealt with the conduct of miners, ore purchasers and the barmaster, and prescribed fines for breaches of the regulations.

Few records of the barmoot courts for the liberties of Hassop, Rowland and Calver or Ashford survive for the first half of the eighteenth century, and so little is known about Robert's activities. However there are records for the 1750s and 1760s which refer to his sons Robert and Samuel Ashton, and which show not only the way in which the courts worked, but also the kind of disputes in which Robert himself must have been involved.

The younger Robert twice brought disputes arising out of lead mining to court. The hearing of the first case was preceded by a request from Robert Ashton to Mr George Heyward, the barmaster of Ashford, stating

> You are desired to arreaast [ie arrest] a Mine upon Seedlow Rake in the liberty of Ashford, all the Tools Meterials Possessions and Mears of Ground Thereunto belonging, The property of the late Thomas Buxton of Wardlow or any person or persons Clameing by from or under him at the suit of me Robert Ashton of Rowland in an Action of Debt to the Sum of two pounds seventeen shillings and eight pence.

Seedlow Rake was a vein of lead which crossed the hills between Rowland and Wardlow. The request to "arrest" the mine was a procedure designed to ensure that the Defendant would "be bound in sufficient Bond and sureties", not only to guarantee that he attended at the court hearing, but also to make sure that there were assets against which any verdict or judgment could be levied.[20]

Robert's claim was heard at the "Small Barmoot Court of the Most noble William Duke of Devonshire holden at Ashford in and for the Liberty aforesaid" on 24th March 1760. A Bill summarising his complaint was prepared and Mark Buxton, a relative of the Defendant appeared, pleading that he owed nothing. Robert was sworn in before the twelve jurors and probably asked: "Is the money for which this Bill is preferred due? Have you demanded it? And have you given lawful Notice of preferring this Bill?"[21]

Robert gave evidence that the particulars contained in the Bill were true. It seems that he claimed that he was owed money for goods supplied to the mine. The total value of them was £3 5s 5³/₄d, but out of that sum 7s 9³/₄d was due to the account of Thomas Hunt. Thomas Hunt, who was in court to give evidence for Robert initially refused to take the oath, but eventually, agreed to be sworn in. Then he said that "he remember that 3£ of candles were delivered by [the Plaintiff] to [the said] Mine." For the Defendant Christopher Howe said "that ab[out] a ffortnight ago he was sent by [the Defendant] to [the Plaintiff] for a Bill of his demands which he refused to give."

The evidence given by Howe was clearly believed by the jurors, and they dismissed Robert's claim with costs awarded against him, apparently on the technicality that he had not given notice that he was preferring the Bill.[22] The "costs" included the amount needed to provide the jurors with dinner! The Bill is endorsed with the words "Verdict for the [Defendant]. Costs 2d + 4d for 12 Men's Dinner".[23]

Five years later, Robert was more successful. He and his "groove fellows" (or mining partners) claimed against William Masden and his partners "for not coming in and keeping company with us at a Groove called Cuckold's Venter" [i.e. venture]. Robert Ashton's claim was that the Defendants had not paid their agreed share of expenses at the mine. The twenty-four jurors of the Great Barmoot Court for the Ashford Liberty held on 23rd April 1765 found the claim proved. They stated:

We do order and say that William Masden or any person or persons claiming under him or them shall pay to Robert Ashton the sum of eight pounds eight shillings and ten pence three farthings due for him or them to pay at a mine called Cuckolds Venter in the Ox Pasture in the Liberty of this Court within ten days next after notice given by the Barmaster thereof or forfeit all his or their shares of mines within the liberty and jurisdiction of this Court.[24]

The minutes of the "Great Barmoot Court" held at Ashford on 28th April 1757, referring to a case brought against Samuel Ashton state:

We do order and say that Mr Samuel Ashton and the rest of his partners shall pay to William Dakin the sum of one pound one shilling and one shilling and fourpence, the charges of the Bill, due for them to pay at [a] mine called Glead Rake within ten days next after notice given by the Barmaster or forfit all their parts or shares of mines within the Liberty and Jurisdiction of this Court.[25]

These court cases show that the younger Robert and Samuel were not only involved directly in mining, but that they also had wider interests. They supplied goods to miners. Their families probably made the candles referred to in the case involving Thomas Buxton with tallow from the sheep that grazed on Longstone Edge. They invested in mines and had shares in at least one mine (Glead Rake) in which they were unlikely to have been active miners. They probably also acted as agents for others, collecting money, trading and perhaps lending money. It was a risky business. Debts were sometimes not paid and although some mines, such as Seedlow Vein, may have been worthwhile, others such as Glead Rake were certainly not and those who invested in them are likely to have lost money. Their way of life was however typical of many families in the Peak District, involving a mixture of farming, mining and trading.

The best impression of the way in which the villagers in Rowland carried on their lives during the older Robert's lifetime is provided by the records of the manorial courts.[26] The contemporaneous minutes record not only the decisions reached by the courts, but also the occasions when the jurors changed their minds and the clerk had to cross out a verdict and replace it with a different decision.

The combined sittings of the Court Baron and the View of Frankpledge were presided over by the Eyres' steward. Normally the court met twice a year, first in April or May, and then in October or November. The dates fixed for the court hearings seem to have varied from year to year and were not related in any way to religious festivals. There are however years when records of only one sitting survive, and later in the century there are records of more frequent hearings. The hearings took place in Hassop, Calver and Rowland in turn. When it sat in Hassop, the court presumably occupied a room in Hassop Hall, but there is no indication as to where the hearings took place when the court sittings were held in Rowland. It is unlikely that any room in any of the cottages was large enough for the tenants from all three manors and so hearings may have taken place in a barn or even in the open air under a tree.[27]

Normally the court consisted of thirteen jurors, although occasionally there were fifteen. Robert Ashton was among the jurors in 1718, 1730, 1733, 1738 and 1739. His brother John was a juror in 1705, 1713, 1717, 1718, 1722, 1728, and 1730. His cousin Francis Ashton was a juror in 1711, 1714, 1717, 1718, 1721, 1724, 1736, 1737, 1738 and 1740.[28] At one sitting in 1718 all three of them served as jurors.

In April every year the court appointed a separate headborough or constable for each of the three manors. The minutes refer to them being "presented" by the jurors and then being sworn into office. Some tenants served as headborough roughly every ten years. Robert's brother John was headborough in 1713, 1723 and 1734 while his cousin Francis was chosen in 1706[29] and 1739. Robert himself did not serve as headborough until 1726, although he was appointed again in 1733. The office seems to have been generally reserved for those tenants who were more actively engaged in farming and who rented the larger holdings in the hamlet.

The headborough's duties included maintaining the stocks, although there is no record of the Rowland court ever ordering anyone to be placed in them. Nevertheless, on 27th October 1703 the headboroughs of Rowland and Hassop were each fined 3s 4d for not keeping their stocks in repair. The courts also appointed a pinder to arrest stray beasts and to confine them in the pinfold, or village pound, until their owners redeemed them by paying a fine.[30]

For the lord of the manor's steward, the most important function of the courts seems to have been to ensure that tenants complied with their obligations and maintained the property which they rented. There are frequent references to tenants being ordered to mend fences, scour ditches, hang gates, etc. These measures were enforced by the court ordering those who transgressed to forfeit a specified sum to the lord of the manor. For example, at the hearing on 25th October 1700, Robert's cousin Francis Ashton was among those who had apparently not been maintaining their fences. The Court directed:

Wee lay a pain that Robert Becks and Ffran Ashton junr do make a suffitient ffence at their yard and adjoyninge to the Pinfold in Rowland Between now and Ladyday next or forfeit to the Lord of the mannour cash of 3s 4d.

Another typical direction was made on 18th April 1723, concerning Robert's brother, John Ashton, when the minutes record the following order:

"We lay a pain that John Ashton & Jon Bland sner [senior] scour up their ditches betwixt them & Francis Ashton['s] Red Meadows before the 10th day of May next or forfiet" three shillings and four pence.

Often tenants complied with these injunctions, but the court records refer to many occupiers who were fined, or "amercied", for breaches.

Another frequent concern of the courts was a tendency for tenants to allow livestock to graze in corn fields before the harvest had been gathered in. On several occasions the courts directed that cattle should not be allowed into fields before particular dates. In April 1709 Francis Ashton was fined one shilling for tenting (or minding) cattle on Breachside before the "corn be gett". The courts also imposed limits on the numbers of sheep and cattle which could be "tented" in the temporary pens which the villagers erected in the fields after harvest.

The courts were careful to ensure that the village's water supply did not become contaminated. In 1704 the court ordered "that no person shall bring or rinse any clothes in Rowland well nor lay any clothes on the well stone", on pain of a sixpenny fine. In 1733 the court directed:

> "We lay a pain that noone shall wash any pudings nor Bissons [basins] any stinking vessalls nor any other thing that shall abase the water, nether at the well nor anywhere betwixt the well and John Booths" on pain of a penalty of one shilling.

In 1742 the court imposed a penalty of nine shillings on any miners fetching water from any shaft well in Rowland, presumably to avoid any risk of lead poisoning or "belland", as it was known locally.

On one occasion in 1704 the court ordered that "every suffitient inhabiter within the Lordship of Rowland shall upon lawful warning given send a suffitient laborer to the Highways" or forfeit one shilling.

Whilst many complaints were initiated by the steward against tenants, allegations were also made by tenants against each other. Much of the court's time seems to have been spent in resolving "neighbour disputes" and preventing and punishing anti-social behaviour. One illustration is the punishment imposed on William Stanley in 1700. He was fined two shillings for "having a dead horse in the highway to the great hazard of goods [ie livestock] by getting diseases".

Another problem was people trespassing on other peoples' land. Robert's brother John was one person affected in this way. Other tenants seem to have taken short cuts to the well in his yard by climbing over and presumably damaging his fence. On 21st April 1702 the court directed:

> We lay a pain that no person or persons do ffetch any water at ye draw well in John Ashton's yard unless [they] come in at ye gate & go down by John's door & not to come over ye ffence in pain to fforfeit for every such offence 1s.

Similarly on 26th April 1705 the court gave the following instructions:

> We lay a pain that no person shall make a foot way down John Ashton croft but shall keep the antient way down the Grove Close, for each offence to forfeit sixpence.
> We lay a pain that Francis Ashton senr shall not make a driveing way with his sheep over Rowland Town field nor Anthony Mosley's field, for each offence to forfeit one shilling.

The manorial courts rarely adjudicated on matters relating to lead mining because they were within the jurisdiction of the barmoot courts. However, at a manorial court hearing in 1700, John Shaw was fined for digging holes in Anthony Gregory's land and not filling them up again.

There are relatively few references to Robert transgressing, presumably because he was not particularly involved in farming. There were however two occasions when he apparently behaved in an anti-social way. In April 1706 the court decreed:

> Wee lay a payne that Robt Ashton shall remove his [aforesaid] midine from Anthony Mosley['s] Croft Wall between this and the 10[th] day of August next or forfit two shillings.

A "midden" was a dung hill. Although Robert seems to have complied with the order, since he was not fined at the next court sitting, he later reverted to his former practice of piling dung and other rubbish against the wall of Anthony Mosley's croft. On 15th October 1720 the court sitting at Hassop made a further, more comprehensive ruling, with a higher penalty:

"We lay a pain that Robert Ashton remove his Muck, Miden or Dunghill from Anthony Mosley['s] croft wall betwixt now and our Lady day next and for the future lay no more dung to the said wall or else forfiet to the Lord" three shillings and four pence.

There was also one occasion when Robert's daughter Elizabeth was fined. In November 1734 the court laid a pain that "noone makes a common foote way upp or downe Thomas Barke['s] stoonham" or forfeit sixpence. A "stoonham" seems to have been a walled enclosure for animals.[31] At the next sitting on 22nd April 1735, Elizabeth was amercied sixpence "for goeing upp Thos Bark Stoonam contrary to a paine ladie Novemb 6 1734". Damage caused by people climbing on dry stone walls in the Peak District is evidently not just a modern problem. (Robert's daughter Elizabeth also transgressed the social norms of the times by being the first Ashton living in Rowland to give birth to a child who was born out of wedlock. Her daughter Mary was baptised on 21st November 1747 and was buried on 6th December 1747. Of the eighty-five Ashton children baptised at Great Longstone before 1800, there were only two other children who were born to mothers who were not married, William the son of Charity Ashton who was baptised in 1787, and John, the daughter of Sarah Ashton who was baptised in 1795. The father of Charity's child was probably William Grafton who was a relative of hers who had been brought up by his grandfather John Ashton and his uncle Valentine Ashton.[32])

Like his mother Mary, Robert Ashton senior paid land tax. He also paid the poor rate which was levied by the churchwardens in Bakewell to provide poor relief in the form of the purchase of food and clothing for those who were unable to support themselves. Rates were assessed annually on every inhabitant and occupier of land. They were the forerunner of local authority rates which were paid by people occupying property until rates were abolished in 1990. The only record of the amount paid by Robert Ashton which survives is the Assessment for 1728. He was assessed to pay one shilling and one penny. His brother John owed payments for two years totalling one shilling and eleven pence. The assessments for the other villagers were:

| | | |
|---|---|---|
| Richard Bland | 1s | 0 $\frac{1}{2}$d |
| John Bland | | 9 $\frac{1}{2}$d |
| Rebeckah Beck (two years) | 1s | 1d |
| John Hardy | | 9 $\frac{1}{2}$d |
| Rowland Bland | | 10 $\frac{1}{2}$d |
| James Jackson | | 6d |
| Thomas Hudson | 1s | 0 $\frac{1}{2}$d |
| George Hulley | | 11d |
| John Goody | 3s | 9 $\frac{1}{2}$d |
| Anthony Barton | | 11d |

Thomas Mossley was recorded as owing four years' rates. It is not clear how these sums were assessed. There was no statutory formula and originally rates were levied according to an estimate of occupiers' ability to pay. Often the amount of rent which tenants paid was taken as a good indication of how much they were able to pay and gradually rates came to be assessed according to an estimated rental value.[33]

Robert probably carried on living in Rowland until his death. It has not however been possible to establish precisely when he died. The minutes of the manorial court hearings in 1749 refer to "Robert Ashton's croft" and in 1752 Robert Ashton was a juror. There is though no reference to his burial in the parish registers. Although a few entries in the registers are illegible, it is most likely that he was buried in 1752 or 1753 or between 1757 and 1767 when there are gaps in the registers. Similarly there is no reference to the burial of any woman who was described as the wife or widow of Robert Ashton.

## Notes

1.  See generally Sidney and Beatrice Webb, *English Poor Law History*, Part 1, chapter 5.
2.  Derbyshire RO (Matlock), XM1/43.
3.  No child of Francis and Sarah Hodgkinson was baptised in Hathersage, although in 1712 Sarah, daughter of Francis Hodgkinson, was buried there. Francis Hodgkinson was buried in Hathersage in 1762.
4.  The marriage of Robert Ashton and Ellin Dale of Fulwood in Sheffield on 18th November 1704 would appear to relate to another Robert Ashton.
5.  Peter Furness, The Family of Eyre of Hassop, 1870, Vol 10, *The Reliquary*, pp 232–6.
6.  FEC1/1139 and Registration of Papists' Estates.
7.  Registration and Enrolment of Papists' Estates, Rowland Eyre, 1749. The later references may be to Robert's son Robert who was born in 1712, but in the absence of a reference to the burial of Robert senior in the Longstone Parish Registers, this seems unlikely.
8.  Although there is no trace of his burial, the last reference to Francis Ashton senior in the manorial court records was on 26th April 1705.
9.  Derbyshire RO (Matlock), Registration and Enrolment of Papists' Estates, Rowland Eyre, 1717.
10. See eg Hassop, Rowland and Calver Articles, para 24 (1st April 1668).
11. See Derbyshire RO (Matlock) D504B LP4 – a Plan of the Mineral Field Belonging to the North Derbyshire United Mining Company 1853.
12. There is a reference in Add MS 6682 fos 107–8, quoted in *Victoria County History of Derbyshire*, vol 2, p 346, to a Robert Ashton who wrote in 1723 to "Morgan of Chesterfield" advising him to become a lead merchant and describing the profit which could be made by transporting lead to London from Chesterfield via Bawtry and then down the Rivers Idle and Trent to the Humber Estuary. His letter stated:

    "You'll please to observe that lead is always bought by the fodder, which is various in almost every place. At the mills you have 23 cwt 3 qrs 16 lb, at Chesterfield and Bawtry I believe it still differs, and here in London 19 half cwt makes a fodder. I say then that

    |                              | £  | s  | d |
    |------------------------------|----|----|---|
    | 23 cwt cost at the mills     | 12 | 4  | 0 |
    | Charges to Bawtry            |    | 14 | 0 |
    | Hull                         |    | 4  | 0 |
    | Shipping charges at Hull     |    | 2  | 6 |
    | Insurance and Commission     |    | 4  | 0 |
    |                              | 13 | 8  | 6 |

    The price in London is £14 6s 7d but expenses of landing and commission on sale amount to 12s 8d."

    There is no description of this Robert Ashton. It is however much more likely that he was an Ashton from Castleton, rather than Robert Ashton of Rowland.
13. See eg paragraph 37 of the Hassop, Rowland and Calver Articles (1664), Brooke-Taylor, L258.
14. Article 30 (1664).
15. Article 27 (1664).
16. As to lead mining in the Peak District generally see Ford and Rieuwerts, *Lead Mining in the Peak District*; Kiernan, *The Derbyshire Lead Industry in the Sixteenth Century*; Pilkington, *A View of the Present State of Derbyshire*; and Stokes, *Lead and Lead Mining in Derbyshire*. Much detailed information can be found in the Bulletins of the Peak District Mines Historical Society and at the Peak District Mining Museum at Matlock Bath.
17. Daniel Defoe, *A Tour Through the Whole Island of Great Britain* (Penguin Classics Edition); pp 460–461.

18. Hassop, Rowland and Calver Articles, Brooke-Taylor, L 258, Article 13.
19. Brooke-Taylor, L 258, 1664.
20. cf Paragraph 24 of the Hassop, Rowland and Calver Articles and notes of L 258 at p 36. The "arrest" of the mine was to "hinder the proprietors from selling any ore or taking off any minerals tools or materials of any kind until the person so arresting is paid." In 1667 the barmoot court sitting at Hassop fined Thomas Rose £1 "for arreasting Bernard Spooner & his ptnrs & not prosecuting", (Derbyshire RO (Matlock) 598M/M3).
21. Brooke-Taylor L 258, p 34, in relation to Hassop, Rowland and Calver.
22. cf Brooke Taylor, L 258, p 34.
23. Brooke-Taylor, L 27.
24. Brooke-Taylor, L 24.
25. Derbyshire RO (Matlock), Brooke Taylor, 504 B/L 24/5. In 1744 the minutes of the Rowland manorial court referred to "Samuel Ashton, limeburner".
26. Sheffield, Bagshaw Collection 344. cf Rowland Parker, *The Common Stream*, chapters 6 to 9.
27. Levett in *Studies in Manorial History* refers to hearings in St Albans taking place under an ash tree (p 119), while Hone in *The Manor and Manorial Records* refers to hearings under an oak tree (p 131). See too the Webbs, *English Local Government: The Manor and the Borough*, Part I, p 65.
28. Either his cousin or his uncle was a juror in 1703.
29. It is possible that this Francis was his uncle, but unlikely. The fact that the court had stopped referring to Francis Ashton "senior" and "junior" seems to imply that Robert's uncle was dead by this time.
30. Nearby Darley Dale still had a pinder at the beginning of the nineteenth century. The parish registers there record the burial of George Clay, pinder of the parish, in 1807.
31. See April 1706 – reference to John Goodey's "cow stoneum". Also *Oxford English Dictionary*, "stoon" = stone and "ham" = "pasture or meadow enclosed with a ditch".
32. See Chapter 6. The general impression gained from looking at parish registers in this part of Derbyshire is that the number of illegitimate births increased as the eighteenth century progressed. See too Peter Laslett and others, *Bastardy and its Comparative History*.
33. Derbyshire RO (Matlock) PO 4/1. Paul Slack, *Poverty and Policy in Tudor and Stuart England*, p 127; Edwin Cannan, *History of Local Rates in England*, 1912, pp 78–9.
34. The entries in the manorial court minutes refer simply to "Robert Ashton", without the suffix "senior" or "junior". It is possible that they relate to Robert Ashton's own son Robert, but this is unlikely in view of the lack of any earlier burial entry. No burials of any Robert Ashtons are recorded in the registers for the nearby parishes of Stony Middleton (1740–58), Baslow (1740–62), Bakewell (1738–53), Darley (1740–55), Edensor (1740–71), Hathersage (typed index to 1774), Tideswell (1740–53), or Ashford (1735–44). The Hathersage parish records include a settlement certificate dated August 1767 certifying that a Robert Ashton and his wife Sarah were legally settled in Wortley, in the West Riding of Yorkshire, but there is nothing to connect Robert Ashton of Rowland with Wortley, and by 1767 he would have been well over eighty if he was still alive. There is no relevant Robert Ashton will. There are references to a Robert Ashton of Hope, but he was a member of a different branch of the Ashton family.

# 4

Henry, Robert's second child, grew up in Rowland and his childhood can have differed little from those of his father or his grandfather. He was married on 4th April 1727, two days after Easter Sunday. The wedding took place at the church on the hillside above Hathersage. Henry was almost twenty-five. His wife was Hannah Froggatt, the twenty-seven year old daughter of Thomas Froggatt of Calver.

Like Rowland, Calver was a manor owned by the Eyre family. It was only two miles away from Rowland and the Froggatt family must have been well known to the Ashtons. There are frequent references to Froggatts attending the same manorial court hearings as the Ashtons.[1] A Thomas Froggatt was presented as pinder for Calver in 1702, 1704, and 1706, and in 1707 Thomas Froggatt "the younger" was fined 3s 4d for allowing his livestock to graze on Calver Peak.[2] An earlier Thomas Froggatt, who was distantly related, had acquired greater notoriety. In 1667 he had appeared at Derby Assizes charged with sheep stealing.[3]

The Froggatts living in Calver had not moved far since the time when English people first started to use surnames. They had clearly acquired theirs from their connection with the hamlet of Froggatt, which was only a mile or so away. When the able-bodied men of Calver had been counted as part of the Militia Muster Roll in 1638, there had been only four male Froggatts living in the village, but, in the intervening period, they had multiplied prodigiously. By the beginning of the eighteenth century there were approximately a dozen branches of the family living in Calver and the immediate neighbourhood. Indeed four different adult "Thomas Froggatts of Calver" were buried at Baslow between 1709 and 1716, but even so, three other Thomas Froggatts were still alive to father children.[4]

Few children who were born at the beginning of the eighteenth century can have had easy childhoods, but Hannah's upbringing, although by no means exceptional, was probably more difficult than most. At the time of her birth, her father was a pauper, dependent upon the parish overseers for "relief". It seems that both her parents died while she was young. Her mother was probably buried during the spring of 1704 and her father in 1712. No doubt Hannah grew up among an extended family of grandparents, uncles, aunts and cousins, perhaps headed by the Thomas Froggatt, who was described as "senex" (old man) when he died in 1716. From a very early age she must have been fully occupied, looking after even younger children, working in the fields and performing household chores.

It is impossible to know how far Henry's parents approved of his marriage to Hannah. Small farmers did not force their children into arranged marriages,[5] especially when their offspring were in their mid to late twenties. However in the small and relatively closed communities of the Peak District in the early eighteenth century, where succeeding generations lived virtually on top of each other, the pressures on children to marry partners of whom their parents approved must have been strong. No doubt families normally discussed, and probably encouraged, blossoming courtships, but in an age when people were very conscious of status, it may well be that Henry's family looked down on a daughter-in-law who had been dependent on parish relief as a child.

It is not clear why the marriage was celebrated in Hathersage, six or seven miles away from Rowland. It does not seem to have been the church attended by Hannah or her family. Although Calver was in the parish of Bakewell, the nearest church was at Baslow, where Hannah had been baptised. There was though, a tendency for some of the other Rowland Ashtons to marry in Hathersage, perhaps because Henry's uncle Samuel was living there. After their marriage, Henry and Hannah lived in Rowland.

Hannah's age on marriage had a significant effect in limiting the number of children that she bore. Unlike her mother-in-law who had married young and who had had nine children, Hannah had six children who were born between 1728 and 1742. They were all baptised at the church in Great Longstone. Only one died young – the first Henry who was baptised on 26th February 1740/1 and buried less than a fortnight later on 8th March.

The number of Hannah's children also seems to have been limited by the length of time that she breastfed each child, since frequent breast-feeding can operate to delay ovulation and so conception.[6] Her first child, Debora, was baptised seventeen months after Henry and Hannah were married. There were then intervals of at least two years nine months between the baptisms of her other children. The only exception to this pattern followed the death of Henry in infancy. Hannah's next child, the second Henry, was baptised only fifteen months after the death of the first Henry. Allowing for a slight delay between the birth and baptism of the second Henry, Hannah conceived again within five months of the birth of the first Henry because, following his death, she had stopped nursing. Breast-feeding must have played an important part in the nutrition of those children who survived until they were at least twenty months old.

Henry Ashton served as a juror at the manorial court for the first and last time in October 1739. It was the only occasion when he was recorded as attending the court, and sometime during 1742 or 1743 Henry, Hannah and their children left Rowland. The land rented in Rowland by the Ashton family had become too small to support the increased number of Ashtons now living in the hamlet. Although Thomas Eyre had granted Henry's uncle, John, a new lease for twenty-one years from Lady Day 1741 in return for a fine of £10 and a yearly rent of £7 10s, the land included was probably only that which he was already farming.[7] Henry's father Robert still rented "a farm or tenement" with an annual rent of £1 10s, but it must have been too small to produce much in the way of crops or livestock. Henry's cousin Samuel, who by 1749 had taken over his father's land, did a little to alleviate the problem by renting almost ten acres in Black Low Piece from the Wrights of Longstone,[8] but this did nothing to solve the difficulties of other members of the family.

The Ashtons faced a serious accommodation problem, even though between them they rented four cottages. Henry paid four shillings a year for a small cottage. His cousin Samuel paid five shillings a year, while the rent which both his cousin John and his uncle John paid each Easter for their respective cottages was seven shillings.[9] A hundred years previously the only Ashtons living in Rowland had been Thomas and Joane and their young children, John and Francis. By 1740 there were about a dozen of Thomas and Joane's adult great grandchildren living in Rowland. Twenty-three Ashton children, all great-great-grand children of Thomas and Joane were born in Rowland during the seventeen years between 1728 and 1745. The shortage of land must also have meant that they had difficulties in producing sufficient food to feed all the members of the extended family. The pressure upon Henry and Hannah to move from Rowland must have been enormous. The move may have been precipitated by the fact that there were "barren years" between 1739 and 1742 when cold or rain led to poor harvests across the country.[10]

They moved to Gorsebank Farm, just to the north of Baslow, a village built on the banks of the River Derwent, where the road for Chesterfield started its climb over the eastern edge of the Peak District. Baslow is situated in the millstone grit part of the Peak District and its cottages, built of the local dark grit stone, are a very different colour to those built of limestone in Rowland.

Gorsebank Farm was owned by the Duke of Rutland, who was by far the largest land owner in Baslow, but rented by Alexander Damme, who was the father-in-law of Hannah's elder brother Robert. He farmed about forty acres of land on Gorsebank.[11] Alexander Damme described himself as a yeoman, but was wealthier than many of the other yeoman farmers in the area. Besides renting land from the Duke of Rutland, he owned several farms in Hathersage, and land and tenements at Fairest Clough (in Eyam), Fulwood (in Sheffield), Shatton (near Hope), Ashgate (in Brampton) and Curbar and Grindleford Bridge (near Baslow). In addition his personal belongings and debts owed to him when he died in 1751 amounted to more than £1,000.[12]

No doubt Henry worked as a farm hand for Alexander Damme, received board and lodging for himself and his wife and children, and, from time to time, was paid small amounts of money for his services. Henry probably felt pleased to be associated with someone who appeared to him to be wealthy. Alexander Damme on the other hand probably expected that he could count on greater loyalty and reliability from someone to whom he was related by marriage. It was the kind of arrangement which was typical in those times when networks of kinship were more extensive and of greater importance than they are today.

Gorsebank was three miles to the east of Rowland. Although it was in the mill stone grit part of the Peak District, it was built on a gentle and reasonably fertile slope in the Derwent Valley. The lower fields were next to the lane leading from Baslow to Stony Middleton, not far from the river. The higher fields, above the farm house, extended up towards the rocky crags and heather of Baslow Edge. The farm buildings were located by a small stream which ran down to the Derwent. Although the stream may have been dry sometimes during the summer months, it provided a source of water at other times. There was also a well, which, by the beginning of the twentieth century, was seventeen feet deep. Henry and Hannah could not see Rowland itself from the farm, but there were views to the west across to the summit of Longstone Edge.

The farm house is said to date back to the thirteenth and fourteenth centuries.[13] The exterior of the house now standing appears to be of later construction, but parts must have been built before Henry and Hannah moved there. It is built of dark millstone grit, with thick walls of coursed ashlar with quoins. It faces southwards.

There are no records describing the kind of farming carried out by Alexander Damme, but a hundred years later,[14] the land at Gorsebank was farmed by his great-grandson, Alexander Froggatt.[15] His forty-two acres of farmland were divided into sixteen fields. Most were either meadow, pasture or fallow, and it is likely that the Froggatts, and Alexander Damme before them, kept both cows and sheep. Three fields were however sown with oats and two with wheat. There may have been a small orchard on the northern side of the farm buildings.[16] The land attached to Gorsebank Farm was about four times larger in area than the fields which the Ashtons farmed in Rowland.

Central England had by this time been spared the ravages of armies marching through the countryside for almost a hundred years. However on 25th July 1745, Charles Edward Stuart, the Young Pretender, landed secretly at Moidart on the west coast of Scotland. He raised his standard at Glenfinnan, at the head of Loch Shiel, on 19th August. The Prince stayed for a while in Edinburgh, and then, with an army of about 5,000 Scottish Jacobites, started to march southwards. On 4th December, after marching through Manchester and Macclesfield and then crossing the Peak District, his soldiers reached Derby. There can be no doubt that

*Fig. 6 – Gorsebank Farm, Baslow.*

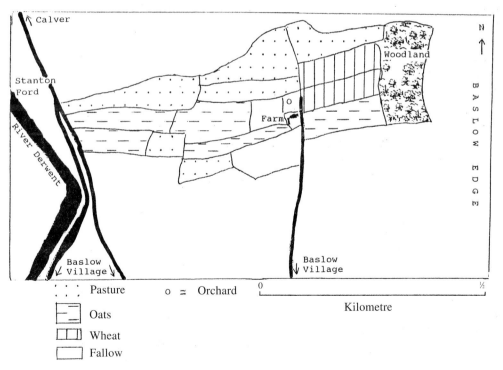

*Map 4 – Gorsebank Farm, Baslow. Although this map is based on the 1839 Tithe Commutation survey, the rotation of crops and field boundaries are likely to have changed little between the 1750s and 1830s.*

the countryside around Baslow buzzed with rumours, but very few Englishmen joined the Jacobite army. Faced with this lack of support and with the desertion of some of his Highlanders, the Young Pretender decided to retreat and, two days later, on 6th December, he left Derby for Scotland and his eventual defeat at Culloden. There is no way of knowing where Henry's sympathies lay. If his grandfather's views still prevailed within the family he may well have hoped that Charles would be successful. On the other hand the prospect of the strife which a long campaign would have caused meant that few Englishmen backed the Young Pretender.

Henry's children were probably the first generation of Ashtons to receive any education at school. The foundation of the Society for the Propagation of Christian Knowledge in 1698 had marked the start of the Charity School movement. From that time donations, particularly in the form of bequests, had been used to set up schools in villages across the country. For example, the Eyre family established a charity school in Rowland, but not until after Henry and Hannah had left the hamlet. The norm was for schools to have a mixture of free and fee-paying places. The first school in Baslow, at Stanton Ford, was set up during the early years of the eighteenth century with money received from several charitable bequests. When he died in 1720/1, the Reverend Joseph Nicholls, curate of Baslow, left £10 to the schoolmaster, "the interest whereof to be paid to him forever for teaching a poor child to be chosen and sent to school by my trustees and the curate of Baslow." (He also left copious instructions on how to care for and' prune his nectarine tree.) Other gifts were made in the wills of Robert Stafford who died in 1728 and Humphrey Chapman. The money given was used to buy land which was rented out to tenant farmers. One piece of land, which was bought in 1756 for £60, was Townend Close in Wheston, near Tideswell. One-third of the income received from it was paid to the master of Ford School. The remaining two-thirds of the rent were shared between the minister of the chapel in Baslow and the overseers of the poor.[17] The chapelwardens in Baslow were responsible for the upkeep of the school building.

The school building was about half a mile north of Baslow village, just down the hill from Gorsebank Farm. It consisted of a school room with two "chambers" above, in which the school master lived. Education was somewhat rudimentary. Masters in charity schools were often not well educated themselves and schooling frequently consisted of no more than trying to teach children to read and write and say their catechism. Moral and religious instruction formed a large part of the curriculum, with an emphasis on Bible reading, prayers and church attendance.[18] There was often a conflict between education and the need for young children to perform menial work on farms or to look after younger siblings. Defoe wrote of children as young as four and five being able to "earn their own bread" through farm work.[19] Many children only spent two or three years at school before progressing to full-time farm work.

Even so Henry and Sarah's children do seem to have benefited from their schooling. In particular Henry's son Thomas learnt to write well. He had a clear and steady hand when he signed his name in the marriage register, both when he was married himself and when he was a witness. More significantly, forty years later, he was able to write out his will in neat handwriting with well-formed letters.

Henry was a well established member of the village community in Baslow. He was not only busy helping his kinsman Alexander Damme to farm the land which he rented from the Duke of Rutland, but, like many other agricultural workers and small farmers, he was also carrying out building work and general odd jobs.[20] In the main details of this work do not survive, but there are records of payments which Henry received from the Baslow churchwardens, or "chapelwardens" as they described themselves in their accounts. The parish fulfilled a local civil government role as well as being an ecclesiastical unit. The churchwardens were not only "the proper guardians or keepers of the parish church",[21] but also had responsibilities towards the poor, and other functions, like paying rewards for the destruction of vermin. They were normally chosen jointly by the Minister and parishioners, unless agreement could not be reached in which case one was chosen by each.

The accounts prepared by the chapelwardens in Baslow for 1750 and 1752 reveal a large number of payments. They included a payment of 6s 6d for a gallon of wine for Whitsun and a payment of two shillings to the clerk for washing the clergyman's surplice. There were also payments to "ye Ringers" for ringing the church bells on the King's birthday, on Christmas Day and on New Year's Day.

On 30th October 1750 Henry Ashton was paid a number of sums by Robert Marple, the chapelwarden who prepared the accounts for the year:[22]

| | | |
|---|---|---|
| for repairing Ford school and Parson's House | 13s | 4d |
| for removing Slate and Lime from School to ye Parson's House | 1s | |
| for removing 2 ladders from Church to School & back again | | 8d |
| for repairing ye Hedge near Derwent | | 4d |

There is no indication of how these payments were calculated, the number of hours Henry worked, or even whether he employed someone else to help him. Rates of pay for work of this kind were generally between one shilling and one shilling and six pence a day[23] and, if that was how much Henry was paid, the payment in October 1750 reflected about a fortnight's work.

The following January the records show the following payments:

| | | |
|---|---|---|
| pd Henry Ashton for work done at our Church | 3s | 4d |
| pd Henry Ashton for Repairing Bakewell Church Yard Wall | 6s | 0d |

On 21st March 1750/1, Henry received six pence worth of ale and was paid two pence for "hair", which was probably horse hair. Although it may have been used in upholstery, it is more likely that the hair was to be used to strengthen mortar or plaster which were made with beaten lime, sand and water.[24] In 1717 the churchwardens had paid another parishioner "for hair and lime for couching church and school".

The chapelwarden's accounts prepared by Robert Froggatt in 1753 show that Henry continued to carry out work for the chapelwardens, although payments were not itemised in the same way. They merely refer to "Henry Ashton's Bill" of "£1 6s 6d".

The accounts show the closely knit nature of the village. Robert Froggatt was the brother of Henry's wife Hannah. He was also related to Sarah Taylor who was to marry Henry's son Thomas. Robert Marple was not related to the Ashtons, but fifty years later one of Henry Ashton's grandsons, also called Henry, married Robert Marple's daughter, Mary. In 1775, after Henry's death, Benjamin Ashton, who may have been one of his nephews, was paid by the chapelwardens for performing odd jobs. His bill was for five shillings.

Henry died during the first few days of 1765 at the age of sixty-two. He was buried on 7th January 1765 at Baslow. Although no grave stone survives, he was almost certainly buried in the churchyard adjoining the River Derwent. The parish register refers to him as "Henry Ashton of Gawsbank". It seems that he had relatively few belongings. He did not leave a will, but his clothes were probably passed onto his sons. The few household belongings which he possessed were probably inherited by his widow.

## Notes

1. Bagshaw Collection 344.
2. There are also references to Thomas Froggatt "smith" being pinder in 1705, and, in April 1730 and 1738, to a Thomas Froggatt who was a miner. See also reference in the minutes for 1700 and 1737 to Thomas Froggatt's "malt house croft" and, in 1704, to a Thomas Froggatt renting land at the "Cliff Edge". Also, in Glover, there is a reference to a monument in the church at Baslow to Thomas Froggatt, yeoman who died on 22nd December 1710 aged 43.
3. Thomas Froggatt of Bubnell. Derbyshire RO (Matlock), ASSI 80/13.
4. Thomas Froggatt of Calver Lane, Thomas Froggatt of Baslow and Thomas Froggatt of Bubnell. Between 1690 and 1705 the Baslow parish registers also refer to the baptisms of the children of Richard, Raphael, William, John junior, and Joshua Froggatt.
5. Houlbrooke, pp 70–72; Alan MacFarlane, *Marriage and Love in England*, pp 294–8; and *The Farming and Account books of Henry Best*, pp 116–7 cf Campbell, *The English Yeoman*, pp 281–88 and 303–4.
6. For discussions on breast-feeding and conception during this period, see Houlbrook, pp 127–8, 132–4; Stone pp 52–4; Peter Laslett, *The World We Have Lost*, p 101, and the French study quoted there; and Chris Wilson, "The Determinants of Marital Fertility", pp 219–26 in Lloyd Bonfield and others, *The World We Have Gained*. For modern studies, see "The Bellagio Consensus Statement, Breastfeeding as a Family Planning Method", *Lancet* 1988; ii; 1204–5, Gray and others, "Risk of Ovulation during Lactation", *Lancet* 1990, vol 335, pp 25–29, and Short and others, "Contraceptive Effects of Extended Lactational Amenorrhoea: Beyond the Bellagio Consensus, *Lancet* 1991, Vol 337, pp 715–17, although comparisons between modern studies and the position during the eighteenth century may not be strictly accurate because of changes in diet, not only of mothers, but also of children. In particuar the lack of a satisfactory eighteenth-century equivalent to modern bottles probably meant that breast-feeding played a more significant part of babies' diets for far longer than today.
7. Derbyshire RO (Matlock), Enrolment and Registration of Papists' Estates, 1749, Rowland Eyre.
8. G T Wright, Longstone Records, p 268.
9. Enrolment and Registration of Papists' Estates, 1749, Rowland Eyre.
10. T S Ashton, *Economic History of England in the Eighteenth Century*, p 4.
11. Details here from Baslow Tithe Award, 1847. Although the survey upon which it was based was made a hundred years later, it is unlikely that there were significant changes. NB also that 1778/1779 land tax returns show Alexander Froggatt as farming Gorsebank. The Baslow manorial court records for the period which are kept at Belvoir Castle almost certainly contain information about the way in which Alexander Damme farmed, but a request to inspect those records was refused.
12. Will at Lichfield JRO, 19th October 1751.
13. Ex rel Mr Thorp, current owner, May 1992.
14. Derbyshire RO (Matlock), XM7/2, Survey carried out pursuant to Tithe Commutation Act 1836.
15. Alexander Damme's daughter Maria Damme married Robert Froggatt in 1713. Their son Henry Froggatt was the principal beneficiary under Alexander Damme's will. Henry Froggatt's son Alexander Damme Froggatt was baptised in 1752. NB reference in Commissioner's Report to Henry Froggatt being grandson and heir of Alexander Damme (p 25) and to Elizabeth wife of Alexander Damme of Gorsebank being buried on 22nd March 1743. Gorsebank was farmed by Froggatts until 1921 when it was sold at auction by the Duke of Rutland for £1,200. Since then it has been farmed by the Thorp family, who have bought additional land to add to the farm and who now keep 1,000 head of cattle.
16. See First Edition Ordnance Survey 25" and orchard today.
17. Reports of the Commissioners to Inquire Concerning Charities and Education, Derby, pp 569–72 for this and other details about the school.
18. See generally Marion Johnson, *Derbyshire Village Schools in the Nineteenth Century*, chapter 1 and in particular the SPCK's "Orders to be observed by its Masters and Mistresses" (pp 21–2).
19. Quoted in Ivy Pinchbeck and Margaret Hewitt, *Children in English Society*, p 310 (separate references in Norfolk, Taunton and Yorkshire).
20. Farey, p 26; Pinchbeck, p 45.
21. Cripps, *The Law Relating to the Church and Clergy*, p 175, quoted in W E Tate, *The Parish Chest*. For the role of churchwardens generally, see Tate, pp 84–108.
22. Derbyshire RO (Matlock), D2380 A/PW 1 (XM1/35 Item 10).

23. cf G D H Cole and Raymond Postgate, *The Common People 1746–1946*, p 76 (in the north of England, labourers one shilling a day, skilled building operatives one shilling and six pence), relying on Arthur Young and Miss Gilboy, *Wages in Eighteenth-Century England.*
24. "Given Henry Ashton in ale 6, pd for hair 2D – 0 0 8d." See R J Brown, *The English Country Cottage*, p 128.

# 5

By the middle of the eighteenth century transport was improving and more outsiders were coming to the Peak District. Better stage coach services were linking the area with the rest of the country and in 1735 the following announcement appeared in the Derby Journal:

> Notice is hereby given that the Nottingham and Derby stage coaches set out from the White Lion Inn in Nottingham every Monday and every Thursday from the George Inn in Derby and from the Bell Inn in Holborn London on the same day. Performed in three days (if God permit) Thomas Smith and John Needham.[1]

Already travellers, attracted by the scenery of the Peak District, were writing glowing accounts about the region. William Bray in 1777 noted "the most varied and picturesque landscape" around Matlock and the "handsome appearance" of Bakewell church.[2] John Lowe writing in 1765 referred to a "very romantic aspect" when viewing the surrounding countryside from Bakewell church tower.[3]

Although these travellers were impressed with the scenery, they seem to have found the living conditions backward. Daniel Defoe, writing in the 1720s, complained about the standard of accommodation in Matlock and was surprised to find a family near Brassington living in a cave.[4] Lowe was distinctly unimpressed with the town of Bakewell, writing:

> . . . the whole (a very few houses excepted) exhibits a very wretched appearance; consisting for the most part, of low, smoaky, mean edifices: the streets are very dirty, particularly the principal, where, to increase the narrowness, which is very considerable, a whole group of shoemakers shops, coblers-bulks, &c are erected on both sides, and present a rude medley of joysts, rafters and beams, whose craggy projections, by thrusting themselves into the street, incomode the passengers, destroy the vistoe, and at the same time fill a traveller with fears, lest these ponderous fabrics should tumble about his ears, and bury him in their ruins.

He described Bakewell market as being "so mean it does not deserve to be mentioned". "A gentleman of the University of Oxford" who stayed in Bakewell in 1797 referred to "an indifferent inn" and to the town itself as being "still more ordinary".[5]

Changes though, were on their way by the middle of the eighteenth century. The population of England was starting to increase and the process of industrialisation which became known as the Industrial Revolution was beginning. Over the next two generations the way of life of the majority of the population was to change dramatically. When Henry Ashton's eldest son, Thomas, was born in 1731 all English production took place in small workshops or, in the case of the manufacture of cloth, in the cottages where the spinners and weavers lived. Apart perhaps from London, there were no industrial centres in the modern sense. Manufacturing was dispersed throughout the countryside. By the time of Thomas's death in 1788 the first large factories had been built. The cotton industry was growing, and spinning in individual cottages was becoming a thing of the past. The migration of people from villages to the new industrial towns had begun to gather pace.

An early example of factory building, which made use of water power, was the new cotton mill which Richard Arkwright built at Cromford, twelve miles to the south of Baslow. It was constructed in 1769. Hands at Arkwright's factory, including children, worked from 7 a.m. to 7 p.m., with a forty minute break at midday. Adults also worked a night shift from 7 p.m. to 7 a.m. By the end of the century, boys aged ten or eleven were paid three shillings and six pence a week. Girls were paid two shillings and three pence. Even so, a visitor wrote that the children "look in general very healthy and [there are] many with fine, rosy complexions."[6] Viscount Torrington visited the area shortly after Thomas Ashton's death. He recognised the beneficial effect that the new factories were having for British trade, but, reflecting the romanticised views held by many eighteenth-century tourists about the countryside and the rural population, wrote:

> . . . yet speaking as a tourist these vales [around Cromford] have lost all their beauties; the rural cot has given place to the lofty red mill, and the grand houses of overseers; the stream perverted from its course by sluices and aqueducts, will no longer ripple and cascade. Every rural sound is sunk in the clamours of cotton works; and the simple peasant (for to be simple we must be sequester'd) is changed into the impudent mechanic; the woods find their way into canals; and the rocks are disfigured for limestone.[7]

By 1789 Arkwright had built another factory at Bakewell which was employing three hundred hands. There was also a cotton mill between Calver and Baslow.[8]

Better transport was one of the factors which led to this process of industrialisation. Roads were gradually being improved. Canals were being built and rivers were being made more navigable. Other catalysts were the rise in the population which in turn provided an increased pool of labour and larger markets, the availability of capital and improvements in technology which meant that sources of power could be harnessed more efficiently.

Thomas would not have recognised, let alone understood, the importance of these changes which were to have a profound effect upon the lives of his grandchildren. He, and even his children, continued to follow an essentially rural existence. They remained largely self-sufficient, growing, rearing and preparing their own food, making their own clothes and selling any surpluses which they produced. Like his forefathers, Thomas was probably more concerned about the weather, unseasonal droughts and floods, and crop prices than about changes in manufacturing methods and their social consequences. He no doubt recalled the night of 22nd August 1749 when there was the "most terrible lightning thunder and rain there was ever known in this age" and the effect which it had upon Alexander Damme's crops.[9] Perhaps he also remembered, when, as a child, during the night of 13th July 1738, there had been an earthquake in Derbyshire which had rocked buildings.[10]

Until his marriage Thomas continued to live with his parents at the farm on Gorsebank near Baslow. In November 1759 he was a witness at the marriage of his relative John Turner and Elizabeth Vickary at the church in Baslow. He was probably also present at the church in Baslow on 29th September 1761 when his sister Martha married Isaac Barratt.

Thomas was himself married on 5th January 1761 when he was a little short of his thirtieth birthday. His wife was Sarah Taylor of Northwood, a hamlet seven miles south of Baslow, in the parish of Darley Dale. She was the daughter of Henry and Ann Taylor and was almost twenty-four.[11] The Baslow parish registers record that:

Thomas Ashton of Baslow in the Parish of Bakewell and County of Derby and Sarah Taylor of the Parish of Darleigh in the County aforesaid were married in the Chapel at Baslow accordinge to the Rubrick of the Church of England being first lawfully published on three preceeding Sundays in the parish Churches of Bakewell and Darleigh aforesaid and married on this 5th day of January 1761.

John Swift, Curate of Baslow

This marriage was solemnised between us Thomas Ashton, Sarah Taylor

In the presence of us Henry Ffroggatt, John Mason.

Both Thomas and Sarah signed their names, as did their two witnesses. Sarah was a distant cousin of Thomas. In 1675 Henry Taylor, Sarah's great-grandfather had married Elizabeth Froggatt, who was related to Thomas's mother. Henry Froggatt, one of the witnesses, was not only one of Thomas's cousins but was also related to Sarah. He was the principal beneficiary under Alexander Damme's will and rented Gorsebank Farm after his death. John Mason was the husband of Sarah's younger sister Mary.

All the indications are that this was "a good marriage" for Thomas which enabled him to move up a rung or two on the social ladder. His father was not even a tenant, whereas Sarah's father was a yeoman farmer owning land of his own. Perhaps more importantly, Henry Taylor had no surviving sons. It was normal for sons, rather than daughters, to inherit from their fathers, but Henry Taylor's lack of male heirs meant that on his death it was likely that his estate would pass to Sarah and her two sisters. The effect of the laws relating to married womens' property would mean that their husbands would become entitled to all the income from the land which they inherited.[12]

Thomas and Sarah's first son, Henry, was born later the same year. He was baptised at the church of St Helens in Darley Dale on 15th November 1761.

After their marriage, Thomas and Sarah lived at Northwood, the hamlet of about half a dozen cottages on a shoulder of land above the Derwent, where Sarah had been born. A steep track, now called Northwood Lane, climbed from the valley floor, past the cluster of cottages which formed the hamlet and then on over the moors towards Chesterfield. Thomas and Sarah's cottage was on the left hand side of the lane. Behind it a stream in a gulley ran down the hill, and beyond the stream were the woods of Northwood Carr.

The Taylor family had lived in Darley Dale since the mid-sixteenth century[13] and had owned part of Northwood since the early seventeenth century. The land which they farmed had originally been bought by Henry Taylor, Sarah's great-great-great-grandfather, from a Richard Senior soon after 1613. In 1784 the historian William Wolley inspected the "ancient parchment copies and original deeds" for the land which dated back to the reign of Edward VI. They were then in the possession of Thomas Ashton. He noted that Richard Senior had bought part of the Manor of Darley in 1613 and that

Soon afterwards Senior sold a little Estate at Northwood in the Parish of Darley to Henry Taylor of Darley & in the conveyance to Taylor there is a Reservation of a right to erect any Buildings Mills &c or take in any quantity of Ground not exceeding 30 statute Acres upon the commons within the Manor of Darley without the interferance of Taylor, his heirs or Ass[ignee]s.[14]

The remaining waste land and woods on the Northwood side of the stream were probably cleared in the first half of the seventeenth century. The older houses in Northwood seem to date from the seventeenth century, and one of the cottages, in which Thomas and Sarah later lived, still bears the mark "H BT 1667".

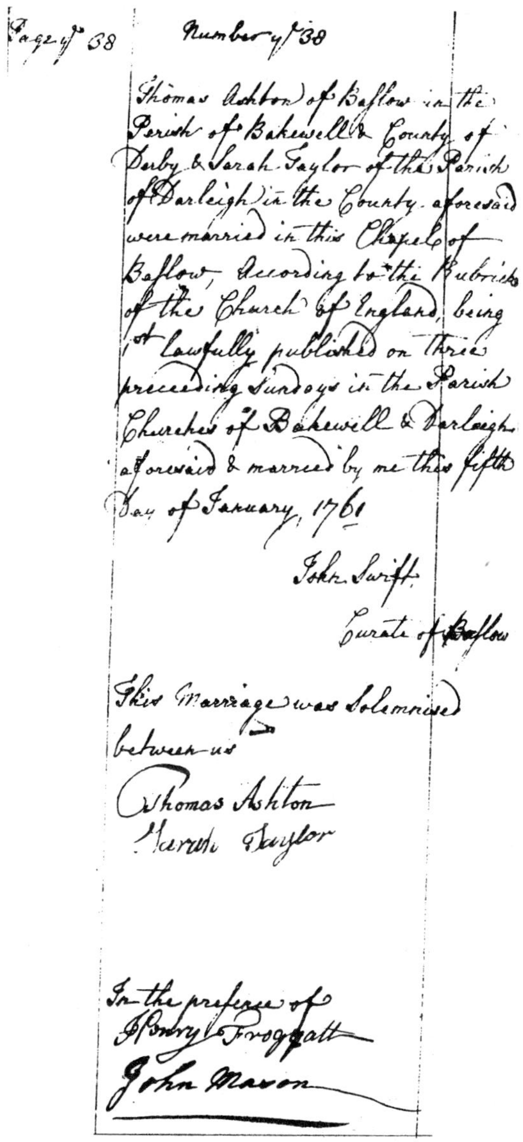

*Fig. 7 – Extract of Baslow parish register showing marriage of Thomas Ashton and Sarah Taylor (1761).*

Thomas and Sarah's second child, Thomas, was baptised at Pentrich, seven miles south east of Matlock on 1st January 1764. It is not clear why he was baptised there, rather than at the parish church in Darley Dale. The parish registers do not provide any clues. Most of the baptisms at Pentrich during this period give a place of residence within the parish, but the entry relating to Thomas made no reference to his parents' place of residence. It is possible that they were living in or near Pentrich at the time, but this seems unlikely. The only apparent connection between Pentrich and Thomas and Sarah is that a Jos Taylor rented land from the Duke of Devonshire in Pentrich.[15]

Sarah gave birth to two more children at Northwood. Charles was baptised at Darley on 28th August 1768. Ann was baptised on 5th April 1772. Thomas and Sarah's children probably went to the village free school which had been set up sometime during the seventeenth century.[16] Children were taught in the old vestry which had been built against the wall of Darley church.[17]

Sometime in the years before 1767, Thomas Ashton acquired the freehold of 2.865 acres of farmland, with a yearly value of forty-five shillings.[18] These fields may have been in Northwood itself, but it is more likely that they were a meadow which ran down to the banks of the Derwent called the Portway, and a couple of fields adjoining the highway from Matlock to Bakewell, not far from the bottom of Northwood Lane. It may be that Thomas used money which he had received as Sarah's dowry, or even that the land itself was given as her dowry. Another less likely possibility is that it had belonged to John Taylor, one of Sarah's relatives, who had died in April 1760 and had been sold to Thomas after his death so that his executors could make payments of legacies contained in his will.[19]

Whatever the circumstances in which Thomas acquired his own small parcel of land, this was typical of the general extension of land ownership during this period. Until the end of the sixteenth century, all of the land within the Manor of Darley was divided between just two families, the Plomptons and the Columbells. In 1781 the number of people owning freehold land in the eastern half of the parish was 77 and by 1830 the number had risen to 116.[20]

No details of the furniture or belongings which Thomas and Sarah had in their home survive. No inventory of possessions was prepared after Thomas's death. However an indication of the circumstances in which Sarah grew up is provided by the inventory made after the death of her grandfather in 1762. (He had also been called Henry Taylor and was ninety when he died.[21]) In the "house place" there were a writing desk (£1), a clock (£3), an oval table, a form and five chairs (£1), a warming pan (£1), a dresser, a case and pewter (£3). In the parlour, besides pots and pans and other utensils, there were a pair of bedsteads and hangings (£2 5s), a bed quilt (15 shillings), an "elbow chair" and a looking glass (£1 15s), a cupboard, three boxes and a close stool (£1). There were also two spinning wheels and a churn. In the "buttery chamber", there were three beds with bedding, (totalling £7 4s), a side-saddle and a pillion (£1 10s), a cheese press and a parcel of oats. The inventory also recorded one waggon and five carts (£14) and two ploughs and three harrows (£2 5s). Henry Taylor's livestock consisted of five horses and "geer" (£25), four cows, five calves and two stirks (ie young heifers) (£20) and thirty sheep (£13). In the barn there were "twelve quarter of oats" (£6), "pease" (£2 10s), a bean stack (£5), a hay stack (£9), an oat stack (£15) and a wheat stack (£24). The value of all the items listed in the inventory amounted to £166 16s 6d.

The quantities of corn, peas and beans, particularly six months after harvest, and the number of carts which he possessed suggest that Sarah's grandfather, although he merely described himself as a "yeoman", was not just a farmer, but was also a corn merchant. There was a small water mill driven by the stream below the hamlet which he must have used to grind corn.[22]

The utensils listed show that like most people in their position, the Taylors made their own butter and cheese and spun wool. It is unlikely that they wove their own cloth, since there is no reference to a loom in the inventory and weaving was becoming less common in private homes, although F M Eden, writing in 1797 about the north of England, stated:

Almost every article of dress worn by farmers . . . is manufactured at home, shoes and hats excepted; that is the linen thread is spun from the lint and the yarn from the wool, and sent to the weaver's and dyer's; so that almost every family has its web of linen cloth annually, and often one of woollen also which is either dyed for coats, or made into flannel etc . . . Although broad cloth purchased in the shops, begins now to be worn by opulent farmers, and others, on Sundays, yet there are many respectable persons, at this day, who never wore a bought pair of stockings, coat nor waistcoat in their lives.[23]

In the absence of an inventory following Thomas's death, comparisons between the Taylors' lifestyle and that of Thomas and Sarah cannot be completely reliable. Although later Thomas and Sarah may have inherited some of the household furniture listed in her grandfather's inventory, it is unlikely that they had as much livestock or corn. When Thomas died, his estate was certified as being worth less than £100. However, in view of the land which he owned, it is likely that Thomas pursued the same kind of mixed farming, growing some wheat and oats and keeping sheep and cattle. According to Pilkington[24] cattle which were fattened in the Peak District were already being sent to market in Manchester and Sheffield. He described the cows of Derbyshire as being "almost universally fully horned, rather large and handsome."

All the indications are that Thomas and Sarah and their relatives in Northwood formed a tightly knit family group who lived and worked closely together. After the death of Thomas's father, his mother, Hannah, came to live at Northwood. Benjamin Ashton, who was probably also related to Thomas, and his wife Mary were also living in Darley.

Thomas's links with his in-laws, the Taylors, were probably closer than those with his own family. Many of Sarah's family lived in Northwood. Her relatives Benjamin Taylor, William Taylor and Henry Taylor all owned or rented land in the vicinity.[25] Sarah's sister Mary and her husband John Mason rented land from Robert Newton nearby. Another relative, also called Mary, and her husband Thomas Holland[26] rented more farmland, not far away, from Mr Christopher Bowers. Indeed many of the families who farmed nearby, including the Gregorys, Pilkingtons, Holmes, Gibbons, Walls and Wildgooses were related to the Taylors by marriage.

Thomas seems to have enjoyed a particularly close relationship with his brother-in-law, Matthew Gibbons, who had married Sarah's younger sister, Ann, at Bakewell on 1st November 1768. Matthew Gibbons farmed land which he rented from the Duke of Rutland in the neighbouring village of Rowsley. He also rented land from the rector of Darley, the Reverend William Ulithorn Wray,[27] who owned land in various parts of the village. Although Matthew Gibbons was in fact Thomas's brother-in-law, Thomas referred to him as his "brother".[28] Later Thomas and Matthew became joint owners of land in Darley. In his will Thomas made Matthew Gibbons one of his executors and on 1st November 1790, after Thomas's death, one of his sons, Charles, married Elizabeth Gibbon, who was probably the daughter of Matthew's cousin, Joshua Gibbon, at Bakewell parish church. Their wedding was a further indication of the close relationship between families which were already associated by marriage. This is not particularly surprising, in view of the relatively small communities in which they lived, where the choice of partners of appropriate social standing cannot have been great.

In some parts of the country, the second half of the eighteenth century saw considerable improvements in farming methods. New crops, such as turnips, were planted. Land was drained. New methods of sowing and manuring were introduced. As a result of improvements in breeding and feeding techniques, livestock became larger. Animals were fed with hay throughout the winter and so farmers no longer engaged in the wholesale slaughter of animals during the autumn. In some areas wheat replaced less valuable cereals such as oats and rye. Agricultural output in the country as a whole increased.[29]

Although these changes had significant effects on larger farms in the flatter areas of England, there is little indication that there was much change in farming methods in the steep upland areas of the Peak District where conditions were more difficult and many farms much smaller.[30] Even so, the quantities of hay in Henry Taylor's barn on his death indicate that his family (and so presumably, after his death, Thomas and Sarah) had enough feedstuffs to keep animals alive throughout the winter. Whereas their ancestors, if they ate any meat, spent the winter eating mutton or pork which was preserved in brine, they were able to eat fresh meat from time to time throughout the year.

The movement towards greater enclosure of commons and waste did however directly benefit Thomas and Sarah to a small extent. Enclosure had been taking place piecemeal since the sixteenth century. From 1760 though, against a background of greater demand and increased prices, there was a dramatic increase in the amount of land enclosed. Between 1760 and 1799 enclosures brought over two million, and perhaps more than three million, acres of wasteland into cultivation.[31] Enclosure also became more systematic, and the earlier ad hoc agreements between local landowners tended to be replaced by parliamentary enclosure sanctioned by private Acts of Parliament. Four thousand Enclosure Acts were passed between 1750 and 1850.

The norm was for the larger landowners, who had most to gain, to petition Parliament for leave to bring in a Bill. The Bill was then drawn up by a lawyer who was appointed for the purpose. Enclosure Acts provided for the appointment of commissioners whose function was to settle awards. They in turn appointed surveyors who measured the existing holdings and allocated land from the commons or waste to compensate land owners for their loss of rights to use the common land which was enclosed. Enclosure was obviously of benefit to existing freeholders who acquired additional land and was a factor which led to improved and more efficient farming. However in some cases it caused problems for labourers and small tenant farmers who lost their rights to keep the odd cow or goose on common land.[32]

In Darley Dale some enclosure had already taken place by agreement between landowners. Indeed the land which Henry Taylor had farmed in Northwood was itself the result of enclosure during the first half of the seventeenth century. Some waste land had been turned into farmland and it may be that the old medieval strip fields in the village had been fenced and reallocated.[33] Even so there was still a significant amount of unenclosed common land on the higher slopes of the valley side to the north east of the village and on the moorland beyond, which, to use the language of the Darley Enclosure Act, "yields but little Profit". Most of this was marginal moorland or waste ground which was between 500 and 1,000 feet above sea-level. The land on the valley sides was steep and is now largely wooded. Although the higher land was flatter, it was bleak and windswept and initially fit for little more than rough pasture.

The Darley Enclosure Act was proposed in 1766 and implemented in 1769. It was one of the first Acts to provide for the enclosure of uplands in Derbyshire. The commissioners appointed by the Act were Bernard Lucas of Chesterfield, Thomas Southern of Wensley and Samuel Brailsford of Hardwicke. They not only decided how the land was to be parcelled out, but also who was to have the responsibility of making and maintaining the fences or walls around each award. Each parcel had to be enclosed within eight months either "by Ditches and Quicksett hedges [i.e. hawthorn] . . . or fenced with poles and nails or other walls in such manner as the Commissioners" should direct. In practice most, if not all, of the land allotted was enclosed with dry stone walls.

The commissioners awarded Thomas three parcels of land, numbered 45, 46, and 61.[34] In total Thomas's new land measured one acre, one rood and twenty-nine perches, or slightly less than one and a half acres. However the three new pieces of land which were allocated to him were dispersed. Parcel number 45, measured one rood one perch. It was on Darley Hillside, to one side of Darley Hall Road, three-quarters of a mile or so south-east of Northwood. The wording used by the commissioners when allocating this land to Thomas Ashton was typical of their awards:

And also we do hereby assign and allott to the said Thomas Ashton his heirs and assigns he being a proprietor of a freehold estate having such right upon Darley Common as aforesaid all that piece of land No. forty five parcell of the said common containing by survey one rood and one perch adjoining south easterly to Darley Hall Road northwesterly to the Allottment No. forty two, northeasterly to Darley Hall Road and southeasterly to old inclosures belonging to Thomas Parks and so we do hereby award order and direct that the said Thomas Ashton his heirs and assigns shall and do make and maintain the fences northeast and southeast against Darley Hall Road and northeast against the allottment number forty two.

Parcel number 46 measured fourteen perches. It was on the other side of Darley Hall Road, more or less opposite parcel number 45. These two pieces of land were very small, and probably of little use to Thomas. They were really no more than narrow strips of land adjoining the lane, and it is unlikely that it was economic for Thomas to bother fencing them. It seems that he sold them, and that the purchasers used them, not as farmland, but as building plots. There is no reference to Thomas occupying them in the later land tax returns, and on the next occasion that a full survey or Darley was carried out, in 1839, there were houses on both pieces of land, although the small plot to the east of the road included a "building in ruins".[35]

Parcel number 61 was however larger. It measured one acre fourteen perches. It was a steep piece of rough land on the northern side of Stonecliff Road, further up the hillside than parcels 45 and 46. It was almost certainly only capable of being used as grazing land, but it was to be farmed by the Ashtons for the next sixty years or so.[36]

The administrators of the estate of Sarah's grandfather, Henry Taylor, were awarded six acres, three roods, seven perches, but it was the largest owners who gained most. Five of them received over one hundred acres each, including the Duke of Rutland who was given additional land because of his rights as lord of the manor and the Reverend William Ulithorn Wray, the rector of Darley, who was compensated for the loss of his tithe on hay which was harvested.

Sarah's father, Henry Taylor, died intestate on 13th January 1781. Thomas gained more land when his estate was shared out between Henry Taylor's three surviving daughters Sarah, Ann (who had married Matthew Gibbons) and Mary (who had married John Mason, but was subsequently widowed). Although Sarah and Ann would have inherited and owned any of his property if they had not been married, the laws relating to married womens' property meant that their husbands became entitled to all the income from the land which they inherited. Accordingly, from 1781 Henry Taylor's land was farmed jointly by Sarah and Ann's husbands, Thomas Ashton and Matthew Gibbons and Mary Mason.[37] By 1786 the three of them had divided up the land and were farming their own individual shares.

By the mid-1780s Thomas owned six or seven acres of land. Although there had been a general tendency over the preceding couple of centuries for farmers' lands to be consolidated and rationalised into compact holdings which replaced the strips which had been scattered among the medieval open fields, Thomas's land was still dispersed throughout the northern

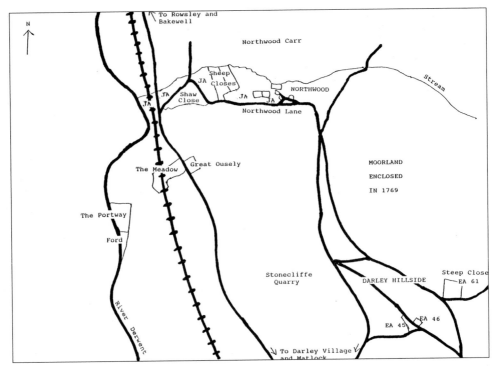

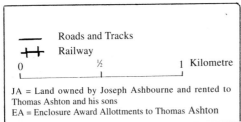

Map 5 – Northwood and Darley Hillside (1760–1850).

part of the parish of Darley. Most of the fields were small, not only by modern standards, but also when compared with the flatter fields handed out in the 1769 enclosure award. In Northwood he owned three houses, each with its own small garden. One was occupied by Joshua Taylor. It had an orchard. The other two houses were inhabited by Mary Mason and by George Higes and his wife. Joshua Taylor and Mary Mason were both related to Thomas's wife Sarah, but there is no indication that George Higes was a relation.[38] Near to the houses there were a stable, a coal house, a swinecote and a yard. A little way down Northwood Lane, there were two steep fields which were later described as "sheep closes". Together they measured a little more than two and a half acres. Half a mile away, next to the Derwent, there was an acre and a half of meadow called the Portway. Also on the floor of the valley there were two meadows on the western side of the highway and an arable field on the opposite side of the road called Great Ousely. Together these three fields measured almost two acres. Near to the road there was a fourth house which was occupied by Marey Wheldon with a "gardin and yard belonging thereunto allso two cow houses and a foder house". Finally, on Darley Hillside there was the steep close which Thomas had received in the enclosure award.[39]

The effect which the land inherited from Henry Taylor had on his holding is demonstrated by examining the payments of land tax paid by Thomas. In 1778 he paid one shilling and five pence halfpenny per quarter. By 1781 he, Matthew Gibbons and Mary Mason were jointly liable for a further three shillings and ten pence. After the three beneficiaries had divided their shares, Thomas was paying a total of three shillings one penny three-farthing in respect of the land which he owned. Although his liability for land tax more than doubled, it seems that in terms of area, the land which he owned only increased by about 50 per cent.

It is unlikely that the fields which Thomas and his relatives owned were sufficient by themselves to maintain the extended family of Ashtons and Taylors who lived together in Northwood. Accordingly, in 1778 or 1779[40] Thomas started to rent other land to augment that which he owned. Most of it was rented from Mr Joseph Ashbourne although he also rented a small field from John Barker. Some of the additional land was next to Northwood Lane, just below the hamlet. The other fields were between the Sheep Closes and the River Derwent. He also rented at least one house in Northwood which he and his immediate family moved into. It was very close to the houses in the hamlet which he owned and was almost certainly originally built by members of the Taylor family in 1667.[41] The land tax which was deducted from Thomas's rent to Mr Ashbourne was eight shillings and two pence and that from the rent which he paid to John Barker was two pence.[42] In view of the amount of the land tax payments, it would appear that the land which he rented from Ashbourne was almost three times as extensive as the land which he owned himself.

Payments of land tax indicate that the combined area of the land which Thomas owned and rented was significantly more than the total farmed by the Ashtons in Rowland, although direct comparisons cannot be completely accurate because the rental values upon which liability was calculated were by then ninety years out of date, and values may have differed from village to village. The land tax return for Rowland made in 1783 showed three Ashtons, Samuel, John and Robert paying a total of five shillings and four pence. In comparison, in the same year, Thomas Ashton was involved in farming land for which the total land tax payments were 13s 7½d. It is clear that, probably as a result of his marriage to Sarah Taylor, his social standing and financial position were better than those of previous generations of Ashtons.

In 1784 Thomas's mother, Hannah, died at the grand old age of eighty-five. She was buried on 2nd April 1784 in the church yard in Darley Dale. Although the existing church in Darley only dates back to the end of the twelfth century, there had been a church on the site in Saxon times and the yew tree near the entrance to the church has been described as being the largest and oldest in the country. In the nineteenth century it had a girth of thirty-three feet and was estimated as being two thousand years old.[43] Hannah's gravestone bears the simple inscription:

Near
this place lie the remains
of Hannah Ashton
who departed this life April 2nd 1784
aged 85 years.

Thomas died in April 1788, aged fifty-seven. He was buried near to his mother on 21st April. The stone mason added to the inscription on her gravestone by carving the words "Also the remains of Thomas Ashton" with the date of his death and his age.

Thomas had made a will on 18th January 1788.[44] It was witnessed by Benjamin Parkes,[45] a neighbouring farmer, John Gibbons, who was Matthew Gibbons's brother, and Thomas Holland. It was three pages long and was written by Thomas himself in a clear and neat hand. By modern standards the spelling occasionally appears idiosyncratic, but it was typical of the rather phonetic forms of the time. Words which would now be considered misspelt included "carrige", "gardin", "medow" and "neaphey", but even so it demonstrates a surprisingly high standard of literacy.

In his will Thomas described himself as a yeoman, a further indication of the social and economic improvement in the family's status over the preceding hundred years since the death of his great-grandfather John. He began his will by stating:

I Thomas Ashton of Darley and county of Derby yeoman do make this my last will and testament Bequeathing and Disposing of my worldly Effects wherewith it hath pleased God to posess me in the following manner.

His executors were his brother Henry Ashton and his brother-in-law Matthew Gibbons. He also appointed them as guardians for his children, although in fact only his son Charles and his daughter Ann were aged less than twenty-one.

He bequeathed to his "dearly beloved" wife Sarah the use of "that dwelling house wherein now George Higes doth live". He intended that his son Charles should live in the house with her and provided that his other sons should pay Charles five shillings a year so long as she lived in the same house as him. Thomas's three sons Henry, Thomas and Charles were jointly to pay Sarah £7 10 shillings by equal payments of fifty shillings "per year and every year so long as she continues unmarried". She was also allowed to "take out of [Thomas's] household goods such goods as she think proper for her own euse during her natureall life whilst she keep unmarried." All the household goods were to be returned if she remarried. His sons Henry and Thomas were also to give their mother "the carrige of her cole to burn" but she had to pay all other expenses. Carrying coal up the steep lane from the floor of the Derwent Valley must have been a considerable burden. Thomas also stated:

It is also my will that my wife Sarah Ashton shall have all the rents and profits that shall be made of my cottage house at Rowland wherein Joshua Bacon now dwell if Mr Eyar [ie Eyre] please to admit her as Tennand for the same.

This was almost certainly the cottage which his father Henry had rented in the early 1740s and which Thomas must have continued renting after his father's death.[46]

Thomas shared out the land which he owned almost equally between his three sons, Henry, Thomas and Charles. He left his eldest son Henry a house, an orchard, a garden and the "steep close". His son Thomas received another house, the garden and yard adjoining it, and three fields, The Portway, The Meadow and The Hillside. Thomas left Charles two houses with a stable, a coal house, a garden and a swinecote, with two pieces of land, Great Ousely and the Little Croft. This equality of division was shown by the amounts of land tax payable in 1789. Thomas and Charles paid quarterly instalments of 1s 0½d, while Henry paid 1s 0¾d.[47]

Thomas left "seaventy eight pounds of good and lawfull money" to his unmarried daughter Ann, to be paid by his sons when she reached the age of twenty-one. Thomas provided that this bequest could be enforced by his executors mortgaging or selling parts of the estate of any sons who defaulted. In view of the fact that the total value of Thomas's personal estate was less than £100, his sons were clearly expected to find at least some of

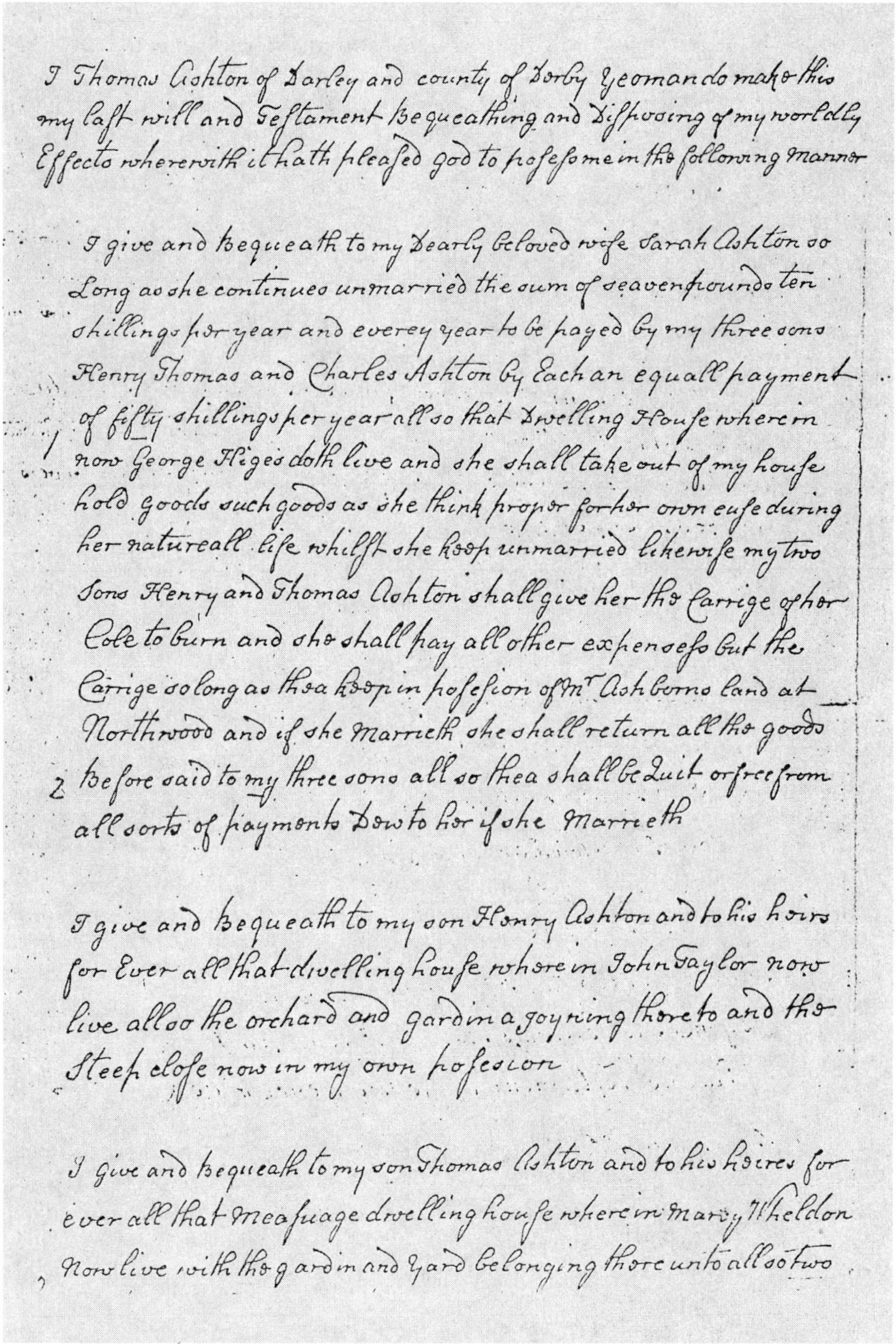

I Thomas Ashton of Darley and county of Derby yeoman do make this my last will and Testament Bequeathing and Disposing of my worldly Effects wherewith it hath pleased god to posess me in the following manner

I give and Bequeath to my Dearly beloved wife Sarah Ashton so Long as she continues unmarried the sum of seaven pounds ten shillings per year and everey year to be payed by my three sons Henry Thomas and Charles Ashton by Each an equall payment of fifty shillings per year allso that Dwelling House wherein now George Higes doth live and she shall take out of my house hold goods such goods as she think proper for her own euse during her natureall life whilst she keep unmarried likewise my two sons Henry and Thomas Ashton shall give her the Carrige of her Cole to burn and she shall pay all other expensess but the Carrige so long as thea keep in posesion of Mr Ashborns land at Northwood and if she marrieth she shall return all the goods before said to my three sons allso thea shall be Quit or free from all sorts of paymonts Dew to her if she marrieth

I give and bequeath to my son Henry Ashton and to his heirs for Ever all that dwelling house wherein John Taylor now live alloo the orchard and gardin a joyning thereto and the Steep close now in my own posesion

I give and bequeath to my son Thomas Ashton and to his heires for ever all that measuage dwelling house wherein Marey Wheldon Now live with the gardin and yard belonging thereunto allso two

Fig. 8 – Extract of Will of Thomas Ashton (1788).

*Fig. 9 – Cottage in Northwood bequeathed by Thomas Ashton to his son Thomas and occupied in 1839 by John Preston.*

this money from their own pockets. Although the giving of dowries was less common among small farmers than it had been a century previously, one of Thomas's aims in bequeathing this sum was to help Ann find a suitable husband. In fact she married a neighbouring farmer, John Wildgoose, at Darley on 11th May 1791, but died only nine years later aged twenty-eight.[48]

Thomas left £5 to his nephew Thomas Ashton, whom he described as being in London, when he reached the age of twenty-one. Although it has proved impossible to find any record of his baptism, it is likely that he was the son of Thomas's brother Henry. He may well have been Thomas's godson. It is not clear what he was doing in London, although it has been estimated that one in eight survivors of births between 1650 and 1750 lived in London at some stage during their lives.[49]

All the indications are that Thomas's body has lain peacefully in Darley churchyard since 1788. This was not however the case with the body of Benjamin Ashton, a distant relative of Thomas, who was descended from Robert Ashton of Stony Middleton. Benjamin Ashton had lived at Hathersage Hall and died in 1725. He was buried in the churchyard at Hathersage.

The circumstances of the exhumation of Benjamin Ashton's body on 31st May 1781 show that there was rather less reverence towards corpses then than there is today. The story was told by the "old woodman Hinchcliff", who had been the son of the Hathersage grave-digger:

After a discussion about making a grave for one of the family, the Major [James Shuttleworth] said "Break up the grave of my uncle Benjamin Ashton, he has been dead above fifty years."[50] This was done, but the body was found entire and sound, as he said, as heart of oak. He was an immensely fat man, and no part had disappeared but the feet and hands, for he died of gout; so antiseptic it appears is the soil in this churchyard.[51]

Another author described the corpse as being "quite white, and petrified, as hard as flint". Dr Spencer Hall wrote that an old woman called Jenny Sheard told him that she

> saw it reared upright in the Church, whilst the grave was preparing for its re-interment. It fell however, along the aisle, when its head broke off. Her father tried to cut a piece out of its back with a saw, to preserve as a relic, but the saw would not make the slightest incision.[52]

## Notes

1. Glover, *History of the County of Derby*, Vol 2, p 610.
2. "A Tour Through Some Midland Counties" in Mavor, *British Tourists*, Vol 2, 1798.
3. *Royal Magazine*, p 235.
4. Daniel Defoe, *A Tour through the Whole Island of Great Britain*, pp 463–5 (Penguin Classics edition).
5. "A journal of a Three Weeks Tour in 1797 through Derbyshire and the Lakes" in Mavor, Vol 5, p 224.
6. *The Farrington Diary*, Vol 1, pp 313–4 (1922 edn).
7. C B Andrews, *The Torrington Diaries*, 1954, Vol 2, p 195.
8. J Pilkington, *A View of the Present State of Derbyshire*, 1789.
9. Cox, *The Churches of Derbyshire*, Vol 2, p 62.
10. Glover, *History of the County of Derby*, Vol 2, p 610.
11. Her parents were married at Darley on 28 April 1732. She was baptised at Darley Dale on 13th February 1736/7. Her mother was buried on 2 July 1776.
12. Blackstone, *Commentaries on the Laws of England*, 1800, Vol I, p 445, Vol II, p 433.
13. In 1588 a Henry Taylor had married Grace Steare in Darley.
14. Wolley MS 6698 ff 11–12. Wolley also noted that in 1784 Thomas Ashton was "owner of part of the Estate at Northwood which was sold by Senior to Henry Taylor".
15. The land tax records for Pentrich in 1781 refer to Jos. Taylor, a tenant of the Duke of Devonshire and to a George Taylor. (Matlock, XM 1/185) However Taylor was such a common name in the area that it is impossible to prove any connection.
16. See burial of Mr William Bradley, school master of Darley, on 22nd February 1687/8.
17. Reports of the Commissioners, pp 598–9, and William Ulithorn Wray by Ernest Paulson, *Derbyshire Miscellany*, Spring 1974, p 10 and pp 15–16.
18. See Enclosure Award, Derbyshire RO (Matlock), Q133 and 133a.
19. Both John Taylor and his father, also called John Taylor, had left wills charging their estates with a large number of legacies to siblings, children and nephews and nieces. (John Taylor senior, after referring to his "ould age", had made his will "knoing and consider[ing] the certainty of death and the time thereof to be most uncertain.") His estate had not been large enough to discharge the specific legacies to his children which amounted to slightly over £28. They remained unpaid on the death of his son John, who was also his executor. John Taylor junior, in his turn, charged his real estate, not only with the unpaid legacies made by his father, but also with legacies to four of his siblings, and to his nephews and nieces. It is possible that one or more of the beneficiaries insisted that the "real estate", which John left to his brother Benjamin Taylor, should be sold to meet unpaid legacies and that Thomas Ashton purchased some or all of it.
20. J C Cox, *The Churches of Derbyshire*, Vol 2, pp 156–59. Land Tax Returns, Derbyshire RO (Matlock), XM1/186 and 201 which only refer to land in High Peak Hundred. The Darley Enclosure Award of 1767 (Derbyshire RO, Q133 and 133a) refers to about one hundred people who owned freehold land in Darley and who had rights to the common land, but that may have included the land in Darley to the west of the Derwent which was in Wensley and Snitterton Hundred, not High Peak Hundred. See too Pinchbeck, p 43; T S Ashton, p 46 (who states that during the period of parliamentary enclosure the number of small farmers actually increased); E Davies, "The Small Land Owner", 1780–1832 in the Light of Land Tax Assessments, *Economic History Review*, Vol 1, 1927–8, pp 87–110, esp. p 94, and J V Beckett, "The Decline of the Small Landowner in Eighteenth and Nineteenth Century England: Some Regional Considerations", *Agricultural History Review* 30, pp 97–111. There were clearly regional variations.
21. He was buried on 14 October 1762. Letters of administration were granted to his widow Mary at Chesterfield on 21 April 1763.
22. There is a reference to the "mill close" in the Schedule to the 1839 Tithe Award (Derbyshire RO (Matlock), Q133 and 133a – item 320 which was farmed by John Gibbon, a descendent of Henry

Taylor), but no reference to the mill itself. The hewn stones which can still be seen in the stream below Northwood are consistent with the existence of a mill.

23. F M Eden, *State of the Poor*, vol i 544–5, cf Pincbeck, pp 8–10, 133 and 158.
24. *A View of the Present State of Derbyshire*, p 300.
25. Land tax returns, 1783, Matlock RO XM1/186.
26. Married 29 May 1766.
27. 1783 land tax returns – Derbyshire RO (Matlock) XM1/186. Rivington, Clerical Guide, 1817.
28. See his will, Lichfield JRO. Some documents refer to "Gibbon", others to "Gibbons". It is clear that they are the same family and that the variations were interchangeable.
29. See eg Chambers and Mingay, pp 54–76.
30. In Farey's *Agriculture of Derbyshire*, 1811, vol 2, pp 360–495, there are long lists of farmers who had carried out "improvements". The only one in Darley was Mr George Barker who had drained some land (p 389). See also Chambers and Mingay pp 45, 57.
31. G R Porter, *The Progress of the Nation*, 1851, quoted in Chambers and Mingay, p 35. See too J Chapman and T M Harris, "The Accuracy of Enclosure Estimates: Some Evidence from Northern England", *VIII Journal of Historical Geography*, 1982, pp 261–4; Michael Turner, *Enclosures in Britain 1750–1830* and John Walton, "On Estimating the Extent of Parliamentary Enclosure", *Agricultural History Review*, 38, 1, pp 79–82.
32. Although the extent of such problems is a matter of controversy – cf Chambers and Mingay pp 77–105; Michael Turner, *Enclosures in Britain, 1750–1830* T S Ashton, *The Economic History of England in the Eighteenth Century*, pp 38–48 and Hammond, *The Village Labourer, 1760–1832*, pp 43–105.
33. NB small area of strip field ridges still visible to west of the A6.
34. Derbyshire RO (Matlock) Q133 and 133a. The reference to perches is clearly to "square perches". A rood was a quarter of an acre. There were forty square perches in a rood.
35. Under the Tithe Commutation Act. It is extremely unlikely that there can have been a building on this land before enclosure and some time must have elapsed between it being built and falling into ruins. cf Chambers and Mingay p 97 and Hoskins, *The Midland Peasant*, p 260.
36. It was described in the Tithe Commutation Act survey carried out in 1839 as "meadow". Derbyshire RO (Matlock), DL 23.
37. See 1785 land tax returns where there is a reference to Thomas Ashton, Matthew Gibbon and Thomas Parker's land being in the occupation of "Themselves/Late Henry Taylor". Like Matthew Gibbon, Mary Mason farmed land in Rowsley.
38. He was born in nearby Beeley in 1762 and married Sarah Stone at Bakewell in 1785.
39. cf Thomas's will and the 1839 Tithe Commutation Act Survey, Derbyshire RO (Matlock), DL23. Great Ousely can be identified from the Tithe Survey.
40. Derbyshire RO (Matlock) XM1/185 – land tax returns.
41. See (a) land tax returns for 1809 and 1810 which show Ashbourne subsequently rented this land to Samuel Fowler and (b) tithe award which shows location of land rented by Fowler. In his will, Thomas did not bequeath the house where he lived, indicating that he must have lived in a rented house. It bears the mark H BT 1667.
42. Derbyshire RO (Matlock) CRO XM 1/183, 1/186.
43. Cox, *The Churches of Derbyshire*, (1875–9), Vol 2, pp 154, 170–2.
44. Lichfield JRO.
45. It may be that Benjamin Parkes married Mary Mason and so was related by marriage to Thomas, but there is no reference to the marriage in the IGI.
46. Although neither the 1783 nor 1788 land tax returns for Rowland make any reference to Thomas Ashton or Sarah Ashton, a survey of Thomas Eyre's land made in 1774 (Derbyshire RO (Matlock), Enrolment and Registration of Papists' Estates) refers to Thomas Ashton renting a cottage for 1s p.a.. (In the 1783 land tax returns the only references to Ashtons in Rowland are to Samuel, John and Robert Ashton, while in 1788 there are only references to Samuel, John and Margaret Ashton.)
47. Derbyshire RO (Matlock) XM1/187. These figures are of no value in assessing the real, as opposed to the comparative values, of their land since assessment was still based on 1693 rental values.
48. She was buried at Darley on 18th October 1800.
49. Houlbrook, p 28.
50. He had been buried on 29th December 1725.
51. Hunter, Hallamshire, 1875, p 3.
52. Dr Spencer Hall, *The Peak and the Plain*, 1853, p 293. See too J C Cox, *The Churches of Derbyshire*, Vol 2, pp 236–8.

# 6

Thomas's two younger sons both married soon after their father's death. On 1st November 1790 Charles married Elizabeth Gibbon in Bakewell parish church. His brother Thomas Ashton was a witness. On 24th October 1792 Thomas was married to Mary Barker by the Reverend William Ulithorn Wray at Darley. His uncle Matthew Gibbons was a witness. The other witness was George Wall who had married Mary Taylor, one of Thomas's mother's relatives who almost certainly lived in Northwood.[1] Although Henry, the eldest son, did not marry for another ten years, he was still very much part of the family group. The small community of Northwood was largely made up of people who were related to him. Besides his brothers and his mother Sarah, there were Taylors, Masons and Gibbons living nearby.

All three brothers carried on farming in much the same way as they had before their father's death. Although their own individual holdings were barely large enough to maintain a subsistence existence, particularly when they had children of their own to support, Henry and Thomas continued to farm the land which their father had rented from Joseph Ashbourne. Charles on the other hand had no share in the land leased from Ashbourne. By 1799 he was renting a small piece of land from his uncle Matthew Gibbons, but he probably still did not have sufficient land to produce enough food or income to support his family. Despite the equal distribution of the fields which his father had owned, he found himself in much the same position as the younger sons of previous generations. He was forced to leave Darley and start a new life elsewhere. In 1803 or 1804 he sold his land and moved to Manchester.[2]

There is no indication that Henry or Thomas tried to augment their holdings by purchasing or renting more farm land while they had the benefit of the lease of land from Joseph Ashbourne. The records of payments of land tax in respect of the land which they owned and rented throughout this period remained constant. Henry and Thomas both paid one shilling and a half penny a quarter for their own land. The payments due on Mr Ashbourne's land remained eight shillings and four pence until he redeemed his obligations to pay by making a lump sum payment in 1800.[3]

Henry was in his late thirties and still unmarried, when Mary Marple, a distant relative, probably came to work for him as a house servant.[4] She was in her teens and was the daughter of Robert Marple of Gate Road, Baslow, one of the chapel wardens who had approved payments to Henry's grandfather for carrying out odd jobs for the parish. Robert Marple had been a widower when he had married Mary's mother, Jane Bramwell. Indeed he was aged seventy-six when Mary was born, and eighty-six when her brother Thomas was born, achievements which were sufficiently remarkable for his age to be noted in the parish register after the entry recording Thomas's baptism.[5] After the death of Mary's father early in 1797, her mother had re-married. Her second husband was Valentine Ashton of Rowland, who was himself a widower. He was the great nephew of Robert Ashton who was in turn Henry Ashton's great-grandfather.[6]

It was not unusual for girls, particularly after the death of a parent, to be packed off to relatives in another village. Probably 60 per cent of the population aged between fifteen and twenty-four worked as servants.[7] Many girls went into service at the age of thirteen, or soon afterwards. Female servants were cheap and sending them away into service gave them some experience of the chores of housekeeping. It also saved their parents the cost of feeding them and provided more space in houses which were often overcrowded.

Henry and Mary became lovers during 1802, if not before. Mary found that she was pregnant during the autumn of 1802 and so they quickly arranged to be married. The ceremony was performed by the Reverend William Ulithorn Wray in the parish church in Darley Dale on 20th December 1802 when Mary was three or four months pregnant. The witnesses were Henry's cousin John Gibbons and a relative of Mary's mother called Stephen Bramwell. As Mary was not yet twenty-one, after the publication of the banns, her mother could have given the rector "Notice of Dissent" and thus prevented the marriage from taking place.[8] However Henry and Mary knew that in view of Mary's pregnancy, there was very little likelihood of her taking that step, even if she disapproved of the marriage. Both Henry and Mary were able to sign their own names in the register. Henry wrote his name in a large clear script with carefully formed letters.

Mary's eldest child Henry was born on 4th June 1803 and baptised on 7th August 1803. In the early nineteenth century sexual relations outside marriage were by no means uncommon. Indeed at least 30 per cent of the brides who were married at St Helen's, Darley between 1800 and 1804 were pregnant at the time of their marriage or had previously given birth to illegitimate children.[9] This is consistent with the results of research in other places which suggests that there were pre-nuptial pregnancies in up to 40 per cent of marriages.[10] Nevertheless there was a great social stigma attached to illegitimacy. There can be no doubt that eyebrows were raised and tongues wagged when baby Henry was born so soon after his parents' marriage. It is likely that the neighbours criticised both parents, Henry for taking advantage of his young maid servant and Mary, either for being too weak to resist his advances or for ensnaring him into marriage. Unfortunately there is nothing to indicate whether those prejudices accurately reflected the circumstances of Henry's conception, or whether there was genuine affection and companionship between two people who had been living in the same house for some time, perhaps with some type of informal betrothal before the wedding.[11]

Although Henry was forty when they were married, his wife was only eighteen. Her age on marriage had a significant effect on the number of children she was to bear.[12] Mary gave birth to twelve children over a period of twenty-four years. Her youngest child, Sarah, was born when she was aged forty-three. Her first six children were born during a period of less than eight years, with gaps of only twelve to fifteen months between most of these births. The only exception was a period of thirty-two months between the baptism of her second child, Ann, and the birth of her third child, Robert, which seems to suggest a late miscarriage, a still birth or the birth of a baby who died before being baptised and whose burial was not recorded. The very short gaps between births seem to indicate that Mary did not breast feed these children herself, but instead used the services of a wet nurse.[13]

In contrast her six younger children were born over a period of fourteen years, with gaps ranging from two to three years. Although Mary's fertility may well have declined as she became older, it is more than likely that she breastfed these children herself and that this meant that she did not conceive again as rapidly as during the first years of her marriage.[14]

Eleven of Mary's children survived infancy. This was more than in any other generation of the Ashton family and mirrored the national pattern of population growth. The fertility of married women between 1810 and 1814 was the highest ever recorded during the times when parish registers were the main source of information about baptisms and the years following 1815 were the period when the English population increased at its fastest rate ever.[15] The only one of Mary's children to die during childhood was the first of two sons called Valentine. He was born during December 1809, but died three weeks later. Her next son, born fourteen months later, was also called Valentine. Both of them were clearly named after Valentine Ashton, Mary's step-father. He was almost certainly their godfather and probably took a special interest in the welfare of the Valentine who survived.[16]

It is likely that some of Henry and Mary's children, particularly the elder ones, went to school. Certainly Henry, Robert, Valentine and Jane could write. Until the 1820s classes in Darley Dale were held in the old vestry at St Helen's church. The lower storey was used as a school room for boys, while girls were taught upstairs. The teachers were paid from income generated by a number of charitable bequests which had been made over the preceding century.

In 1821, the rector thought that 270 boys and girls aged between seven and thirteen required "cheap or gratuitous instruction", but the school was only able to educate eighty children. However when Parliamentary Commissioners visited Darley a few years later, even that limited education had ceased. The Commissioners noted that "the instruction at the school . . . has been suspended for some years, in consequence of the age and infirmity of the late master who died in November 1826. At the time of our inquiry, his successor has not been appointed."[17] It was perhaps not surprising that the school master, a Mr Gregory, had given up teaching by the 1820s. He had first been appointed as school master in 1764 and was aged ninety-three in 1826.

In 1824 the rector, the Reverend Benjamin Lawrence, made an application for a grant from the National Society for Promoting the Education of the Poor which had been founded ten years previously. He sought £100 towards the estimated cost of £625 for building a new school. The balance was to be given by subscriptions, principally from the rector himself and Arthur Heathcote, the wealthy owner of Stonecliffe Quarry. Lawrence proposed that the new school should have two rooms, each measuring twenty feet by twenty feet. Parents would be expected to pay two pence or three pence per week towards the education of their children, according to their means.

In April 1824 the Committee of the National Society approved a grant of £100. In return for the grant, the Reverend Benjamin Lawrence signed an undertaking that the children "would be instructed in the Liturgy and Catechism of the Established Church, and constantly attend Divine Service at their Parish Church or other place of Worship under the Establishment . . . on the Lord's Day." He also gave an assurance that "No Religious Tracts shall be used in the school, but such as are contained in the Catalogue of the Society for promoting Christian Knowledge."[18]

The standard of education received by those of Henry and Mary's children who attended school was extremely basic even after the school reopened in its new building. No assessment of the quality of teaching was carried out during the first quarter of the century when they were at school, but when the Reverend John Allen inspected 184 Derbyshire schools in the year 1842–3, he found only fifty-one children present at Darley school. Whilst most could read words of two syllables, only fifteen were "able to read with ease". Twenty-one children were learning basic arithmetic, but only one child had progressed beyond the first four rules.[19]

The quality of education given to those children who went to school may not have been high, but the number of children who did not go to school at all was even more significant. Many parents either did not think that education was important or needed their children's labour, either to earn money or to perform household chores. It is reasonable to assume that almost all children who spent at least some time at school would have learnt to write their own names, but many children in Darley Dale could not even do that. Between 1800 and 1804 half of the people who lived in Darley Dale and who were married at St Helen's church could not write their name, and instead made a mark in the marriage register – normally a cross. There was however a noticeable contrast between the ability of men and women. Two-thirds of men could write their names, whereas only one-third of women could do so. Despite the existence of the village school, two-thirds of girls and one third of the boys received no education.[20]

The house the Ashton children grew up in has been greatly altered over the years, and so it is not possible to describe it, except to say that it was built of the local millstone grit. Typically though, the houses of farmers in Darley Dale at this time had ground floor rooms which were laid with flags or paving stones. Often the internal walls were whitewashed annually. Many farmers' wives, rather than cooking over open fires, as they had done a generation or so earlier, used square iron boilers with lids which were set at the end of fire grates. In 1815 one contemporary writer noted that these iron boilers had "spread so amazingly, that there is scarcely a house without these ovens, even of the cottages of the first class."[21]

In 1809 or 1810 Thomas and Henry's lease of the farmland which they rented from Joseph Ashbourne was terminated. Instead the farmland was rented by Samuel Fowler.[22] The reasons for the change of tenant are not clear. It is possible that Henry and Thomas surrendered their interest because they refused to pay the increased rents which, in view of the inflation brought about by the wars against France, most landlords were demanding. On the other hand it is possible that they neglected the farm or failed to pay their rent and were evicted by Ashbourne.

Henry's brother Thomas seems to have tried to compensate for the loss of the lease. By 1827 he had bought a small amount of extra land from Messrs Twigge.[23] He was also renting other land jointly with Abel Holmes and Samuel Taylor from Messrs Twigge. The new land which Thomas rented seems to have been larger in area than the farm which had been leased from Ashbourne. In 1827 the land tax deducted from the rent which Thomas Ashton, Abel Holmes and Samuel Taylor paid was seventeen shillings and four pence.[24] Later Thomas bought a close on Darley hillside called The Bank from James Turner.[25] By 1839 he was renting three pieces of land from Thomas Stanley Potter. Shaw Close (at the bottom of Northwood Lane), Derwent Lanes (alongside the river) and Ford (adjoining The Portway) comprised about three and a half acres.[26]

Henry's holding in contrast seems to have reduced further. By 1830 he had disposed of some of his land to Arthur Heathcote, the owner of Stonecliffe Quarry, and although he initially rented it back from him, this arrangement only continued for a short period. Henry's annual payment of land tax was reduced from four shillings and two pence to three shillings and seven pence.[27]

The first few years of the nineteenth century had been a prosperous time for farmers. Like his father, Henry was probably making a reasonably good living during these years, when agricultural prices, particularly those of wheat, rose steeply as a result of the wars against France, a run of bad harvests and increasing demand. All but the least efficient farmers prospered. It is likely that, with the benefit of the land which he had rented from Joseph Ashbourne, Henry was able to profit by selling some surplus crops.

However after the end of the war in 1815, demand fell, unemployment rose, farm prices dropped dramatically and there was an agricultural slump. Wheat prices, which had averaged over ninety-one shillings a quarter from 1810 to 1813, plummeted from a high of 126s 6d in 1812, to 65s 7d in 1815 and, after some fluctuations, reached a low of 44s 7d a quarter in 1822.[28] Although prices then began to rise gradually, partly as a result of the new Corn Law, which was introduced in 1815 and which prohibited the sale of imported wheat when the price was below £4 per quarter, they did not return to their war time levels. Many small farmers sold their interests during the 1820s and the number of such smaller holdings declined. The twin effects of the depression and growing industrialisation, with a corresponding decline in traditional cottage industries, brought about the break-up of the self-sufficient peasant society in which Henry's ancestors had lived.[29]

There can be no doubt that Henry suffered. A combination of the prevailing economic climate, including increased taxes and higher poor rate contributions,[30] the division of Thomas's property among his three sons on his death, the loss of the lease from Joseph Ashbourne and the sale of part of Henry's land, must have meant that his economic position and social standing declined so that they were considerably inferior to those of his father. He was probably reduced to little more than subsistence farming. Henry no doubt blamed the external factors over which he had no control and which it was hard for him to combat. Certainly he lacked the capital which farmers needed to make improvements or increase their holdings, and by the time of the post-war slump he was in his mid-fifties with a large family. Even so, it may well be that he put less energy into farming and was not as concerned about bettering his position as his father. As Chambers and Mingay point out[31] "in the final analysis much depended on the enterprise and efficiency of the individual farmer." Henry's father Thomas seems to have been an impressive figure, both in terms of the way in which he improved his social and economic standing and his literacy. In contrast Henry may well have been an unenterprising and inefficient farmer who was unable to overcome the difficulties which he faced.

Although there had been some improvements in farm implements by the early nineteenth century, generally, there was little in the way of mechanisation. Drilling machines for sowing corn had been invented, but few farmers used them, particularly in areas with small steep fields such as those which Henry farmed. The Ashton family almost certainly still sowed, harvested, threshed and winnowed by hand. The most important farm implement which Henry possessed was probably a plough. By 1815 many ploughs in Derbyshire were wheeled. The nearest plough-wright to Darley was Mr Peter Hibbert in Baslow who charged £3 or more for a plough. A plough drawn by two horses could usually plough an acre a day. Like his ancestors, Henry almost certainly rotated his crops, leaving fields fallow for perhaps one year in three.[32]

Friday was market day in Bakewell. However in the early years of the century, farmers like Henry bought and sold cattle and sheep at fairs which took place twice a year at Darley Flash, on the moorland to the east of the village. They were held on May 13th and October 27th each year, until they were discontinued in the 1840s.[33] They were probably similar to the fair at Matlock described by Dr Spencer Hall, who saw:

Herds of kine and flocks of sheep; and dealers among them, with broad red faces, broad hats and broader dialect – all vociferation, bustle and eagerness; shows of wild beast, mountebanks, giants, dwarfs and conjuroros, loudly proclaimed by drums and gongs, bugles and clarionets, and slang orations; mock auction cats with their wide-mouthed auctioneers; and stalls of toys and gingerbread, enough to supply a whole county . . .[34]

An annual village feast was held in Darley Dale on the fourth Sunday in August.[35]

Henry's mother, Sarah Ashton, who had been living in Northwood, died in June 1812. She was aged seventy-five. She was buried in the churchyard in Darley Dale on 11th June 1812. The same year another relative died in rather more traumatic circumstances. Mary Mason, the eight year old daughter of Robert Mason, who lived in Northwood, was burnt to death.

Another death which affected the family was that of Valentine Ashton, Mary Ashton's stepfather, who died on 20th February 1820. He had been baptised in Rowland on 26th February 1737/8 and was presumably born on St Valentine's Day, hence his name. Although he described himself as a "yeoman" of Baslow, he worked primarily as a tailor. He also owned land in Baslow, Tideswell, Little Longstone and The Ridge Flats, Great Longstone and was awarded land in the Longstone enclosure award.[36] Apart from disposing of his land, his will also contained bequests to various people totalling £75. These included sums of £10 to his stepdaughter Mary and £20 to Henry and Mary's son Valentine, which was to be paid to him when he attained the age of twenty-one. In the meantime interest on that sum was to be applied for his use and education.

During his lifetime the elder Valentine Ashton's economic position had appeared reasonably secure. Although he could not write his name, he had income not only from his work as a tailor, but also from the land which he owned. He also benefited from marrying a widow who had inherited some money from her husband.

However the way in which misfortune could strike, and how families could fall on hard times, is demonstrated by what happened to William Grafton. He was Valentine Ashton's nephew, the son of his sister, Mary Grafton, née Ashton, and so descended from Thomas and Joane Ashton who had lived in Rowland during the 1630s and 1640s.

When William Grafton was thirty-one he sought poor relief from the parish overseers in Longstone. They, like most overseers, were very careful not to pay relief to anyone unless they were legally obliged to do so. Whether or not a person was the responsibility of a particular parish depended upon his or her "settlement". Parish overseers had power to remove poor people to other parishes if they were not settled in the parish where they sought relief.

Accordingly on 5th July 1800 William Grafton was examined on oath by Thomas Denman[37] and Bache Thornhill,[38] two justices of the peace, who were to investigate whether or not he was the responsibility of the Longstone overseers. This must have been an intimidating experience. In response to their questioning he gave an account of his life history. He described how, when he was very young, his father went to live in Holmesfield, a village six miles north-west of Chesterfield, where he rented a farm jointly with his brother-in-law William Ashton, paying a rent of approximately £50 a year. William Grafton's mother, Mary Grafton née Ashton, had died when he was about six and his father had then made an agreement with William's grandfather, John Ashton of Rowland,[39] that he would take care of William and two younger children. When he was eleven, his grandfather in turn had made an agreement with Valentine Ashton to teach him "the business of a tailor". This seems to have been like an apprenticeship, but the justices found that there was no formal indenture. William served Valentine Ashton for two or three years in Rowland, and when he moved to Baslow, lived with him there until he was twenty-one. Valentine Ashton "found him meat, drink, washing and lodging and cloaths and all other necessarys and sometimes gave him a little money for pocket money." William married a relative, Charity Ashton, in Bakewell Church in 1790, but clearly fell on hard times.

After examining him, the justices submitted their account of his testimony to John Balguy, Recorder of Derby, for him to determine which parish he should be removed to. He found that the informal nature of his service with Valentine Ashton was insufficient to establish a settlement in Rowland or Baslow and that accordingly he had derived his settlement from his father.[40] As his father had been settled in Holmesfield because of the farm which he had rented there, Balguy ordered that William and his family should be removed to Holmesfield, a village in which he had not lived since he was six. However he cannot have stayed there long, if indeed he ever complied with the order. In 1802 he was living in Baslow, probably

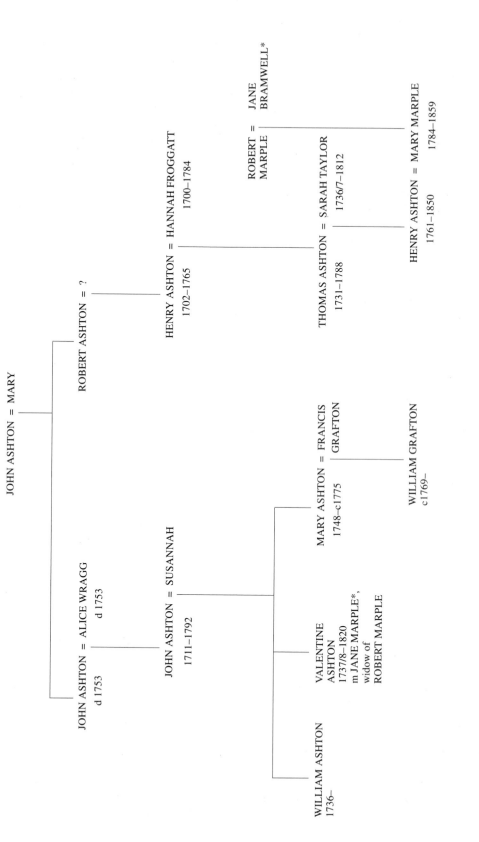

Fig. 10 – Family tree showing the relationship between William Grafton and the Ashtons.

under the patronage of Valentine Ashton. In that year his wife gave birth to a son who was called Valentine Grafton, presumably as an indication of William's respect and gratitude towards his former employer.

Nationally, the years from 1780 to 1850, which roughly corresponded with Henry's adult life, were a period of rapid population growth and industrialisation. Although the population of England and Wales rose from seven and a half million to eighteen million,[41] Darley Dale remained a predominantly rural and agricultural area. In 1789 Farey found that there were 196 houses in the liberty of Darley and lordship of Little Rowsley. By 1801 this had increased to 229 houses of which 210 were inhabited. By 1851 there were 294 houses, of which 19 were uninhabited.[43] At the beginning of the century, the population of Darley actually declined, dropping from 1,077 in 1801 to 990 in 1811, presumably due to migration to cities, particularly Manchester and Sheffield. Later though, it increased gradually, rising from 1,175 in 1821 to 1,375 in 1851.

In 1830, Stephen Glover, author of The Peak Guide, described Darley Dale as a small rural village. Although a large flax spinning mill using water power had been built at Sydnope on the eastern side of the village in 1826,[44] he found that "agriculture and the mining business [were] the chief supports of the inhabitants."[45] The lead mines were at Snitterton and Wensley, on the western side of the valley.[46] Gritstone was extracted from Heathcote's quarry at Stonecliffe, between Darley and Northwood.

This view of Darley is confirmed by the occupations given in the 1841 census. By far the largest number of residents were employed in agriculture. In those parts of the parish of Darley Dale to the east of the Derwent there were almost fifty farmers and slightly more agricultural labourers. Over forty people were employed in the flax mill, either as flax dressers, flax spinners, or bleachers. They tended to be younger people, generally in their teens or twenties. The only sign of any remnants of domestic textile work were four stocking makers and one straw bonnet maker. About a dozen men were employed as stone cutters, presumably at Stonecliffe Quarry. Apart from these three main types of employment there were a handful of craftsmen or traders whose jobs were connected with agriculture and building, including six wheelwrights, five butchers, two cordwainers, three blacksmiths and a whitesmith, a waggoner, ten joiners and carpenters and six stonemasons.[47]

Although Darley Dale was still predominantly countryside with a rural economy, its occupants were not self-sufficient in the way that the Taylors had been eighty years previously, or John and Mary Ashton had been in Rowland in the seventeenth century. The development of more industrialised textile manufacture meant that fewer farmers' wives spun and hardly any farmers wove their own cloth. The growing tendency of farmers to employ labourers, who did not live in with them, also meant that an increasing number of farm workers did not have their food supplied directly by their employers.[48]

These factors, and the declining role of fairs, meant that there had begun to be a need for shopkeepers. Money was beginning to play a far more important role, even in the lives of small farmers. By 1835 Darley Dale had two bakers, a boot and shoe maker, a druggist and George Picklington, who was described merely as a shopkeeper. There was also an auctioneer.[49] The 1841 census refers to a draper, two tailors, a surgeon and a druggist. In 1846 there were four boot and shoe makers, three blacksmiths and two shopkeepers. Darley Dale had five public houses, The Crispin, The Nag's Head, The Plough, The Square and Compass and the Three Stags' Heads.

John Young, one of the two bakers, was also the village post master. In 1835 letters arrived by mail cart from Bakewell at two o'clock each day and were despatched at five o'clock every afternoon.[50]

From 1808 to 1838 the rector of the parish church of St Helens was the Reverend

Benjamin Lawrence, a wealthy absentee cleric who relied upon curates to administer to the day to day needs of his parishioners.[51] Unlike modern clergy, he did not receive a regular stipend, but depended upon income from the glebe lands and tithes paid by parishioners. Incumbents were entitled to one tenth of the produce of the land in the parish. Originally this was paid in kind, but gradually the giving of beasts and crops had been replaced by monetary payments. By the beginning of the nineteenth century the clergy in the areas around Darley and Matlock, had adopted a practice of employing surveyors to carry out annual appraisals of the crops growing in fields before harvest. The surveyors assessed the amounts of tithes payable per acre depending on the different crops grown by each occupier. These varied between 2s 6d and 4s 6d per acre for hay, 7s and 10s 6d per acre for oats and 12s and 14s per acre for wheat.[52] Farmers also paid one penny for each sheep, cow, foal or swarm of bees sold and a halfpenny for every calf sold.[53] Depending on the crops which he grew in any particular year, Henry probably paid something in the region of five to ten shillings per annum. Although that may not have been much, the income from tithes from the parish as a whole was substantial. In 1650, when there had been two rectors of Darley, one for the northern half of the parish and the other for the southern half, their joint incomes had been £150 per annum.[54] By the time that the Reverend William Ulithorn Wray was rector (1764–1808) the estimated income from tithes and the glebe lands in Darley was in the region of £1,000 per annum. This was one reason why the social standing of the clergy in English villages was often second only to that of the squire. A living in a prosperous agricultural parish provided a good means of income for the younger sons of the gentry, such as Wray, who was in fact the grandson of the twelfth Baronet of Glentworth.[55]

However the lack of any national system for the assessment of tithes led to anomalies, and in 1836 Parliament passed the Tithe Commutation Act. The Act established a Tithe Commission which was empowered to effect a commutation of tithes in kind to an annual monetary payment. It was hoped that this would normally be effected by agreement between the clergy and the local landowners, but a mechanism was provided for compulsion in the absence of agreement. In such circumstances assistant commissioners held a local enquiry and then recommended an award which became legally binding upon all. This involved detailed mapping and surveying of all land in the particular area.

A full survey of Darley Dale was carried out by George Nuttall, a valuer from Matlock, during the first half of 1839. A report was also prepared by Thomas Smith Woolley, an Assistant Tithe Commissioner. He found the land in the valley around Darley to be "rich" and "deep". The meadows adjoining the Derwent were "low, but extremely productive". The upland meadow was "highly manured and produce[d] a large quantity of the very finest description of Hay". However he was far less impressed by the "high moor", the area on the east of the parish which had been enclosed in 1769. "A few straggling patches only are cultivated – a considerable tract is planted and the remaining and much larger proportion is in its natural state, grouse preserve only."

When he came to describe the farms and their occupants, he stated:

> The farms are very small. The occupiers generally a remarkably industrious class, farming with an utter disregard of everything approaching to system, the only grain grown is wheat or oats, the high grounds producing oats only – of bad quality, ripening very late.[56]

Small farmers generally lacked the acreage or capital to improve the quality of their stock or grasslands. They also tended to be more ignorant and conservative.

According to the survey, Henry Ashton owned and occupied two houses in Northwood, a cowhouse, a garden, an orchard which was also used as pasture, two sheep closes and some rough woodland. Together these pieces of land amounted to two acres, three roods, seventeen perches. As a result of the apportionment by the assistant commissioner, the amount which was to be paid by him to the rector was to be five shillings and three pence halfpenny each year. His brother Thomas, who owned five acres thirty-seven perches, was to pay eleven shillings and six pence. Altogether the rector was to be paid £261 each year, split between one hundred and twenty-nine owners of land in Darley and Little Rowsley.[57]

Another financial obligation which Henry and Thomas Ashton had to meet was the poor rate. After the introduction of the Poor Law Amendment Act of 1834, local parishes ceased to be responsible for poor relief. They were replaced by poor law unions and elected boards of guardians who collected rates in their place. These rates, which were calculated according to the gross estimated rental of land, were paid by all occupiers of land. In 1840 the gross estimated rental of Henry's land was £7 18s 6d per annum. Its rateable value was £7 0s 5d. The gross estimated rental of land occupied by Thomas was £3 15s 8d and its rateable value was £3 9s 4d. By this time however much of Thomas's land was farmed by his son-in-law John Derbyshire. The gross estimated rental of the land which he occupied was £12 3s 1d.[58]

Even before the Great Reform Act of 1832 extended the Parliamentary franchise, Henry and Thomas, as forty shilling freeholders, had the right to vote. However until the 1830s, the infrequency of contested elections meant that in practice it was a virtually meaningless right. In the previous 135 years there had only been three contested elections in the Northern Division of Derbyshire, which included Darley. They had taken place in 1701, 1734 and 1768. On other occasions North Derbyshire's two Members of Parliament had been returned unopposed and without an election. In the long term the Reform Act was the most important of the reforms introduced by Lord Grey's government, but even after it became law, the franchise was still very limited. No women were entitled to vote and only one man in six had the vote. There were still no secret ballots and, as a result, votes could be bought and corruption was still widespread.

The first election after the passing of the Reform Act was called in December 1832. There were three candidates for the two seats in the North Derbyshire Division, Lord Cavendish of Hardwick Hall, Sir George Sitwell of Renishaw Hall and Thomas Gisborne of Howich Hall. They all rode into Bakewell on 17th December, escorted by supporters on horseback, with flags and to the sound of music. Cavendish's colour was orange and his slogan "Reform for Ever". Sitwell's colour was pink and his slogan "Independence". Gisborne's colours were pink and white and his slogan "Union and Victory." All three addressed the crowds and then a show of hands was taken. There appeared to be a significant majority for Lord Cavendish and Thomas Gisborne, but Sir George Sitwell did not accept the result and demanded a poll. Polling began on 20th December, and was due to last for two days, but on the evening of 20th December, Sitwell conceded defeat. The voting was:

| Cavendish | 3,377 |
| Gisborne | 2,384 |
| Sitwell | 1,193 |

It is impossible to know whether or not Henry Ashton was among the noisy throngs of men from the outlying villages who had crowded into Bakewell. Although both he and his brother Thomas Ashton would have been eligible to vote, neither of their names appeared in the electoral register.[59] Perhaps they were not interested in the election or thought that the result was a foregone conclusion. It is even possible that there was some manipulation of the register. Whatever the reason may have been, Henry and Thomas Ashton were not the only men in the area whose names failed to appear in the register. In 1832 the names of only fifty-seven men in Darley and Little Rowsley were listed.

In the 1837 election, there was again a choice of three candidates, with two MPs to be returned. The Hon. George Henry Cavendish, a relative of the Duke of Devonshire and George Arkwright of Sutton Hall, were elected. The defeated candidate was William Evans of Allestree. George Henry Cavendish was to be Member of Parliament for the seat until shortly before his death in 1880. Henry Ashton's name still did not appear on the electoral register, but his brother Thomas voted for Cavendish and Evans.[60]

From 1838 the names of both Henry and Thomas Ashton appeared regularly in the Register of Electors. By 1841, the number of men in Darley and Little Rowsley listed in the electoral register had increased to one hundred and fourteen, but this was still less than a quarter of the adult male population of Darley and Little Rowsley.[61]

By the time that the 1841 census was taken, Henry and Mary's household, was reduced to just four people. Henry, who by now was in his eighties, and Mary who was in her fifties, lived with one unmarried daughter, Ellen, and their illegitimate grandchild, Hannah. She was the daughter of Harriet Ashton and John Hawley, a blacksmith, and had been born in March 1838. Henry was listed as having "independent means" although Bagshaw's directory in 1846 still described him as a farmer. Their youngest daughter Sarah was living next door as a house servant with the Preston family. According to the 1841 census, John Preston was a labourer, although in 1846 Bagshaw's Directory described him as a wheelwright. Sarah died four years later on 11th September 1845 at the age of eighteen.

Henry's younger brother Thomas died on 12th July 1845 in Northwood, aged 81. Most of the land which he had farmed, although left to his widow Mary "for and during her natural life for her own use and benefit", was in fact farmed by his son-in-law John Derbyshire who was married to his daughter Elizabeth.[62] His widow Mary lived in a cottage, called "The Meadow" on the road from Darley to Rowsley.

In 1846 Thomas's widow Mary found that her land was in the path of a railway line which it was proposed should run from Lancashire, through Buxton, Bakewell and Matlock to Ambergate on the North Midland line slightly north of Derby, a route of just over forty miles. The company, the Manchester, Buxton, Matlock and Midland Junction Railway, surveyed a route for the line prior to seeking Parliamentary approval for their plans. The map prepared shows the proposed railway line, with a permitted "limit of deviation", slicing through the meadowland just to the east of the River Derwent. The survey listed Mary as being the owner of a house, a stable, a cart shed, a pigsty, a road, a yard, offices, an orchard, gardens and appurtenances. All of these, apart from the cottage where she lived, were recorded as being in the occupation of John Derbyshire.[63] The Act of Parliament required to permit the building of the line was passed on 16th July 1846 and authorised the company to raise capital of £1,650,000. However the company had difficulty raising this sum, and the following year put forward a Deviation Bill which would allow the proposed line to follow a cheaper route at the northern end of the line. A revised survey was prepared during 1847 and land owners were canvassed for their views on the proposed changes. They did not affect Mary Ashton and her views were recorded as being "neuter". However the land which in 1846 was farmed by John Derbyshire was in 1847 recorded as being in the occupation of John Ashton, her eldest son, who was born in 1807.[64]

The first stage of the line, from Ambergate to Rowsley, which was eleven and a half miles long, opened on 4th June 1849, with a station in Darley Dale, about half a mile south-east of the church. By 1857 there were five passenger trains and one goods train running between Rowsley and Ambergate each day,[65] but the connection through from Rowsley via Millers Dale to Manchester was not finally completed until 1867.

Henry Ashton died on 9th March 1850, at his home in Northwood, at the age of eighty-eight. His wife Mary was present, but no doctor attended to certify the cause of his death. He was buried in the churchyard in Darley, near to the gravestones of his parents and his brother. When Mary reported his death to the Registrar in Matlock three weeks later, the cause of death was recorded as "decay of nature".

Soon after Henry's death, his widow Mary moved to Darley Hall Farm. The Farm and its fifty-seven acres were rented by John Derbyshire, who had married Elizabeth Ashton, one of the daughters of Henry's brother, Thomas Ashton. Mary and Thomas's widow, also called Mary Ashton, lived with John, his two sons and his second wife, Hannah.[66] The land in Northwood which Henry Ashton had farmed was sold[67] and the proceeds of the sale used to buy an annuity for his widow Mary. The 1851 census described both Mary Ashtons as annuitants and "visitors". They were aged sixty-six and eighty-two respectively. Between them they had given birth to twenty-one children. Their lives had undoubtedly been hard and it may be that this was the first period when they were free from the combined burdens of rearing children, running homes and performing their share of the farmwork.

Thomas Ashton's widow died on 12th June 1854 aged eighty-one. On her death, in accordance with the terms of her husband's will, his land and other possessions, which had provided an income for Mary while she was a widow, were shared between her children George, John, Samuel, Harriott, Ann and Elizabeth. After her death, Henry's widow, Mary, moved to Wichnor, a hamlet in the Trent valley, five miles north-east of Lichfield. She lived there with one of her sons, Henry, and his wife Ann, who farmed 178 acres of land.[68]

Mary died on 2nd June 1859 of old age. Her body was brought back from Wichnor to Darley where she was buried four days later in the same plot as her husband. Their gravestone reads:

> In remembrance
> of
> Henry Ashton
> of Northwood in this parish
> who died March 9th 1850
> aged 88 years.
> Also Mary, wife of
> the above who departed
> this life June 2nd 1859
> aged 75 years.
> God grant as we have been partakers
> of His death and passion so may we be
> of His resurrection.

Neither Henry nor his widow left a will. Probably they had no assets to dispose of.

For the Ashtons, Mary's death marked the close of an era and the end of a way of life which had evolved gradually over the centuries. Their connection with the rural agricultural communities of Derbyshire was over. By the time that the 1861 census was taken two years after Mary's death, none of Henry and Mary's children was still living in Darley Dale.[69] They had been swept up by the Industrial Revolution and transported to the new cities. The family had ceased to be a simple, largely self-sufficient economic unit, and instead became part of the complex economic structure of today, involving factories, service industries, agricultural producers, wholesalers and retailers. If ever there was a generation gap between Ashtons, it was between Henry and Mary and their children.

## Notes

1. See marriage at Darley, 13 February 1769.
2. He was not listed as occupying any land in Darley in the 1805 land tax returns. Derbyshire RO (Matlock), XM 1/195. There is no evidence that his brothers acquired Charles's land. XM/1/196. Alice, the daughter of Charles and Elizabeth Ashton, was baptised at Manchester Cathedral in 1809. There is no IGI reference to any marriage of a Charles and Elizabeth Ashton in Lancashire.
3. Land tax returns, Derbyshire RO (Matlock), XM 1/187, XM 1/194, XM 1/196 and XM 1/197.
4. This seems to be the most likely explanation for the circumstances which led to Mary and Henry being married five and a half months before the birth of their eldest child.
5. There are however examples of men becoming fathers at even more advanced ages. In July 1991 the wife of 92-year-old Australian Les Colley gave birth to a baby boy. There are also reports of a Brazilian man aged 112 who fathered a daughter. (*Independent* 2nd August 1991, *Guardian* 3rd August 1991)
6. See page 75.
7. Ann Kussmaul, *Servants in Husbandry in Early Modern England*, 1984, p 3.
8. "An Act for the Better Preventing of Clandestine Marriages" (Lord Hardwicke's Marriage Act), 1753.
9. Darley Parish Registers 1800–04. The baptismal register gives dates of birth. Thirty-five couples were married during the period. Two brides had already given birth to illegitimate children and a further nine gave birth less than seven months after marriage (one in Wirksworth). No baptismal entries were found in relation to nine couples, either because they did not live in Darley after marriage (other parishes not searched) or because they had no children or because there was a significant delay before the baptism of their first child. Obviously these nine may have included brides who were pregnant on marriage.
10. Lawrence Stone, *The Family, Sex and Marriage in England 1500–1800*, pp 385–388 (on occasion over 40%); J R Gillish, *For Better, For Worse, British Marriages*, quoted in Rogers and Smith, *Local Family History*, p 46 (30 per cent in Culcheth, Lancs in the early nineteenth century); David Levine, *Reproducing Families*, pp 77, 89 and 122 (rise from 15 per cent in 1680 to 35 per cent in 1880); and R M Smith, "Marriage Processes in the English Past" in Lloyd Bonfield and others, *The World We Have Gained* pp 85–92 (where he makes the point that the percentages of brides who were pregnant understate the numbers of women who were sexually active before marriage). cf Peter Laslett, *The World We Have Lost*, pp 130–1 and 139–45 ("sexual intercourse outside marriage was universally condemned.")
11. Alan MacFarlane, *Marriage and Love in England*, pp 299–301 and 304–7.
12. See David Levine, *Reproducing Families*, pp 79–90 and 115–7.
13. Stone, pp 52–4.
14. See note 6 in Chapter 4.
15. David Levine, *Reproducing Families*, pp 131 and 139–40.
16. See also his will, p 74 below.
17. Reports of the Commissioners to Inquire Concerning Charities and Education, Derby, pp 598–9.
18. J C Cox, *The Churches of Derbyshire*, Vol 2, p 156; Bagshaw, History, Gazetteer and Directory of Derbyshire, p 473 and records of the National Society.
19. Quoted in Marion Johnson, *Derbyshire Village Schools in the Nineteenth Century*, pp 92–3. By 1857, the number of pupils at the national school had increased to 150 (White).
20. Darley Parish Registers 1800–04. Thirty-five couples were married. Omitting those people who did not state that they lived in Darley, twenty men could write their names, while nine placed their mark in the register. Only eleven women could write their names. Twenty-two women entered their mark.
21. Farey, *A General View of the Agriculture of Derbyshire*, 1815, Vol 2, pp 15, 19 and 20.
22. Land Tax Returns, Derbyshire RO (Matlock), XM 1/197.
23. There is no reference to them in any contemporary directory, but the surname is local.
24. Land Tax Returns, Derbyshire RO (Matlock), XM/1/200.
25. Thomas Ashton's will.
26. Derbyshire RO (Matlock), D2360/DL 23.
27. cf Derbyshire RO (Matlock), XM 1/201 1830 and 1831.
28. B R Mitchell, *British Historical Statistics*, 1988, pp 756–7; Lord Ernle, *English Farming, Past and Present*, 6th ed., 1961, Appendix III p 489; Chambers and Mingay, pp 113 and 125; and G D H Cole and Raymond Postgate, *The Common People 1746–1946*, p 191. The comparable figures for oats were 44/6d (1812), 23/7d (1815) and 18/1d (1822).

29. In many communities enclosure played a significant part in the destruction of the self-sufficient peasant society, but the effect of the 1769 enclosure in Darley was probably negligible. The land enclosed was waste, and was probably not used much for grazing.

30. The total poor rate contributions for Darley rose from £232 in 1801 to £348 in 1811, to £473 in 1813 and to £531 in 1814. Although they subsequently reduced, they never returned to their pre-war levels. (Derbyshire RO (Matlock), Poor Rate Township Returns, QAG, p 92.)

31. p 130. cf Hoskins, *The Midland Peasant*, pp 265–272, describing "the end of a peasant society" as a result of enclosure and agricultural depression in a very different village.

32. Farey, Vol 2, p 43, p 94.

33. Farey, Vol 2, p 457. Bagshaw, p 473.

34. *The Peak and the Plain: Scenes in Woodland, Field and Mountain* (1853), p 260. The fair described was held on 9th May 1826.

35. White, *Gazetteer and History of Derbyshire*, 1857.

36. Made in 1810.

37. He was the grandfather of Lord Denman (1779–1854), Lord Chief Justice, and "for many years he practised as a surgeon" in Bakewell. Foss, *Biographical Dictionary of the Judges of England*.

38. See letter from Robert Thornhill, 30th November 1970.

39. This John was the nephew of Robert Ashton, described in Chapter 3. William Ashton, Valentine Ashton and Mary Grafton were his children and the great grandchildren of John Ashton (1638–90) described in Chapter 2.

40. Balguy referred to the earlier decision in *R v. The Inhabitants of Margam* (1793) 5 Term Reports 153 as authority for this finding. For the development of "derivative settlement" (i.e. derived from the settlement of parents, or even grandparents), see Webbs, English Local Government, *English Poor Law History*, Part 1, The Old Poor Law, pp 333–4.

41. Kenneth Morgan, *The Oxford History of England*, p 477, cf Wrigley and Schofield pp 534–5, who give comparative figures of 7 m and 16½ m by back-projection.

42. Farey, *A View of the Present State of Derbyshire*, p 464.

43. Schedules to 1801 and 1851 censuses. These figures do not include Wensley and Snitterton to the west of the River Derwent, which were in Wirksworth Hundred and which were listed separately.

44. Bagshaw's Directory, 1846.

45. Stephen Glover, *The Peak Guide*, 1830. See too the list of occupations in Pigot, 1835. See too White in 1857.

46. Farey, *A General View of the Agriculture of Derbyshire*, 1811, Vol 1, p 252.

47. HO 107 184. These figures have to be viewed with some caution. Parts of the census microfilm are illegible. Often the term "labourer" is used without giving any indication of the type of work involved and I have made no attempt to count the number of domestic servants. These figures do however give a "broad brush" impression of the types of employment available in Darley in the mid-nineteenth century. cf the lower ratio of farmers to labourers quoted in David Levine, *Reproducing Families*, pp 62–3. The small number of labourers employed in Darley would seem to be an indication that small-scale, self-sufficient farmers clung on to their traditional way of life for longer than farmers in some other parts of the country.

48. See Chambers and Mingay, p 19.

49. Pigot and Co's *Directory of Derbyshire*, 1835, p 38.

50. Pigot, p 38.

51. Bagshaw, p 474, and "William Ulithorn Wray", by Ernest Paulson, *Derbyshire Miscellany*, Vol VII, Part 1, Spring 1974, p 10 at p 38. Residence requirements for clergy were not introduced until the Pluralities Act of 1838.

52. Farey, vol 2, p 27. Cash payments were common elsewhere – see eg Chambers and Mingay, p 46.

53. PRO, IR18/888.

54. Lambeth Palace Library, COMM. xii a 6 427–8.

55. Wray succeeded to the baronetcy four years before his death, but because of his spendthrift characteristics, his cousin Sir Cecil Wray barred the entail, depriving him of any income. "William Ulithorn Wray", by Ernest Paulson, *Derbyshire Miscellany*, Vol VII, Part 1, Spring 1974, pp 10–39.

56. PRO IR 18 888.

57. Derbyshire RO (Matlock), D2360/DL 23.

58. Derbyshire RO (Matlock), 504B AP2.

59. Register of Electors, Matlock Local Studies Library, 1838–9, 1841–2 and 1844–5.

60. Poll Book, Institute of Historical Research, London. [He was described as "of Torrside". On the

25" OS Map Tor Farm adjoins "The Meadow" where his widow Mary later lived. NB Off Licence called The Meadow on the A6.]

61. In 1841 there were 483 males aged over twenty in Darley (including High Peak and Wirksworth hundreds).
62. See will of Thomas Ashton, 1845.
63. House of Lords RO, M21.
64. House of Lords RO, M232.
65. White, *Gazetteer and History of Derbyshire*, 1857.
66. See census HO 107 2150 and baptisms in Darley of Thomas Ashton Derbyshire (15th November 1835) and Henry Derbyshire (22nd October 1837). Their mother was Elizabeth Derbyshire. They were born in Manchester.
67. There is no reference to any auction of the land in the *Derby and Chesterfield Reporter* between 15th March 1850 and May 1851. Nor are there any auctioneer's particulars relating to the sale at Derbyshire RO (Matlock).
68. HO 107 2012 fo 406 and will of Henry Ashton 1860. (cf HO 107 976 and RG9 1967 – no reference to Henry Ashton in Wichnor in 1841 or 1861 censuses.)
69. RG9 2541.

# 7

Robert, Henry and Mary's third child, left Northwood for Manchester sometime during the late 1820s or the first half of the 1830s. It may be that he had visited Manchester previously, perhaps to visit his uncle Charles, or to sell boxes of vegetables or fruit from the family's small orchard on the fringes of one of the markets. On Saturdays Manchester's Smithfield Market in particular was frequented by farmers and country people with farm produce to sell.[1]

There are no records of the date of his departure, or of the means by which he travelled. He may have walked all the way to Manchester, a journey of almost forty miles which would probably have taken him two days. On the other hand, he may have been a passenger on one of the horse-drawn stage coaches which plied daily between Derby, Nottingham and Manchester, along the road running beside the River Derwent at the bottom of Northwood Lane. If he did so, it is likely that he sat on one of the cheaper seats on the roof of the coach. In 1829 five stage coaches passed through Bakewell on their way to Manchester each day. The Royal Mail coming from Sheffield left Bakewell at seven o'clock each morning. The Lord Nelson from Nottingham and The Bruce from London both departed at eleven o'clock. The Peverel of the Peak and The Times which both started their journeys in London left at three o'clock each afternoon.

Whether he went on foot or by coach, Robert would have travelled along the wooded valley of the Wye, up over the moors by Taddington, and then through the limestone gorges of the Upper Wye valley to Buxton, which was already a well established spa town with elegant Georgian buildings frequented by the fashionable and the rich. After Buxton, the road descended via Stockport into the recently developed industrial area just to the south of Manchester.

Robert was following a well-trodden path. The first half of the nineteenth century was a period of massive migration from the villages to the new industrial cities. Principally people came to work in Manchester from other parts of Lancashire and from nearby counties, such as Cheshire, Staffordshire and Derbyshire, but Mrs Gaskell's novel, *Mary Barton*, describes labourers travelling to Manchester from as far away as Buckinghamshire.[2]

For Robert, there were few reasons to stay in Northwood. He had grown up during the twenty years of agricultural depression which followed the end of the wars against the French. He had seen the traditional self-sufficient way of life, which his ancestors had followed, become untenable. The land which his father owned was too small to provide a good living for his family, and Robert no doubt assumed that if his parents still owned the farm and land when they died, the small fields would be shared out between his brothers, and possibly sisters, so that the parcels which each of them inherited would be minuscule. In addition, the invention of the power loom and the growth of factories meant that it was no longer possible for small farmers to supplement their income by spinning and weaving. The standard of living in the countryside had declined. In contrast there were far better prospects of work in Manchester, where wages were higher. Robert had no doubt heard about these, perhaps from his uncle, Charles, and his elder brother, Henry, who were both already living in Manchester.[3] His elder sister Ann travelled even further. After marrying a man called John Shepheard in Manchester on 29th April 1823, she emigrated to the United States of America.[4] Later Robert's younger brothers and sisters, Valentine, Charles, Jane, Ellen and Hannah, all moved to Manchester.[5]

By 1841 the population of Manchester was approximately eight times greater than it had been in 1774. During less than seventy years the combined population of Manchester, Salford and Chorlton-cum-Medlock had risen to 354,142. Between 1831 and 1841 it increased by almost 80,000.[6]

Manchester and the surrounding area were dominated by industry, and in particular by tall red brick textile mills. The town and the neighbouring area were famous for the manufacture of cotton, silk and linen. Increasingly machinery was driven by steam and by the 1830s power looms were largely replacing the labour of individual handloom weavers. In 1841, factories in Manchester exported 258 million pounds of yarn.[7] There were also important engineering and tool-making works. The French visitor Leon Faucher noted that during the daytime, in many parts of town, the roads were deserted and silent apart from the noise of machinery emanating from the factories. The streets only became packed with people when workers came out of the factories.

The Manchester of the 1830s and 1840s was perceived throughout the country, and in Europe, as one of the foremost examples of a modern manufacturing city. Disraeli was able to describe it as "a Lancashire village [which] has expanded into a mighty region of factories and warehouses" which was "as great a human exploit as Athens".[8] The money generated by industry was being used to erect many handsome buildings. New hospitals and public buildings were being built in a neo-classical style. The institutions of a modern city were beginning to appear. A new town hall had been built in 1832. The gas works which had been constructed in 1817 already supplied gas for lighting to many parts of the town. There were public baths. The Manchester and Salford Water Works Company, which had been established in 1808, had laid seventy miles of iron mains. Even so, in the poorer areas, the inhabitants almost invariably used communal pumps in courtyards or streets, which were liable to contamination from neighbouring cess pools, or rain water collected in butts, which was so blackened by soot that it could not be used until it had been allowed to settle. A police force had been established. In 1841 its 390 officers apprehended 13,345 criminals. The fire brigade had seven engines. There were nine different banks, a savings bank and a number of building societies. There were already many shops, and Faucher noted "*les magasins ouverts au luxe*" in Picadilly. Five different newspapers had a total average circulation of over 18,500. There was a concert hall and a choral society. There were even zoological gardens in Higher Broughton with elephants, monkeys and polar bears.[9] Even so many streets were still unpaved. In the early 1830s of 687 streets, 284 were not paved at all and 53 were only partly paved. 352 streets contained "heaps of refuse, stagnant pools, ordure etc."[10]

There was a huge gulf between the rich and poor. The Reverend R Parkinson, Canon of the Collegiate Church in Manchester, said:

There is no town in the world where the distance between the rich and the poor is so great, or the barrier between them so difficult to be crossed.[11]

This was epitomised by the way in which life expectancy varied between the classes. A professional person or member of the gentry could expect to live for thirty-eight years. However the life expectancy of shop-keepers was twenty years and of factory workers and journeymen only seventeen years. According to Faucher:

*Les ouvriers de Manchester sont pâles et grêles, leur physionomie n'a pas cette animation qui est la signe de la force de la santé. La beauté des femmes disparait, et la vigueur des hommes, qui décline, est remplacée par une enérgie fébrile.*[12]

Queen Victoria, visiting Manchester in 1851, noted the "painfully unhealthy looking population which she saw." The rate of mortality in Manchester in 1839/40 was 1 in 28, whereas in England and Wales as a whole it was almost 1 in 45.[13] In 1840 half of all deaths in Manchester were of children aged less than four.

Domestic sanitation was still largely limited to the old system of earth privies. Although Manchester's Paving and Soughing Committee laid thirty-four miles of sewers between 1830 and 1844, they did little to improve the more critical problem of the disposal of night soil and other household refuse. Water closets were extremely uncommon. In some of the poorer districts, even privies were rare. Inhabitants either deposited their night soil on "communal" privy middens, or else emptied their chamber pots clandestinely in the streets. (The Manchester police statistics for 1845 include details of the number of prosecutions for Emptying Chamber Utensils in the street.) In some areas privately employed night soil men were paid by property owners at the rate of three shillings for each two ton load of night soil which they took away, and sold to farmers for use as manure. However, from 1846, the Borough Council, bearing in mind not only the implications for public health, but also the annual profit of £6,300, which they believed that they could make from the sale of 60,000 to 70,000 tons of human excrement, employed seventy night soil men with twenty-four carts to do the job.[14]

Housing conditions were often appalling. Love, who generally wrote positively about life in Manchester, admitted that:

The dwelling houses of the operatives of Manchester need great improvement. Many houses are without back doors, or any outlet except the front door. This opens frequently into a narrow street containing thirty or forty similar dwellings, which street is made to serve not merely the purpose of a thoroughfare, but of an exposed main sewer.[15]

Many families lived in dark, cramped, poorly drained and unventilated cellars. Often these cellars lacked furniture,

bricks, logs of wood, and other contrivances being frequently used as substitutes for tables and chairs, while the bag of shavings or litter of straw is laid in some corner, to be occupied nightly by the miserable tenants . . . Frequently different families occupy opposite corners of the same room, the sexes being no further separated than by the few feet of space which lie between their respective beds of straw.[16]

Mr Buckland, a missionary to the poor, described the suffering of one family:

In a house almost destitute of anything in the shape of furniture or things of domestic convenience, lived a man and wife and three small children. The husband had been ill for a long time, so that the family was supported by the labour of a woman and what little the eldest child not ten years of age could do. For the last twelve months their whole income has not, I believe, exceeded six or seven shillings a week . . . Last Sunday fortnight the husband died. The little boy was weaving till past eleven o'clock on Saturday night, and the woman was washing the childrens' few bits of clothes. Soon after midnight the poor man, who was lying on what was intended for a bed in the same room was suddenly taken worse; it was evident that he was struggling with death; the little boy was dispatched to a relative, a short distance off, almost in a state of nudity, having only an old cloak over him. This was about one o'clock on Sabbath morning, and the poor man was a few minutes afterwards released from his poverty and his sufferings by the friendly hand of death. I cannot describe the scene which I witnessed next day, or rather the same day. No words can represent it. The simple facts which I have stated will speak for themselves.[17]

The fear of such destitution and the dire consequences of poverty must have rested in the backs of the minds of all who lacked the security of the professional and upper classes. The literature of the time frequently refers to respectable and decent folk who fell on hard times. Robert however was young and able-bodied and initially seems to have had no difficulty in finding employment. He worked as a house servant, probably in Longsight.

Although servants worked long hours, Robert did find the time to start courting a young Scottish woman, Ellen Steel.[18] She was one of many Scots in Manchester. By 1841 the population of Lancashire included 21,000 Scots and over 105,000 Irish.[19]

During the autumn of 1836 Ellen found that she was pregnant. The nineteenth century was undoubtedly a period when sexual relations outside marriage were condemned by a large proportion of the population, not only for religious reasons, but also because illegitimate children and their mothers almost inevitably became a charge on the poor law authorities. Indeed it has been said that "the combined result of early bastardy legislation and its obsession with guilt was to stigmatize and ostracize both mother and child and inflict an often unbearable cruelty which compelled concealment, abortion, desertion and infanticide and the later horrors of baby farming."[20] Rates of infant mortality were also higher among illegitimate children. Even so sexual relations outside marriage were by no means uncommon. The proportion of illegitimate children born rose during the 1830s and 1840s, with the Registrar General estimating in 1845 that 7 per cent of children were born out of wedlock, and those statistics do not take into account the large number of pregnant women who married before their children were born.[21]

Robert did marry Ellen, but their marriage did not take place until virtually the last moment before the birth of their child. They were married at St Mary's Church, a stone's throw away from the River Irwell, on 20th March 1837, just five days before their eldest daughter was born. They were married by William Keeling, a curate at the church, in the presence of Robert's younger brother Valentine and Thomas Clarke, a clerk who organised and witnessed many of the marriages at the church. Both Robert and Ellen were able to sign their names, although it was still not uncommon for couples who had been married to place their marks in the form of crosses in the register. Indeed in 1839, 41 per cent of the population of England was illiterate.[22] The mere fact that Robert and Ellen could write their names was not necessarily proof that either could write confidently or read fluently.

It is only possible to speculate why Robert and Ellen left it so late before they were married. It may be that this was an indication of Robert's fecklessness and the difficulty that friends and relatives had in forcing him to honour his obligations. On the other hand they may have wanted to marry earlier, but had to postpone the wedding for some reason, although it is hard to imagine what could have delayed it for so long.

Robert and Ellen's first daughter, Mary, was born on 25th March, but was not baptised until 11th June 1837, the month of Queen Victoria's coronation. She was baptised at the Collegiate Church which was to become Manchester Cathedral when the town was made into a city. 105 other children were baptised on the same day as Mary. This was typical of the number of children baptised on Sundays at the Collegiate Church. On 31st March 1839, the Easter Sunday when Robert and Ellen's second child Henry was baptised, two ministers baptised 160 children. This may have been due to the simple fact that fees for performing marriages and baptisms at the cathedral were cheaper than in the surrounding churches.[23] The parish register relating to Henry's baptism in 1839 recorded that Robert was still working as a servant, but had moved to Chorlton-cum-Medlock. It may be that he was living and working with his brother Valentine who gave his address as Brook Street, Chorlton-cum-Medlock when he was married in December 1839.

Ellen was to have a total of ten children, six girls and four boys. They were born roughly every two years. There were relatively long periods between the births of some of her children and their baptisms. This was particularly so for the younger children. The longest delays were before the baptisms of Anne (three years) and Margaret (almost two and a half years). Margaret was baptised at the same time as her younger brother Thomas. It has been said that after the Industrial Revolution practically no-one in the cities went to church and that Christianity belonged to the rural world which the new city dwellers had lost.[24] The time lag between the birth and the baptism of Robert and Ellen's children may be an indication that Robert and Ellen did not go to church regularly. It may be that Robert worked every Sunday and simply did not have the time to go to church. On the other hand it may be a further indication that Robert was feckless. Unfortunately it is impossible to know for certain.

In 1839 or 1840, Robert Ashton stopped working as a servant and tried to better himself by renting a grocer's shop at 51, Dickinson Street. In 1841 he was listed in Pigot and Slater's Directory as "a shopkeeper and dealer in groceries and sundries". The owner of the shop, Robert's landlord, was a Mr Matthew Corbett. He lived in Pimlott Street, Pendleton, and owned three other properties in Dickinson Street. Robert probably thought that the shop, which was at the Portland Street end of Dickinson Street was in a good location. It was only a couple of hundred yards away from the new town hall. Nearby, in the same street, there were a cotton spinning firm, a boatbuilder, a joiner, a hairdresser, a couple of merchants, Pickford and Co who were described as "carriers by Railway and canal", a lodging house, a couple of beer retailers and an organ builder.[25] Robert and Ellen lived above the shop, but sublet one room to William McGriffie, a cabinet maker, and his wife Sarah.[26]

The shop itself was probably dimly lit, perhaps with a window made from small panes of bottle glass. In the middle of the nineteenth century, window displays in shops were rare and prices of goods were not marked. It was normal for customers to haggle about prices. The walls of the shop were probably lined with jars, barrels, chests, drums, and drawers containing Robert's merchandise. In those days retailers were far more involved in the preparation and packing of food than at any time during the twentieth century. For example, Robert probably blended tea, mixed herbs and spices, cleaned and washed dried fruit, cut and cured bacon and chopped and ground cones of sugar. Adulteration of food by shop keepers was common, and if he was a typical grocer, Robert probably added "smouch", a mixture of dried ash leaves, to his tea and brick dust to his cocoa powder.[27]

In 1841, Robert, as the occupier of the shop, was assessed to pay a poor rate of £1 11s 6d per annum. This was based on a gross estimated rental of £16. Although gross estimated rentals for rating purposes did not always correspond with the actual rent paid, the estimated rental for rating purposes gives a rough indication of how much rent Robert was to pay to Mr Corbett each year. Manchester poor rates were levied at two shillings and four pence in the pound, a figure which would have been far higher if the overseers had not adopted a strict policy of avoiding making payments of poor relief to the many newcomers who had not acquired settlement.

While Robert and Ellen were living in Dickinson Street, Ellen gave birth to their third child, John. He was born on 1st March 1841.

Robert's hopes for the shop were soon dashed. He had chosen a very bad time to set up in business. Although the first half of the nineteenth century was generally a time of economic expansion, 1841 and 1842 were years of severe economic depression. The rapid growth of the preceding years had outstripped demand and, with inadequate transport to distribute goods and exploit new markets, there were surpluses, with the result that prices of manufactured goods began to fall. In Manchester large numbers of workers were laid off in the mills and factories. Others suffered substantial reductions in wages. By March 1842, 116 mills and factories had closed and there were 5,492 empty houses.[28] The effect of unemployment and short time working were aggravated by the fact that, as a result of a series of bad harvests, food prices were higher than at any time since 1819. The decade later became known as the "Hungry Forties". Many people became destitute. Many families pawned their belongings.[29] Sickness, among a population weakened by malnutrition and, not infrequently, starvation, spread. In 1841 the Bedding and Clothing Fund relieved 10,132 families, providing beds, counterpanes, blankets, sheets, petticoats etc.

The interests of tradesmen were closely connected with those of the labouring classes.[30] As their customers became unemployed and ceased to have money to spend, shopkeepers too found themselves in financial difficulties. Provision dealers and retail shopkeepers were particularly badly hit by the slump.

A meeting of the "shopkeepers, innkeepers, tradesmen, and retail dealers of Manchester" was held at the Town Hall on 16th June 1841. The meeting had been requisitioned by 233 shopkeepers. They wanted to make known publicly the "exceedingly depressed state of their trade". At the meeting "the most appalling statements of commercial decay and distress were made". Butchers told of how they were unable to sell prime beef costing between seven pence and nine pence a pound even at reduced prices of two pence halfpenny. They said that much meat went bad and that butchers were making losses of between £2 and £4 each Saturday. Many traders were not covering their rent.

A further meeting was held at the Spread Eagle Hotel, Hanging Ditch on 1st July when

Resolutions declaratory of the existence of unexampled distress, and of the utter hopelessness of improvement without legislative interference, were carried, and a deputation appointed "to wait upon Sir Robert Peel and such other members of Her Majesty's Government and Members of Parliament as may be practicable, to lay before them, on behalf of the shopkeepers and traders of the borough, the appalling facts which have come to their knowledge of the state of trade, and which are so undeniably manifest and to entreat them to adopt some means that shall give immediate and permanent relief. . ."[31]

A petition was prepared and signed.

By March 1842 681 shops had closed.[32] Those grocers and butchers who managed to continue trading reported that daily sales had been reduced by 40 per cent.

The effect which the slump had upon Robert's business was disastrous. He fell into debt. He found that he was unable to pay the full amount of the rates levied by the overseers for the poor. When a new rate was made in 1842, Robert Ashton was listed as having arrears of nine shillings due from the previous year. His predicament was however by no means unusual. In the rating years 1842/3, the occupiers of nine of the twenty-one properties at the southern end of Dickinson Street failed to pay some or all of the rates due.

Like many other small shopkeepers he was forced to give up his shop, probably sometime during 1842. It is not clear whether Mr Corbett forfeited the lease because Robert was not able to pay the rent, or whether fear of the debtor's prison forced him to close down.[33]

Whatever the immediate cause of Robert's departure was, Mr Corbett was unable to re-let 51, Dickinson Street for some time.[34]

Robert returned to work as a servant. He was described as a servant on the baptism of Ellen's next two children, Jane and Robert, who were born in 1843 and 1845. However, his growing family meant that it was no longer possible to live in at the premises where he worked. From 1843, he rented a terraced house at 26, Meredith Street, near Boundary Lane, in Hulme. His landlord there was William Jebson who owned two other houses in the same street. The rent which he paid was probably in the region of £11 per annum.[35] The house cannot have been finished long before Robert and Ellen moved in. It was one of many homes which were being built at the time for Manchester's rapidly expanding population. When Robert and Ellen lived there, it was right on the southern edge of the densely built up area of the Manchester conurbation. To the south was Greenheys, then a pleasant suburb with large houses and spacious gardens, and beyond, there was open countryside. Even so housing conditions in Hulme were still not good. Engels described Hulme as "really one big working-class quarter". He said that even in the less densely populated parts where "the houses are of more modern construction and more open to the fresh air . . . most of them are surrounded by filth. In general the cottages are damp."[36]

It is easy to assume that in moving from small villages to large cities people like Robert became isolated and lost the support provided by the extended network of relatives which existed in the countryside. The distance from Manchester to Darley, the hours which Robert worked, and the lack of holidays in the modern sense, meant that once he moved to Manchester he rarely saw his parents. However throughout his time in Manchester, Robert remained in touch with a number of his brothers and sisters, including his younger brother Valentine, who had been a witness at his wedding.

Valentine had been rather more successful than Robert. In 1839 he had set up in business as a cab proprietor, perhaps putting the £20 left to him by his godfather towards the capital needed to buy horses and a cab. It was a natural choice of occupation, allowing him to be his own master, and making use of the knowledge of horses which he had presumably acquired as a child in Northwood. As the years passed his business expanded. By 1843 he had a yard and stable in Sidney Street, off Oxford Street, although he lived at number 5, Fairfield Street, in Chorlton. By 1845 his younger brother Charles, who lived at 6 in No. 3 Square, Mason Street, had started working for him as a driver. By November in the same year, Robert had stopped working as a servant and he too was driving a cab for Valentine. In 1861 Valentine employed a stableman and six drivers and by 1871 nine men worked for him.[37]

Until 1842, hackney carriages and their proprietors were regulated by the Manchester Watch And Hackney Coach Committee. Watch committees had been set up throughout the country with responsibility for ensuring that the streets were safe, and it was under their auspices that the first police forces were established. Indeed the early minutes of the Manchester Watch Committee contain many references to police officers being fined for being asleep or drunk on duty and for buying drinks for prostitutes. The Committee also summonsed beer retailers for "keeping company" out of hours and refusing to open their doors when raided.

As the number of hackney coaches in Manchester increased, the Committee granted licences to their proprietors and made rules as to their conduct. In 1838 licences were granted for sixty-seven one- and two-horse hackney coaches.

On 28th October 1839 the Committee resolved to grant additional licences for twenty-six one horse cabriolets to ply for hire, making a total of ninety-six licensed hackney carriages. Cabriolets, which by the 1830s were generally known as "cabs", were light, two-wheeled carriages drawn by one horse. They had hoods of wood or leather and an apron to cover the legs and laps of their occupants. They were allowed to carry two adults and one child of up to two years old. Licence number sixteen was granted to Valentine Ashton. His licence which cost five shillings was renewed annually. He worked from the cab rank in St Ann's Square, off Deansgate, one of nine such ranks in Manchester. Twenty-one other hackney carriages were based at the same rank.[38] In 1842 fares for cabs carrying two people were one shilling for the first mile and three pence for every succeeding third of a mile, or if they were hired "for time" nine pence for the first quarter of an hour and four pence for each succeeding quarter of an hour. Night fares, between midnight and seven o'clock in the morning were double.[39] These fares were high when compared with ordinary wages and the people carried in cabs can only have been members of the richer sections of society. It has been estimated that the average weekly wage of a Lancashire cotton worker in 1840 was about ten shillings.[40] It is hard to determine Valentine's outgoings, but apart from the purchase of the cabs themselves and his horses, they cannot have been large. Although the horses needed feeding and stabling, these costs, and the wages which he paid his men, were probably relatively low.

In the first half of the nineteenth century, hackney coachmen enjoyed a poor reputation. In 1827, one writer stated, "Extortion is so prevalent . . . that a mild and passive passenger who hires [a hackney carriage] is almost certain to be cheated or insulted."[41] The regulations, made by the Watch Committee, which came to be embodied in the "Bye-Laws relating to all Coaches, Chariots, Cars, Cabriolets and Such Like Carriages", were a determined attempt to prevent passengers from being overcharged or otherwise exploited by cab drivers or their proprietors. They give some indication of the way in which Robert, Valentine and Charles Ashton worked. Owners' names were to be printed in letters not less than one inch in height on the outside of every carriage. Licence numbers were to be painted both on the outside and inside of the carriage in letters not less than two inches high. Drivers were obliged to provide all passengers with tickets which included their licence number for use "in case of complaint". Carriages were to be "ready to take a fare at the stand to which they shall have been appointed, from nine o'clock in the morning until twelve o'clock at night." The bye-laws also provided that "every driver shall be sober, and conduct himself in an orderly and respectful manner, and obey the reasonable orders of the person or persons hiring his carriage." Any owner or driver demanding more than the authorised fare was liable to a fine not exceeding £5. Offences against the bye-laws could be heard and determined by a single Justice of the Peace. If fines were not paid, they could be recovered by distress and sale of the offender's goods, and if distress was not successful, the bye-laws provided that "the offender or offenders shall be committed to the house of correction for the hundred of Salford, for any time not exceeding six weeks nor less than fourteen days."[42]

During the year ending 14th October 1839, nineteen drivers were fined for offences of overcharging. Nineteen drivers were punished for being drunk and disorderly. There were seventeen cases of "furious driving", thirty-one cases of plying for hire without a licence and three cases of failing to return articles left in coaches. Three drivers were prohibited from driving as a result of misconduct. For example, on 2nd December 1839 the Manchester Watch and Hackney Carriage Committee resolved that "Robert Mackay be prohibited from driving any carriage licensed by the Committee, he having been drunk on the stand on two days in succession."

By 1848 Robert and Ellen had moved to 2, Sunnyside, a house in a terrace overlooking the River Irwell in Lower Broughton.[43] Broughton had remained largely unaffected by Manchester's growth until the 1840s. During the first twenty years of the century, it had been a small village with a population of between 800 and 900. Even during the early 1840s Louis

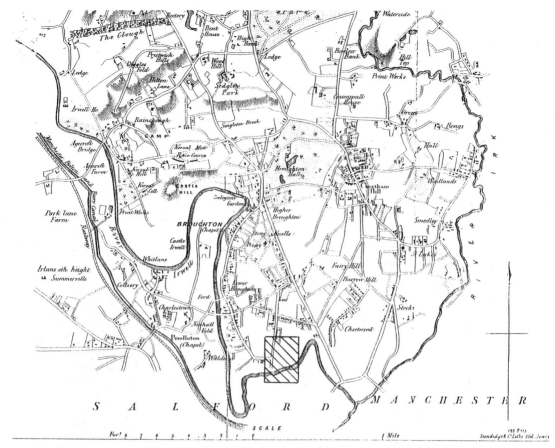

*Map 6 – Broughton and Cheetham Hill (1850). The box in the southern centre of the map represents
the area depicted on the map on the following page.*

Hayes was able to describe walking down Broughton Lane as being "very nice and sweet"
and to refer to wild flowers, summer houses and arbours nearby and to children swimming in
a clean sandy stretch of the River Irwell. From then onwards though, Broughton expanded
rapidly to house Manchester's overflowing population. In 1841 the population of Broughton
was 3,794 and by 1849 it had risen to 6,094.[44]

The policy of the Clowes family, who were lords of the manor and owned much of the
land there, was to restrict development to larger houses which they hoped would be occupied
by "a superior class" of residents. However at the southern end of the township, adjoining
the Irwell, the housing was more cramped and less salubrious. Indeed Sunnyside seems to
have been an attempt by a builder to try to make an extremely unattractive location appear
more pleasant than it actually was. The terrace of houses, which was built in a field which
had been called The Great Meadow, was sandwiched between the Elton Street Dye Works to
the west and a manure depot to the east. Directly in front of the house, which faced
southwards, there was a bank of a few feet leading down to the river. Leon Faucher referred
to the "*eaux noires et puantes*" (black and stinking waters) of Manchester's rivers.[45] Another
contemporary writer described their waters as "thick, black and filthy".[46] Engels wrote about
one Manchester river which had "a series of the most revolting blackish-green puddles of

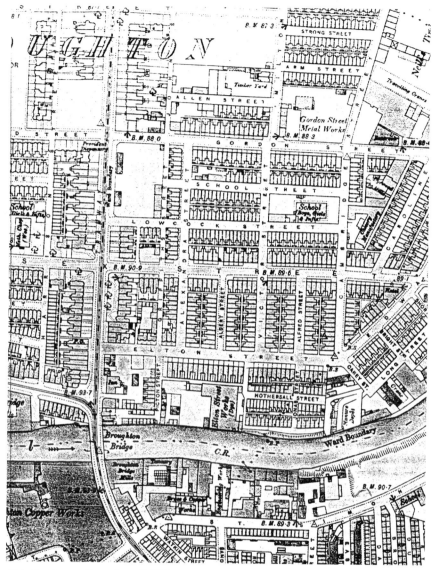

*Map 7 – Lower Broughton (1892).*

slime from the depths of which bubbles of miasmatic gases constantly rise and create a stench which is unbearable even to those standing on the bridge forty or fifty feet above the level of the water".[47]

The land on which Sunnyside was built was low lying and the river often burst its banks after heavy rain, flooding the ground floor of Robert and Ellen's home.[48] Nearby there were the Hopefield mills which manufactured worsted, the Broughton Copper Works, the Broughton Bridge Paper Mills, a tannery and an iron and brass foundry. To the rear of the house there was a very small yard with a privy and, like all of the houses in the area which were not built "back to back", a narrow alley, which was used by the night soil men. This became the typical lay-out of houses in the Manchester and Salford area after the Building and Sanitary Relations Committee of the Manchester Borough Council decided in 1844 that all new houses should be built with a privy and an ash-pit behind them.[49]

Sunnyside cannot have been a healthy environment in which to raise young children. At times of the year the air must have been particulary damp and smoky. Nevertheless none of Robert and Ellen's children died while they were living there and, in material terms, they were probably better off than they would have been had they not moved from the countryside. The wages which Robert earned enabled them to buy things which the predominantly subsistence existence which his father had followed would not have permitted. Paradoxically, the family probably also had what they considered to be a better diet. Engels referred to the better paid workers in Manchester having "meat every day and bacon and cheese for the evening meal."[50]

By 1851 Robert and his family had moved to 11, Sunnyside. Robert's sister Ellen was living with them.[51] At that time at least four of the twelve houses in Sunnyside were uninhabited. Next door to Robert and Ellen at number 10, their neighbour was Ann Fildes, a sixty-one year old widow from Newton, who lived with her unmarried son who was a warehouseman and her daughter who was a dressmaker. On the other side at number 12, another widow, Mrs Percival from Prestwich, worked as a charwoman. She lived with sons, a mechanic and a tailor, and a daughter who worked as a cap maker. Other neighbours living in Sunnyside had employment as a journeyman joiner, a smallwear weaver, a blacksmith and a mechanic.

During the 1850s Robert and Ellen moved to 19, Elton Street, Lower Broughton, about one hundred yards away. The street was probably developed by members of the Elton family. Jos Elton was a toll collector and builder who lived at Broughton Spout. (Nearby Broughton Bridge was still a toll bridge.) Mrs Ann Elton, who may have been his widow, lived first at 6, Irwell Terrace, Broughton Lower Road, and then at Elton's Yard, off Elton Street. In the 1861 census she was described as a "Proprietress of Houses". She was probably the landlord to whom the Ashtons paid their rent. In 1866 Robert and Ellen moved across the road to number 10, Elton Street, and then, about three years later, to number 28. The houses in Elton Street were slightly larger than those in Sunnyside, with small front gardens, rear additions and back yards. Numbers 10 and 28 were overlooked to the rear by the dye works which separated them from the River Irwell.[52]

Although Elton Street was only just round the corner from Sunnyside, it definitely represented "a step up in the world". Other people living in the same street in 1861 included two book-keepers, the manager of a print works, a retired brewer, a commercial clerk and accountant, the manager of a bank, a salesman in a Manchester warehouse, a master engineer, an importer of foreign provisions and a fancy box maker employing eight women, three girls, a boy and an agent. Of the twenty-five heads of household living in Elton Street who were listed in the 1861 census, only seven were born in Manchester or Salford. William Thomson, a fifty-seven year old book-keeper/accountant living at number 10 was born in Ireland and James Nelson, a fifty year old joiner living at number 18 was born in the Isle of Man. Besides Robert, three other heads of household hailed from Derbyshire.

Ellen's last child was born in November 1857 when she was forty years old. She was called Violetta. She was the only one of Robert and Ellen's children not to survive to adulthood. She died less than a year after her birth, on 20th October 1858. The cause of her death was whooping cough/pneumonia.

Although Elton Street was a little further away from the river than Sunnyside, the Ashtons were still affected when the Irwell flooded. The river had burst its banks in 1840, 1843 and 1852, and was to do so again in 1869, 1872 and 1881, but the most serious flooding occurred in 1866.[53] According to the *Manchester Weekly Times*:

The occasional overflow of the river for some distance from the banks is a periodical misfortune at intervals of a few years in the lower parts of Broughton and Salford, but the inundation of yesterday [16th November] was of a character to which those minor floods formed no precedent. The consequences to some hundreds of inhabitants who before night were obliged to leave their homes and depend upon the civic authorities for shelter will render this a somewhat memorable calamity . . . Early in the morning the waters had spread over a great part of Lower Broughton and by midday the whole district . . . was totally submerged . . . Those with no other place of refuge were taken to the Town Hall and lodged on the basement floor.

In view of the location of Elton Street, there can be no doubt that Robert, Ellen and their children were forced to leave home, although it is impossible to know where they stayed until the waters subsided.

As a result of the flooding, few of the people listed in the 1861 census stayed in Elton Street for long, and gradually the tone of the neighbourhood began to decline. Those who could afford the rents elsewhere chose to move to higher and more salubrious ground. In 1871 only five of the families who had been living in the street in 1861, besides the Ashtons, remained. By 1881 only one other family had lived in Elton Street for twenty years. Widow Sheldon who lived at number 22 throughout this period was a brewer's widow who was born in Bakewell and who took in lodgers. By 1881 almost all the people living in Elton Street were craftsmen. They included another coachman, a shoemaker, a barrel maker, a chemist, a warder at Strangeways Prison, a brass finisher, two iron turners, a bricklayer, an engine driver, a French polisher, a plasterer, a costermonger, two labourers and an estate agent's clerk. Robert and Ellen, perhaps because they did not have the means to pay more rent, stayed where they were.

Throughout this period, and even before the 1867 Reform Act extended parliamentary suffrage in towns to all male householders, Robert was eligible to vote in elections. The house which he rented had a "yearly value of not less than Ten Pounds" and so his name appeared regularly in the "List[s] of Persons entitled to vote in the Election of a Member for the Borough of Salford, in respect of property occupied within the Township of Broughton-with-Kersal, by virtue of an Act passed in the Second Year of the Reign of King William the Fourth" (i.e. the Great Reform Act of 1832). Also, as a male occupier of three years standing he was entitled to vote in municipal elections, provided that he paid the rate which was levied for poor relief.[54] Although secret ballots were not introduced until 1872, there are no records which indicate who Robert voted for, or even if he voted at all.

Sometime after 1872, Robert's employer and brother, Valentine moved out of Broughton and went to live at Patricroft, five miles to the west of central Manchester.[55] Robert probably retired as a coachman when Valentine gave up his business before moving. Certainly by the time of the 1881 census, Robert was described as a "retired coachman". He died on 26th May 1886 at 25, Elton Street. He was aged seventy-eight. His daughter-in-law [Sarah] Ellen Ashton of 1, Farrell Street was present when he died. He was buried three days later at the parish church of St John, Higher Broughton, a lofty Victorian Gothic church which had been consecrated in 1839. The causes of Robert's death were certified by Dr G H Pinder, MRCS, as pulmonary congestion and cardiac dilatation.

By 1889 Robert's widow, Ellen, had moved to 4, Alma Street, Eccles. This was a small red brick terraced house in a cul-de-sac of about forty houses. There was a bay window on the ground floor at the front which looked out onto a little front garden. At the back there was a rear addition and a small back yard which opened onto a back alley which was used by the night soil men. In 1891 she was living there with her three unmarried children, Henry, who was not described as having any occupation, Robert, who was working as a billiard marker, and Jane, who was described as living off her own means.

Ellen died in Alma Street on 25th June 1894, aged seventy-seven. The cause of her death was certified by Dr W Race, MB, as senectus (i.e old age), congestion of the lungs and syncope (i.e. weakness). Her daughter Sarah Parkinson of Oswall Road, Chorlton-cum-Hardy was present when she died. Like her husband, she was buried at St Johns, Higher Broughton, although the parish register described her as living in Eccles.

Neither Robert nor Ellen left a will. It is unlikely that they enjoyed sufficient income during their lifetimes to acquire any property or possessions to leave to their children.

## Notes

1.  B Love, *Handbook of Manchester*, 1842, p 242. For details of stage coach journeys along this route, see George Head, *A Home Tour Through the Manufacturing Districts of England in the Summer of 1835*, pp 92, 114.
2.  Penguin Classics Edition, p 43.
3.  Henry afterwards ran a shop in Longsight on the eastern edge of Manchester.
4.  See will of Henry Ashton of Wichnor, 1861. Their names do not appear in Filby and Lower's *Passenger and Immigration Lists*, 1st edn or the cumulative supplements 1982–5, 1987, 1988 or 1989. Robert's cousin Elizabeth also moved to Manchester temporarily, while her husband John Derbyshire worked there – see baptisms of their sons on 15th November 1835 and 22nd October 1837.
5.  Jane was witness at Valentine's marriage. Hannah was buried in 1893 at St John's, Broughton aged 70. Ellen lived with Robert in 1851 census. Charles lived in Rugby Street – 1861 census.
6.  Love, *Handbook of Manchester*, pp 21/3. These figures included Manchester, Salford and Chorlton-cum-Medlock.
7.  Love, *Handbook of Manchester*, 1842.
8.  Coningsby, Book IV, Chapter 1, page 2. For a contemporary description of Manchester and the surrounding towns, see Engels, *The Condition of the Working Class in England* (1958 edition), pp 52–8.
9.  Love, pp 243–83.
10. Dr J P Kay, *The Moral and Physical Condition of the Working Classes Employed in the Cotton Manufacture in Manchester*, 1832, p 30, quoted in Faucher, p 362 and Engels, *The Condition of the Working Class in England*, (1958) edition, p 76.
11. Quoted in Love, p 85.
12. *Etudes sur l'Angleterre*, 1845, p 369. ("The workers of Manchester are pale and thin. Their faces do not have that liveliness which is the sign of strength and health. The beauty of the women disappears, and the robustness of the men, as it declines, is replaced by a feverish energy.")
13. Faucher, p 369; Briggs, *Victorian Cities,* p 112; Love, p 26.
14. A Redford, *History of Local Government in Manchester*, pp 147–60.
15. p 104.
16. Joseph Adshead, *Distress in Manchester – Evidence of the State of the Labouring Classes in 1840–2.*
17. Adshead, p 28. See also Engels, pp 53–87.
18. All the censuses up to and including 1881 merely state her place of birth as "Scotland". However the 1891 census states that her place of birth was "Newcastle, Durham". Her name was spelt variously Ellen, Helen and Hellen. The IGI contains references to a number of Helen Steels (or Stills) born in 1817 in places as far apart as Aberdeen (1817), Brechin (1817), Edinburgh (1816 and 1819), Glasgow (1819 and 1820) and Eastwood, Renfrew. One of these entries may relate to Robert's wife, but there is simply too little information to be sure. There are no relevant IGI entries for Durham or Northumberland.
19. Leon Faucher, *Etudes Sur L'Angleterre*, 1845, p 325.
20. Ivy Pinchbeck, "Social Attitudes to the Problem of Illegitimacy", *British Journal of Sociology*, 1954, p 309 at p 316. See too the description of how Mary Barton's sister drifted into prostitution after being abandoned by the father of her illegitimate child, Penguin Classics Edition, pp 208–12.
21. Quoted in Henriques, *Bastardy and the New Poor Law, Past and Present*, Vol 37, 1967, p 103 at

p 121, although these statistics should be treated with caution. Faucher stated that rates of illegitimacy were higher in the countryside than in the towns, although this may merely be because it was easier to conceal illegitimate births in the towns where there was greater anonymity. See also Chapter 6, page 70.

22. Cole and Postgate, p 308.
23. For a description of marriages at "The Old Church", see Head, *A Home Tour Through the Manufacturing Districts of England in the Summer of 1835*, pp 70–3.
24. Laslett, *The World We Have Lost*, p 72.
25. Pigot and Slater's General and Classified Directory of Manchester and Salford, 1841.
26. Census, 1841, HO 107/570, Book 20, Folio 13.
27. James Jefferys, *Retail Trading in Britain 1851–1950*, pp 2–7, 126–7; Engels pp 80–7; and Reay Tannahill, *Food in History*, pp 292–5.
28. Faucher, p 458.
29. Adshead, p 17. See too *Mary Barton*.
30. Joseph Adshead, *Distress in Manchester – Evidence of the State of the Labouring Classes in 1840–42*, p 9.
31. Adshead, p 54.
32. Faucher, p 458.
33. See Blackstone, vol II, p 414 on the writ of "capias ad satisfaciendum".
34. *Pigot's Directory* did not list any occupiers in 1843 and 1845, although the Rates Books for 1844 and 1846 respectively list George Savage and William Jones as occupiers of number 51.
35. Based on Gross Estimated Rent for rating purposes. Rates Book, Manchester Archives.
36. 1850 5 feet to the mile Ordnance Survey Map, Manchester Local History Unit. See the description of Greenhey in *Mary Barton*, p 39. For a description of Hulme, see Engels p 73.
37. Census returns, RG9 2909 Fo 98 and RG10 4014 Fo 120.
38. Manchester Archives M9/30/5/4. Minutes of the Hackney coach etc Committee, esp pp 177, 327, 332, 369, 446–7 and 539.
39. Love, p 284.
40. G H Wood, quoted in Cole and Postgate, p 302.
41. Frederick Skoberl, *The World in Miniature*, vol III, p 254.
42. Slater's *Manchester and Country Directory*, 1841 p 145–6 and 1848, pp 101–2.
43. Slater's *Manchester and Country Directory*.
44. *Reminiscences of Manchester from the Year 1840*, 1905, pp 51 and 61, and Robert Rawlinson, Report of the General Board of Health on a Preliminary Enquiry as to Sewerage, Drainage and Supply of Water and the Sanitary Condition of the Township of Broughton, 1850.
45. Leon Faucher, *Etudes Sur L'Angleterre*, 1845, p 316.
46. B Love, *Handbook of Manchester*, 1842.
47. Engels, p 60.
48. Redford, p 371, 377–400 and ex rel. Bernard Hales. See too *Manchester Weekly Times*, 17th November 1866 and the correspondence columns of the *Salford Chronicle passim*. The Ship Canal opened in 1894.
49. Description based on Ordnance Survey, first edition, 1892 (25") CIV.6. Redford p 149.
50. p 85.
51. 1851 Census, PRO, HO 107 2222 Fo 17 p 13.
52. Details again taken from Burgess Rolls, Electoral Registers and Ordnance Survey Maps. All rate books for Salford seem to have been destroyed during the last war and so it is impossible to be certain about the identity of the Ashton's landlord.
53. Tom Bergin, *Salford A City and Its Past*.
54. See Reform Act 1832 section 27 and Municipal Corporations Act 1835 sections 9 and 29.
55. See Census and Burgess Rolls.

# 8

Robert and Ellen's nine surviving children grew up in Broughton in the 1850s and 1860s. This was a time when, apart from the brief "cotton famine" of the early 1860s, when the American Civil War prevented the import of the large quantities of cotton which the textile industry required, Manchester and Salford prospered. It was the hey-day of the British manufacturing industry. Coal from the nearby Lancashire coalfield provided steam power to drive machines. There were plentiful supplies of raw materials from the Empire. Factories were busy. The British population was increasing. There were not only more workers to manufacture goods in the factories, but also an expanding market where they could be sold. Towns were still growing rapidly and builders were busy constructing row upon row of terraced houses. Manchester was in the centre of one of the most successful manufacturing districts in a country which was the leading economic power in the world.

In this environment fortunes were made, but not by any of the Ashtons. Perhaps the opportunities never came their way. Perhaps the education which they received at school until they were twelve or thirteen was inadequate.[1] They may have lacked the personal qualities needed to make money. Probably though the openings simply did not exist for the children of a hackney carriage driver. In the very class-conscious society of Victorian England, their horizons must have been severely limited. They would have said that they knew their place in society. It was hard to cross the boundaries which separated the classes and for many there was no alternative to factory work. Perhaps the summit of their expectations was to set up in business as shop keepers.

Saintsbury, writing in 1887, but looking back to the Manchester of the 1860s, said:

> The great commercial progress . . . created a class of enormously wealthy men, [but] it created a much larger class of men and women who were at the best in a better position than country labourers pecuniarily . . . [They] had a certain quickness of intelligence, but . . . either by the fluctuations of commercial prosperity or by their own ill-considered efforts to better their position, were too often doomed by the severest sufferings.[2]

There is no evidence that any of Robert and Ellen's children suffered severely, but initially they did not prosper either. Mary, their eldest daughter, did not immediately go out to work after leaving school. Probably she stayed at home to help look after the younger children. She lived in Elton Street until 1869 when, at the age of twenty-eight, she married a grocer called James Blears. They went to live in Eccles.

Robert and Ellen's eldest son, Henry, did not marry and lived with his parents until they died. In the 1860s and 1870s he worked as a "billiard marker". In 1881 the census enumerator described him as "an agent", although *Slater's Directory* for the same year listed him as the proprietor of a billiard room in Burn's Chambers in Market Street. His great-nephew Bernard later said that he was a good billiard player, but that he could be put off his game by whistling.

On leaving school Jane, who had been born in 1843, became a cotton-winder in a factory, but she spent much of her life as a lady's maid working for a member of the Montefiore family. She was the only daughter in the family who did not marry.

Robert was initially apprenticed to a blacksmith and in 1861, when he was sixteen, was described as a blacksmith's journeyman. Like his brother Henry he continued living at home and did not marry. Later he also found work as a billiard marker, perhaps working with his brother. In 1871 he was out of work, with the census enumerator describing him as an unemployed billiard marker.

Tom was the most successful of the sons. Although he also worked as a billiard marker in his early twenties, by 1881 he was living at 37, Hilton Street, Higher Broughton and was described as a commission agent. He had offices at 64, Corporation Street. According to his great-nephew he developed a successful business as a bookie, but was "a loveable character always helping the lame ducks in the family." Later he moved out of Manchester to live in Macclesfield.

Margaret and Sarah, who were born in 1848 and 1852, had both left home by 1871, probably to go into service. Margaret married William Turner in 1881 when she was aged thirty-three. Sarah married John Parkinson, also in 1881, when she was twenty-nine. John Parkinson had various jobs, working at different times as the manager of a mill and as a station-master of a small country station. They too ended up living in Macclesfield.

Annie, who was Robert and Ellen's youngest daughter to survive childhood, initially worked as a burler, removing knots and other imperfections from cloth. By 1881, when she was aged twenty-five, she was working as a waitress.[3] She married a man called Richard Carpenter in Chorley in 1889 when she was thirty-five, but was widowed only a few years later. After her husband's death she lived at Walton near Warrington with her two sons, Eric and Howard.

Robert and Ellen's second son, John, was also apprenticed to a blacksmith after leaving school. Although no records relating to their employment survive, it may be that John and his brother Robert were introduced to their apprenticeship master by their Uncle Valentine who must have used the services of at least one blacksmith. Like his brother, John was working as a blacksmith's journeyman when information for the 1861 census was obtained. He was then aged twenty.

John soon gave up working as a blacksmith. He had thought that his employer was an old man until one day he asked him his age. John was shocked when the blacksmith said that he was only forty. He did not wish to become prematurely aged in the same way and so decided that a blacksmith's life was not for him. Like his father, John went to work for his uncle, Valentine, as a hackney coach driver. For the time being he continued to live at home with his parents.

On 24th May 1870 John was married to Elizabeth Ashburner, at the Church of St John the Evangelist, Higher Broughton by the rector, the Reverend F B Wright. Elizabeth, who had been working as a domestic servant in Broughton, was born in Leece, a small village with about thirty houses near Barrow-in-Furness, on 23rd January 1844. She was the daughter of Charles and Elizabeth Ashburner. Her father had been a cordwainer,[4] but had died some time before her marriage.[5] No doubt most of John's brothers and sisters were present in church when they were married. The witnesses who signed the register were his brother Thomas Ashton and his sister Annie Ashton. All those who signed the register were able to write their names. John was aged twenty-nine, while his bride was twenty-five.

On their marriage John and Elizabeth moved to 85, Hilton Street, next door to the house where Valentine Ashton, John's uncle, lived with his wife Ann and her mother, Betty Brockenhurst (who was aged eighty-one), two other coachdrivers and a general domestic servant (who was aged sixteen).

John and Elizabeth took in a lodger, presumably to help with the rent, but he left in late March or early April 1871, shortly before Elizabeth was due to give birth to her first child. She had conceived within two months of her marriage and went into labour at 85, Hilton Street on 18th or 19th April 1871. Doctors were not routinely called when women went into labour and the most likely people to have been present at the birth were John's aunt, his mother and a mid-wife. A baby boy was born on 19th April. John and Elizabeth called him Henry Ashburner Ashton. Henry had been the name given to the eldest Ashton boy child for the three previous generations. However this was the first time that the Ashton family had given a child a second Christian name – "Ashburner" in honour of Elizabeth's family.

John's joy at the birth of a son was however short-lived. Little Henry died almost immediately. Such deaths were by no means uncommon – of every thousand children born in the early 1860s, 263 died before they reached the age of five.[6] More seriously Elizabeth never recovered from what had probably been a long and difficult labour. She died a fortnight later, on 3rd May 1871. The cause of death was certified as "Weak heart. Fatal syncope" (i.e. weakening). In 1870, 2,383 women in England and Wales died in childbirth. Such deaths represented almost 6 per cent of all the deaths of women aged between 25 and 45.[7]

John had called in a doctor sometime before Elizabeth died, and the scene may well have resembled one described in Mrs Gaskell's novel *Mary Barton*, which accurately represented life in the Manchester area in the middle of the nineteenth century. One of the central characters, John Barton, ran to fetch a doctor as his wife lay dying in childbirth:

> The doctor was very long in hearing the repeated rings at his night-bell, and still longer in understanding who it was that made this sudden call upon his services . . . Barton absolutely stamped with impatience, outside the doctor's door, before he came down; and walked so fast homewards, that the medical man several times asked him to go slower.
>   'Is she so very bad?' asked he.
>   'Worse, much worser than ever I saw her before,' replied John.
>   No! she was not – she was at peace. The cries were still for ever. John had no time for listening. He opened the latched door, stayed not to light a candle for the mere ceremony of showing his companion up the stairs, so well known to himself; but in two minutes was in the room, where lay the dead wife, whom he had loved with all the power of his strong heart. The doctor stumbled up the stairs by the fire-light, and met the awe-struck look of the neighbour, which at once told him the state of things. The room was still, as he, with habitual tip-toe step, approached the poor frail body, whom nothing now could more disturb . . . The husband stood like one stupefied. The doctor questioned the neighbour in whispers, and then approaching Barton, said, 'You must go down stairs. This is a great shock, but bear it like a man. Go down.'

John did not remain long on his own in the house in Hilton Street. He resolved to make a fresh start. In 1872, he moved to Farrell Street, a short cul-de-sac between Elton Street and the River Irwell. He took a grocer's shop and beer-house, called the Vine Tavern, at numbers 1 and 2, Farrell Street.[8] There was living accommodation above the shop. There was no other building in the street apart from the Lancashire Raw Cotton Dyeing Company's factory. It was only half a dozen houses away from his parents' house and had probably been built sometime around 1862 by Farrell and Brownhill, builders. Patrick Farrell lived at 1, Broughton Terrace.[9]

John submitted an application to the police for the transfer of the licence for the Vine Tavern from the previous licensee, Samuel Yeardley, to himself. Then, on Wednesday 28th August 1872 he went to the Police Court, which was held at Salford Town Hall, for the annual Brewster Sessions, where the formal transfer would take place. The court was crowded, and amongst those present were "a number of gentlemen interested in the temperance movement." The court was presided over by the mayor, Thomas Barlow, with eight other magistrates. They heard the chief constable report that there were 117 public houses and 508 beer houses in the Borough of Salford. (The policy of the Clowes family had been to restrict the number of public houses which were built in Broughton, but by the turn of the century Broughton alone had twenty public houses with licences to sell beer and wine, thirty-one beer and ale houses and 107 off licences which sold beer.[10]) The chief constable also announced the number of people apprehended for drunkenness during the previous year – 1478 men and 599 women – an increase of 434 on the previous year. 281 people had been convicted of committing assaults of various kinds when drunk. Notwithstanding these statistics, and the presence of the temperance lobby, the magistrates allowed all of the transfers and granted several new licences. John's licence was for the sale of beer for consumption "on and off" the premises and had to be renewed annually. There is no evidence that John ever brewed his own beer. Certainly by 1900 the Vine Tavern was owned by Boddingtons whose brewery was less than a mile away at Strangeways.

John lived and worked in Farrell Street as a provision dealer and beer retailer for the next quarter of a century. His prospects were very different to those of his father in his ill-fated attempt to run a shop thirty years previously. The second half of the nineteenth century was a period of rapid and almost continuous economic advance. Apart from the period of the "cotton famine" in the 1860s, Manchester and Salford continued to prosper. For retailers there was an expanding market. The population was growing. Factory workers had no means of producing their own food or beer. Real wages were rising and consumption of most commodities increased. In 1850 the average annual consumption of tea per person was 1.8 lbs. This rose to 3.8 lbs in 1870 and to 6.1 lbs in 1900. The comparable figures for the consumption of sugar were 24.8 lbs in 1850, 47.2 lbs in 1870 and 87.1 lbs in 1900.[11]

This period also saw changes in the ways in which grocers worked. More foodstuffs were packed by manufacturers and wholesalers. Goods began to be given brand names and to be advertised by their manufacturers. Shop-keepers started displaying their wares, either in their windows or by hanging up samples outside their shops. Retailers started openly pricing goods, with the result that haggling died out and some competition based on price differentials developed between shops. As transport and distribution improved, a greater range of imported food became available. Despite these changes, virtually all retail sales of groceries were made by small shop-keepers. Even in 1900 the proportion of sales by large scale food and household stores was only 10 per cent. This was the golden age of the corner shop.[12]

John remarried on 15th March 1876. His second marriage was celebrated at the Church of the Ascension, a Victorian red brick church on the other side of Great Clowes Street, which was consecrated in 1869. The wedding was performed by a curate, the Reverend W H B Tucker. John's bride was Sarah Ellen Ward. Although he was by now thirty-five, she had been born in Birkenhead on 23rd August 1855 and so was not quite twenty-one. She was the daughter of Daniel and Eliza Ward. Her father Daniel was described on the marriage certificate as a waterman and later Sarah Ellen was to describe to her grandson Bernard how as a child she had "run up the rigging like a monkey." Besides working as a boatman, Daniel Ward and his wife had also run a butcher's shop in Chester and at one time had lived in Oswestry. However Sarah Ellen's mother had died young and she was brought up by her grandmother.[13] On their marriage Sarah Ellen was described as living at 28, Elton Street, John's parents' address, but it is likely that this was merely a temporary address prior to the wedding. The witnesses recorded in the register were John's sister, Sarah Ashton, and his brother, Robert Ashton. Robert could not write his name and so signed with his mark, a cross. Sarah was able to write her name.

John and Sarah Ellen had a typically large Victorian family of eleven children. They were born between July 1877 and June 1896 at roughly two yearly intervals. All were baptised at Manchester Cathedral and the dates of their births written down in the Family Bible. Five of their children died in childhood.

John and Sarah Ellen's two eldest sons, Bernard and Bertram both died away from their parents' home in Farrell Street. Bernard died in November 1881 at 9, Sunnyside. He was aged two years three months. His death was reported to the Registrar of Births Marriages and Deaths by Amelia Pearce who was present when he died. Doctor G Pinder, a Member of the Royal College of Surgeons who practised in partnership with Doctor M Johnson certified that the cause of death was tubercular meningitis. (Doctors Pinder and Johnson of 122, Great Clowes Street were to treat the family for the next thirty-five years.) Bertram died in March 1884 aged seven months. Doctor Johnson certified that the cause of his death was pertussis (i.e. whooping cough), broncho-pneumonia and pulmonary congestion. He died at 45, Alexandra Street, Broughton. His death was reported by Mary Missett.

Amelia Pearce was the wife of a dyer who does not seem to have had any children of her own, but lived with an adopted son aged nine and a boarder. Mary Missett was born in Carlisle and was the wife of an Irish musical instrument maker. They lived with five children aged between six and twenty-two.[14]

It seems likely that Amelia Pearce and Mary Missett were "baby farmers" who were paid to look after Bernard and Bertram. (In view of the risk of infecting Mary Missett's children and Amelia Pearce's adopted son it seems unlikely that Bernard and Bertram were taken to their houses merely because they were ill and to avoid passing on the illnesses to John and Sarah Ellen's own children.) Although the practice of wet-nursing was becoming far rarer,[15] baby farming was still common in the late nineteenth century, particularly where mothers were factory workers. In 1849 the "going rate" for nursing a young child during the day-time was three shillings and six pence a week. Children were often poorly looked after and given unsuitable food. Sometimes they were drugged with opiates such as "Godfrey's Cordial" or "Mother's Quietness".[16] The rate of child mortality was significantly higher among children who were not looked after by their own parents. Although Sarah Ellen is not recorded in the census entries for 1881 or 1891 as having any occupation, there can be no doubt that she worked long hours helping John to run the shop and the tavern, and so needed help with the children. Even so, to modern eyes, it appears strange that the children were away from home when they were so seriously ill, and that their deaths were not reported by their parents.

John and Sarah Ellen's third daughter, Annie, died in Farrell Street on 1st February 1891. She was only twenty-one days old. The cause of her death was certified as pulmonary congestion and convulsions. The other two children who did not survive, Robert and Ellen, died within eight days of each other in Farrell Street during the spring of 1896. Robert died on 27th March 1896 aged four years. Doctor Pinder certified the causes of his death as rubella, pertussis and broncho-pneumonia. Ellen died on 4th April 1896, aged two years. Doctor Johnson certified the causes of her death as rubella and pertussis. All the children who died were buried in the graveyard of St John the Evangelist in Higher Broughton. Historians have referred to the "extraordinary equanimity with which our ancestors viewed the illness and early deaths of their children as almost inevitable",[17] but it is hard to believe that John and Sarah Ellen were not deeply saddened by these five deaths.

John, Sarah Ellen and their children lived with a general domestic servant. In 1881 she was Emma Clark who was aged sixteen and who had been born in nearby Hulme. In 1891 the servant they employed was Sarah J Waterhouse, who was aged fifty-three and born in

*Fig. 11 – Photograph of John Ashton (c.1887).*

Manchester.[18] There was nothing unusual in people of their social standing employing a servant. In 1891, among a population of almost twenty-four million, there were approximately two million domestic servants.[19] John's daughter-in-law Lucy (his son Jack's wife) later complained that the boys had been "waited on hand and foot", perhaps an understandable maternal reaction on the part of Sarah Ellen after the death of five children. The "menfolk" in the house used to expect the best of everything, but even so Sarah Ellen economised, for example by buying cheap unbranded cocoa and putting it in the tin of a more expensive brand. No-one ever noticed the difference.[20]

Sometime around 1887 John went to the photographic studios of J L Hackett at 59, Picadilly, in the centre of Manchester. The picture which was taken was a "carte de visite" size photograph of the type first introduced in the 1860s. It shows a bearded man with receding brown hair. His mouth is almost entirely hidden by a long moustache. His eyes staring straight at the camera, his expressionless face and a slightly wooden posture probably reflect the length of the exposure used in taking the photograph. He was wearing a morning coat and a high buttoned waistcoat. There is no sign of a watch or watch chain.

The family were regular church-goers. All the boys sang in the choir of St Albans, a Victorian Gothic Church on Waterloo Road, and Sarah Ellen later talked about how she regularly washed, ironed and starched their surplices. Tom in particular had a very good soprano voice and sang solos in Christmas choral services. John was appointed as a sidesman at the church and helped the church warden perform his functions. The family were clearly well thought of. In 1916 the St Albans Parish Magazine referred to John as "our highly esteemed sidesman" and acknowledged a donation of two shillings and six pence to the Clergy Fund from Mr and Mrs Ashton.

Despite this, John did have one brush with the law. He was summonsed to appear at Salford Police Court[21] on 7th November 1890 for selling beer during prohibited hours. The *Salford County Telephone* included brief details of the case in its weekly column of court reports headed "FRIENDS IN TROUBLE" underneath a lurid sketch of a scruffily dressed man in the stocks. Its headline for the case was "THE DEMON OF DRINK OUT OF HOURS". The *Salford Reporter* carried a more factual account. After giving details of another case, it stated:

John Ashton indoor beer house keeper, Vine Tavern, Farrell-street, Broughton was summonsed for a similar offence. Mr Holmes [the Deputy Town Clerk] appeared in support of the information, and called Police-constable McPherson, who said he and another constable watched the house after 11 o'clock on the night of [Saturday] 18th ult. During the time they were watching they observed two women and a boy enter the place. The women on their return appeared to be carrying beer in their jugs, and the boy had some beer in his possession. The police returned to the house with the parties, whereupon the wife of the Defendant said, "Yes I served him and he gave me $1\frac{1}{2}$d for it, and as the beer was drawn I thought there was no harm in it." Mr Makinson [the Stipendiary Magistrate] said he did not think it was a bad case, and imposed a fine of 10 shillings and costs of the summons, or seven days imprisonment.

In 1899 or 1900 John and Sarah Ellen moved from Farrell Street and bought two houses at 190 and 192, Great Clowes Street, close to the junction with Upper Camp Street. They were still in Lower Broughton, but further from the river and on slightly higher ground. The premises in Farrell Street were initially taken over by a woman called Mary Pearson, but there were then three further changes of licensee before 1907 when the justices refused to renew the licence and the Vine Tavern closed down.[22] Sarah Ellen later told her grandson Bernard that they had moved because of the unhealthy location near to the Irwell, and the deaths of five of their children. These factors undoubtedly played a part. However another reason for the move may well have been the Jewish immigration into the area in the years approaching the turn of the century, caused by the pogroms in Russia and eastern Europe. Many Jews settled in Lower Broughton during this period. Jacob Moses, a silk waste dealer, had lived at 14, Elton Street since the mid-1880s. He had been born in Germany but was a naturalised British subject. By 1898 there were three Jewish families living in the street, headed by Myer Silverstone, a machinist and Marx Simonson and Jacob Goldman who were both tailors. However, in 1899, ten of the sixteen inhabited houses between numbers 8 and 46 on the south side of Elton Street were occupied by Jewish families. All, apart from John Cohen, who was described as a householder, and the machinist, Myer Silverstone, were tailors.[23]

The Ashtons were convinced that the area was "going down hill". Their son Jack, who maintained some anti-semitic prejudices throughout his life, said that the Jews had "changed" the area. In fact the Jewish immigrants were settling in what was already an unhealthy area with relatively poor housing. The occupations of John and Sarah's neighbours show that the social composition of the street had already changed before the arrival of the Jews. The Ashton's attitudes, born of conservatism, fear and lack of understanding, were unfortunately not unusual among all levels of Victorian society, but were particularly prevalent among the small shopkeepers and other members of the petit bourgeoisie of the

*Fig. 12 – 192, Great Clowes Street (c.1910).*

time. Indeed the Jewish immigrants of the late nineteenth century met the same kind of hostility and prejudice as most other immigrants, both before and since. A generation earlier, similar prejudices had been directed against Irish settlers. As has often been the case, it was people like shopkeepers and skilled labourers, who were a small way up the social ladder, who felt they had most to lose. They felt threatened by a culture about which they knew next to nothing and by the fear that the neighbourhood was being "taken over".[24]

It seems that John bought 190 and 192, Great Clowes Street from William Young, a surveyor. He acquired long leasehold interests with a yearly "chief rent" of £5 0s 4d on each property. From those rents he deducted property tax for which the freeholder was liable, but which, as the lessee, he was obliged to pay directly to the collector of taxes in Broughton. (For example in 1918 tax on number 190 was assessed at the rate of six shillings in the £ and John's executors paid two instalments of £1 10s to the Inland Revenue.)

In social terms the upper part of Great Clowes Street was a better area than the streets adjoining the Irwell in Lower Broughton. The Clowes family had sold off land in large plots to individual buyers, intending to create a high class residential suburb. The large Victorian houses which remain in parts of Higher Broughton are a marked contrast to the tightly packed cottages which were built in Lower Broughton. By the turn of the century, Higher Broughton was becoming less genteel, but, judging by the occupations of other residents, John and Sarah Ellen still found that they had moved to a better area. In 1904, the occupants of the other houses between 158 and 214, Great Clowes Street included a druggist, a clerk, a clergyman, a school-master, a cloth agent, an estate agent, a pawnbroker, an African merchant, a corn merchant, a draper and two engineers. Nine householders were not listed as having any occupation and so were presumably living off savings or some other form of unearned income. There were very few people with manual jobs and no families with surnames which were likely to be Jewish.[25]

Numbers 190 and 192 were part of a terrace of large flat fronted red brick houses which had been built during the first half of the century. In the 1840s part of the terrace had been used as a school run by a Mr Jackson, but by the turn of the century, it had long since reverted to residential use.[26] Each house had a ground floor and two upper storeys, with cellars below. There were gardens to the front and rear. John and Sarah Ellen's grandson Bernard remembered a stone flagged hall or lobby floor which was covered with linoleum. The house at 192 where the Ashtons lived did not have a bath. The adjoining house, which did have a bath, was rented out. Initially the tenant was Mrs Lydia Peel who was described merely as "a householder". Later the house was rented by Mrs Hannah Woods, a teacher of dress-making and Aaron Woods, a cashier, who was probably her son.

In 1909 John and Sarah Ellen were joined in their house in Great Clowes Street by the children of their daughter Violet. She had married George Ernest Hale during the summer of 1902, and had given birth to four children, Eric, Winifred, Phyllis and Bernard, between 1903 and 1909. Violet died of "milk fever" six weeks after Bernard was born. Although their father looked after them occasionally, the main responsibility for bringing up the children fell upon Sarah Ellen. Bernard was a sickly baby and she was up with him night after night.

Although John and Sarah Ellen intended to resume trading after the move to Great Clowes Street, they never did so. They lived on their savings, the rent from 190, and income from shares. John had bought shares in the Manchester Ship Canal (five hundred units of 4 per cent perpetual debenture stock and thirty ordinary £1 shares), the Fine Cotton Spinners and Doublers' Association Ltd (ninety-four £1 shares), and the Mersey Docks and Harbour Board ($3\frac{1}{2}$ per cent Debenture Stock worth £730.16.7d) and War Stock (worth £1,920 10s).[27] Although they had more income than John's parents, Robert and Ellen, ever received after their retirement, the inflation associated with the First World War meant that their small income did not go far. This is perhaps borne out by the fact that in the final years of his life, John borrowed money from his relatives. His brother Thomas lent him £25 in cash in Macclesfield in 1913. His son Val loaned him £20 in September 1914 while his son Jack lent him £24 in March 1915. None of these sums was repaid before his death.

John and Sarah appear to have been the epitome of a respectable petit bourgeois Victorian family. They worked hard, lived frugally and went to church regularly. In contrast, the life of John's elder brother Henry reflected the seedier aspect of society and demonstrated the hidden side of Victorian morality. He had worked as a billiard hall proprietor. Just before the turn of the century he was employed at Diggle's Billiard Saloon in the Criterion Billiard Rooms, 82, Market Street.[28] He did not marry, and at some stage caught syphilis. Although there is obviously no way of knowing how he contracted the disease, it is likely that it was from a prostitute. Victorian Manchester was notorious for its prostitution. In 1841, 448 publicans and beer house proprietors had been convicted of keeping disorderly houses. When Faucher had visited Manchester in the 1840s, he had found five or six hundred prostitutes working each

*Fig. 13 – George and Violetta Hale*
*with Eric, Winifred and Phyllis*
*(c.1908).*

night in the streets around the Exchange, which was at one end of Market Street.[29] In the age before the discovery of penicillin, Henry's syphilis went untreated. He developed tabes dorsalis or locomotor ataxia, the extremely unpleasant tertiary stage of the disease when its organisms destroy the sensory nerves and normally cause severe stabbing pains in the legs, an unsteady gait, a loss of bladder control and, in some cases, blurred vision as a result of damage to the optic nerves. Henry became a nervous wreck. By 1891 he had been forced to give up work. His brother Tom "paid doctors a small fortune until they admitted they could do nothing useful." After his mother's death, Henry was admitted to the Northern Counties Hospital for Incurables at Heaton Norris, near Stockport, where he died on 23rd August 1909.

Another relative to die was John's uncle Valentine. After moving out of Broughton, he lived at 165, New Lane, Patricroft. He had prospered, to such an extent that in his will he described himself as a "gentleman". He did not have any children. He died on 9th September 1898, aged 87, at Winton. His effects were valued at £1,327 18s 5d.

*Fig. 14 – Sarah Ellen with grand-
daughters Winifred and Phyllis Hale
(c.1910).*

John Ashton died at 192, Great Clowes Street on 21st September 1916 after having a stroke. His son Jack was with him when he died and the cause of his death was certified by Doctor Johnson. Later on the day of his death, his daughter Lizzie called on her brother Jack with the family bible and asked him to write in particulars of the death. The family all believed that the real cause of his death was that he lost the will to live after his youngest, and favourite, son George had been killed in action at Thiepval during the Battle of the Somme on 1st July 1916. Doctors Pinder and Johnson had called to treat John several times during the year before his death. Their bill for the period from 24th November 1915 to 21st September 1916 was £6 2s 6d. The family also paid a specialist, Doctor Steel, two guineas. The District Nurse was paid a "gratuity" of twelve shillings and sixpence for her attendances.

John was buried at three o'clock on 25th September at St Johns, Higher Broughton. The undertaker was James Kirkham of the "Salford and Broughton Funeral Establishment" whose bill indicated that he also supplied "Wedding Carriages" and arranged cremations. It referred to John being buried in a "Best Saxony Flannell Shroud" and a "man's Best Oak paneled Coffin". The cortege included a glass case and carriage and a single horse brougham. The passing bell at the church tolled. James Kirkham's fees which included the sums paid to the church for a "First Class New Grave" came to £22 17s. The family also paid one guinea for acknowledgements and announcements of the death in the Births, Marriages and Deaths column of the *Manchester Evening Chronicle*. The entry, which appeared on Friday 22nd and Monday 25th September, read:

ASHTON On the 21st inst. suddenly at 192, Great Clowes Street, Broughton, John, the dearly-beloved husband of Sarah Ellen Ashton in his 76th year – "His end was peace."

John's solicitor, Edward E Hankison, had prepared a will which John had executed on 9th August 1916. He appointed his sons John, Valentine and Thomas and his widow Sarah Ellen as executors and executrix. He directed that his widow should have the use of his household furniture and goods during her life time and that the rest of his property should be held on trust for Sarah Ellen during her life and then shared equally between all his sons and daughters who attained the age of twenty-one.

His widow also received the benefit of a life assurance policy taken out on the joint lives of John and Sarah Ellen which had been purchased from the Refuge Assurance Company. The proceeds which were paid to Sarah Ellen amounted to £127 5s 4d.

After John's death, Sarah Ellen became responsible for paying the rates which he had paid as a householder during his lifetime. Although Salford had been incorporated as a municipal borough in 1844, Broughton did not become part of the borough until 1853.[30] From that time the revenue received by the borough from the rates went towards the cost of local government services such as the paving and lighting of streets, the provision of police and fire services and measures to promote public health. Such rates were payable by all householders. In addition the Board of Guardians, who were responsible for poor relief in the parliamentary borough of Salford and Pendleton, levied a further rate, known as the poor rate. The amount of rates payable was calculated by multiplying the rateable value of each property, which was calculated roughly according to its rental value, by the amount in the £ of the rates levied in any particular year.

In 1916–17 the County Borough of Salford levied a rate of four shillings in the £, of which slightly over one shilling and seven pence was for educational purposes. Residential occupiers also paid a general district rate of two shillings and five pence in the £ and a highway rate of five pence in the £. The total of the rates payable to the County Borough in respect of 190, Great Clowes Street was £7 0s 11d. The equivalent amount for the other house at 192, Great Clowes Street, which had a lower rateable value, but for which an additional payment was due because it had a bath, was £7 5s 3d. The Overseers of Broughton, in the Salford Union, "demanded" a poor rate for 1916–17 of one shilling and eight pence in the £. The amounts payable for the two houses were £1 15s 5d and £1 18s 4d. The water rates which were payable to the Manchester Corporation Water Works were £1 8s 3d for 190 which had a bath and £1 1s 3d for 192 which did not. Although the water rates did not increase during the three years which followed, by 1919–20, the borough rates payable for 190 had increased to £11 13s 10d and the poor rate payable for the same house had risen £2 9s 10d.

By 1919 Sarah Ellen wanted to move from Broughton. She and her three surviving sons Jack, Val and Tom, who as trustees had held the two houses in Great Clowes Street since the death of her husband, agreed to sell them. Both houses were sold to neighbours. Number 190 was sold to Hyman Jacobs, a tailor, who lived at number 194. Number 192 was sold to Nathan Berg, another tailor who lived at 188, Great Clowes Street. The trustees paid their solicitors, Richard Hankinson and Son, £6 and £7 10s which were respectively their charges for deducing title and completing the conveyance of the two properties.

The new house which the trustees bought for Sarah Ellen was 11, Church Road, Urmston.[31] They acquired a 999 year lease with a yearly ground rent of £5 8s 2d from Mr A Quayle and others. Sarah Ellen moved in October 1919 and the trustees paid their solicitors £7 10s for acting in the purchase.

Sarah Ellen's new home was one of eight reasonably substantial semi-detached houses. It had a small front garden with stone steps leading up to the front door. At the side a flight of steps with an iron railing led down into a larger back garden which had a children's swing. There were cellars with windows at the back below the ground floor. One large tiled cellar was used for washing and had a coal-fired boiler, dolly tubs and mangles. There were also cellars for storing coal and meat. Inside there were two main floors with bay windows at the front. There were further rooms in the attic with windows at the side and under the front gable. Sarah Ellen's granddaughter Mildred remembers the house having large heavy furniture made from a dark wood. There were electric lights. The contrast between this house and the small terraced house where her mother-in-law Ellen ended her days was very marked. It represented not only the increased opportunities open to John and Sarah Ellen's generation, but also the fruits of many years of hard work.

Sarah Ellen's daughter Lizzie and son Tom moved with her and Violet's four children to Urmston. Lizzie was a kind and loving soul who was anxious and unsure of herself. She knew little of life beyond the house and never married. Her relatives described her as "not being very bright" and Sarah Ellen felt that she needed to be protected. She was never encouraged to have paid employment outside the home, but in effect she worked as an unpaid servant. She did the washing and cleaning, and it was her responsibility to light the boiler in the wash cellar on Monday mornings. Tom carried on living in the house for a while even after he was married on 7th June 1924. He and his wife Gertie moved out when they bought their own home in Davyhulme in 1927.

Sarah Ellen also brought two of her sisters-in-law to live at 11, Church Road. They were Mary Blears, the eldest of Robert and Ellen's children who was now a widow, and Jane Ashton, who was a spinster. Before moving to Urmston, they had been living at 186, Barton Lane, Eccles. The sisters wore white frilly caps and lived in the large front bedroom where they shared a four poster bed. Jane teased her sister Mary who had "delusions". Sarah Ellen's grandson Leslie witnessed a "tremendous row" between them, in which one forced the other out of the room, shouting furious abuse. Mary's husband had been a grocer, and after his death the business was sold and a nephew called regularly to bring her the interest which the proceeds earned. She would give him something for his trouble and Sarah Ellen would give him some refreshment.

Jane died on 7th February 1926, aged eighty-two. She left an estate worth £1,926 5s 1d. The executors appointed by her will were her nephews, Eric Ashton Carpenter, Jack Ashton and another relative, Walter Turner.[32] Her estate was shared between her surviving sisters, Annie Carpenter, Mary Blears, Margaret Turner, and Sarah Parkinson and her sister-in-law Sarah Ellen Ashton. Mary Blears died on 20th February 1931, aged ninety-four. She did not leave a will. Her nephew, Jack Ashton, took out letters of administration in respect of her estate which was valued at £364 4s 3d.

The household was visited by several other relatives. Sarah Ellen's son, Jack, had tea there every Wednesday after leaving his office. Her brother-in-law Tom Ashton, who had moved out to Macclesfield, called less frequently. His daughters Lucy, Margaret and Ann came to stay from time to time. Another visitor was Eric Ashton Carpenter. In economic terms he was to become the most successful of the relatives. After his father's death, he had attended Warehouseman and Clerk's orphanage school in Cheadle Hulme. He then rose from being an office boy to become managing director and chairman of the board of Gregg Brothers, a Manchester firm of cotton manufacturers and merchants. He was elected President of the Manchester Chamber of Commerce in 1948 and knighted in the New Year's Honours List in 1951.[33]

In her later years Sarah Ellen remained upright in stature, but her dark brown hair, which she wore in a bun, turned grey. She wore ankle-length skirts and high-necked blouses. She also wore steel-rimmed glasses. Her daughter-in-law, Lucy regarded her with respect and affection. Her grandchildren had differing impressions of her character. Bernard, who was brought up by her, described her as "a wonderful woman" who "saved [his] young life." Leslie recalled her as having a "fierce disposition." Mildred remembered her as a determined and strong-willed woman, who was also kind and affectionate. She gained the impression that her grandmother had controlled the household finances during her marriage when money was tight. Sarah Ellen was however generous after the death of her husband. She bought Mildred a beautiful dolls' pram, as well as two pairs of combinations which were at least four sizes too big for her. She also bought an expensive black silk eiderdown for her daughter-in-law Lucy. Her son Jack, however, had the feeling she was spending too much money. In particular he commented on the new carpets and furniture which she bought not long before her death.

She died at 11, Church Road on 16th March 1932, aged seventy-six. A Doctor Tootill certified the causes of her death as cardiac muscle failure, senile decay and pleurisy.

Her will, which, like that of her husband, was drawn up by Edward E Hankinson, had been executed on 1st July 1925. She left all her estate and effects to her daughter Lizzie. Her personal estate was valued at £270 11s 11d. The house, which was not valued, was still held in trust in accordance with the provisions of her husband's will.

During their lives both John and Sarah Ellen had wanted to replace the headstone over the family grave at St Johns. It was in need of repair and the names of some of their children who died had been omitted. Due to "lack of funds [Sarah Ellen had been] unable to gratify [her] desire" to buy a new gravestone during her lifetime. However, after her death, her surviving children paid Hilton and Sons of Barlow Moor Road, Manchester £43 to erect a new "British Granite Headstone" which read:

IN MEMORY OF
JOHN ASHTON
Died September 21st 1916, in his 76th year
and of SARAH ELLEN, His wife, who
Died March 16th 1932, in her 77th year
Also their children
BERNARD
Died November 13th 1881, aged 2 years 3 months
BERTRAM
Died March 27th 1884, aged 7 months
ANNIE
Died February 1st 1891, aged 1 month
ROBERT
Died March 27th 1896, aged 4 years
ELLEN
Died April 4th 1896, aged 2 years
GEORGE
16th (Service) Batt. Lanc's Fus.
Killed in action, Thiepval, France
July 1st 1916, aged 20 years.[34]

After Sarah Ellen's death, her daughter Lizzie went first to live with her brother Tom and then later with her nephew Bernard at 7, Kenwood Avenue, Gatley. Jack and Tom, as John Ashton's trustees, tried to sell the house, but it was the middle of the Depression and they were unable to find a purchaser, even after placing the following advertisement in the *Manchester Guardian*, the *Manchester Evening News* and the *Dispatch*:

> URMSTON – To Close Trust: SEMI: 3 mins station: will accept low price: what offers?
> F H Coller, Estate Agent, Urmston, phone 2472.[35]

The house was empty from March 1932 until 1st October 1936 when they let it to a tenant, Mr H Hartley, at a rent of £12 per quarter. He however fell into arrears with the rent. In March 1942 he owed £158 15s 11d. The trustees instructed a solicitor, Percy H Barker, who took proceedings to evict him. His fees were £2 12s 6d. The house was again put on the market and, this time, was sold in June 1942 for £300. John's remaining stocks and shares were sold and the balance of John Ashton's estate was then distributed among Jack, Tom, Lizzie (to whom Val had given his share) and Violet's surviving children, Eric, Winifred and Bernard who each received one-fifteenth. Including interim payments which had been made, Lizzie received £1,521. Tom and Jack's shares were each £760. Violet's surviving children each received £253.

## Notes

1. HO 107/2222 fo 31 and RG9/2909 fo 115.
2. G E B Saintsbury, *Manchester*, 1887, p 101.
3. RG 9 2909 fo 115, RG10 4013 fo 49 and RG 11 3953, Slater's Directory 1881, p 16.
4. Or leather worker.
5. She was not living in Leece in 1851. Her family were not there in 1841.
6. Robert Barker in *Parliamentary Papers*, 1864, XXII p 699, quoted in Pinchbeck and Hewitt, pp 349–50.
7. *Annual Report of the Registrar General of England and Wales*, 1870. See generally Schofield, "Did The Mothers Really Die? Three Centuries of Maternal Mortality" in Lloyd Bonfield and others, *The World We Have Gained*, where he quotes a maternal mortality rate of 4.6 per 1,000 births in 1856–60.
8. Bernard Hale described it as a "grocer's cum licenced tavern". *Salford Chronicle*, 31st August 1872 for details of the Salford Brewster Sessions. The *Salford Chronicle*, 8th November 1890, said John's house was "also a greengrocer's shop". John's name appeared on the Burgess Roll for Salford for the first time in 1873/4. (Salford Local History Library.)
9. *Slater's Directory*, 1858. The first licence for the Vine Tavern was granted in 1862, County Borough of Salford Register of Licence Holders.
10. County Borough of Salford Register of Licence Holders. See Monty Doblin, *Broughton and Cheetham Hill*, pages 12 and 25–6.
11. Jefferys, *Retail Trading in Britain 1851–1950*, pp 9 and 128.
12. Jefferys, pp 6–14, 30–37 and 126–31. In contrast, by 1991, five groups of stores (Sainsburys, Tesco, Argyll, Asda and Co-ops) accounted for over 50 per cent of all grocery sales. (*The Guardian*, 12th October 1991)
13. Letter from Bernard Hale.
14. 1881 Census, RG11 3963 Enumeration District 34, RG11 3953, Enumeration District 16.
15. It is extremely unlikely that either child was wet nursed. Amelia Pearce seems to have had no children of her own and so would not have had any milk. There was no death of a Missett child during the nine months before Bertram's birth or death and so it is unlikely that she would have been in a position to wet nurse.
16. I Pinchbeck and M Hewitt, *Children in English Society*, pp 406 and 613–8 and Valerie Fildes, *Wet Nursing, A History from Antiquity to Present* pp 199–200.
17. Pinchbeck and Hewitt, p 349.
18. RG12/3152.

19. OPCS, Extract from 1891 census.
20. Ex rel my mother. In 1916 John paid his wife £2 2s 6d per week house-keeping money.
21. *Salford Reporter* 15th November 1890; *Salford County Telephone* 15th November 1890; *Salford Chronicle* 8th November 1890. The courts presided over by magistrates were known as "Police Courts" until the implementation of the Magistrates' Courts Act 1952.
22. Slater, 1902 and County Borough of Salford Register of Licence Holders. The editions of the *Salford Chronicle* which reported the Brester Sessions in 1899 and 1900 did not record the transfers of licences.
23. *Slater's Directories*, 1897, 1898 and 1899.
24. cf the attitudes of London East Enders in Bethnal Green described by Peter Sanders in *The Simple Annals*, p 162–5 and William J Fishman, *East End 1888* pp 131–76 for an account of the conditions in which Jewish immigrants lived.
25. *Slater's Manchester Directory*, 1904.
26. Louis M Hayes, *Reminiscences of Manchester*, 1905, p 68. Numbers 190 and 192 have been demolished, but number 208/210 (now the Presidential Hotel), which seems to have been of a similar construction, is still standing.
27. Details taken from deed of gift by Val Ashton of his share under John Ashton's will to Lizzie Ashton.
28. His nephew Jack said that he worked at Diggle's. Diggle was a famous billiards player of the 1890s. See Slater, 1895 and 1898.
29. Love, *Handbook of Manchester*, 1842; Faucher, *Etudes sur L'Angleterre*. See too Elizabeth Gaskell's *Mary Barton* and the portrayal of Mary's sister's life.
30. See generally, T Bergin, *Salford A City and Its Past*, 1975, pp 90–5; Sidney and Beatrice Webb, *English Local Government*, Vol 2, chapter 2.
31. The following advertisement in the *Manchester Evening Chronicle* on 22nd September 1919 probably refers to the house which was purchased:
    URMSTON – Compact HOUSE, close to Station: 3 bedrooms, bath, drawing-room, dining-room, kitchen, scullery +c: garden.
32. See letter from Bernard Hale.
33. Ex rel. Bernard Hale and *Manchester Evening News*, 9th February 1948.
34. All headstones have been removed from the churchyard at St John's, but Jack's instructions about the wording of the new stone survive.
35. *Manchester Evening News*, 14th October 1932. On that day that paper carried 149 other advertisements of houses for sale in the Manchester area.

# 9

John and Sarah Ellen's children, growing-up during the last years of the nineteenth century, were among the first generation to benefit from free compulsory education. Until the passing of the 1870 Education Act, most schools had been set up and run by voluntary school boards. These local charitable bodies were often connected with churches and most were strictly denominational. Although increasingly they received money from central government, there was no national responsibility for education. Indeed the earliest statutory provisions relating to education were not Education Acts but Factory Acts. The 1844 Act, for example, had prohibited the employment of children aged less than eight in cotton mills. It had also limited the working day for children aged between eight and thirteen to six and a half hours and required them to spend one session a day in school.

Without any national education system, the number and quality of schools had varied greatly. While some areas had sufficient school places, others were poorly served. The Education Act of 1870, by establishing a national responsibility for schooling, aimed to bring education within the reach of every home. It gave voluntary school boards six months in which to ensure that there was adequate provision in every area. If they failed, elected school boards were to be set up. These new boards were given power to levy a rate for the building and maintenance of schools. It was then only a matter of time before the 1876 Act made schooling obligatory for all children up to the age of twelve and the 1891 Act dispensed with the need for parental contributions towards the cost of their children's education.

There can be no doubt that these reforms meant that John and Sarah Ellen's children were better educated than any preceding generation of Ashtons. For example, Jack, the eldest son to survive childhood, "took in" a large amount of "general education" and his grounding in the "Three Rs" was probably superior to that of any generation since. Reading and writing became second nature and the children did not suffer the difficulties of not being able to read fluently or fumbling with a pen which previous generations probably experienced. Indeed some of their children stayed on at school after they reached the compulsory school leaving age. Jack went on to Manchester Central School in Whitfield Street. He stayed there until he was sixteen.

These improvements in education in turn widened the children's horizons in terms of the jobs available to them when they left school. Jack, Val and Tom all found work which needed these better standards of literacy and numeracy. Val was the most adventurous. In 1906, at the age of nineteen, he answered an advertisement placed in *The Times* by Reggie Stafford, the British Consul in Arequipa, Peru. He travelled out to South America, and worked as a field agent for Stafford and Company, who were involved in exporting alpaca and collecting rubber from estates in the valley of the River Beni in Bolivia. The explorer Colonel Fawcett stayed with Val twice, between 1910 and 1912, at San Carlos and Marte on the Tambopata River.[1] Jack and Tom, in contrast, stayed in Manchester. Tom worked as a clerk for Jaffe and Son, a firm of shipping merchants with offices at 101, Princess Street.

Jack also found work as a clerk. From 1906 he worked for Christys, a firm who manufactured towels.

Jack was about five feet ten inches tall, with brown hair and brown eyes. He took great pride in his appearance and dressed smartly. His daughter remembers him buying good ties, wearing pig skin gloves and carrying a carefully rolled umbrella. His shoes were always well polished and he was meticulous about shaving and washing.

In the early years of the century, Jack and Lucy Jane Lowe, a dressmaker, began "courting". No one can now remember how they first met, but probably it was at St Albans, the church in Waterloo Road where Jack had been a choir boy. Lucy was much shorter than Jack, with long thick brown hair. She was the youngest of four daughters. Her father, Charles Hugh Lowe, had been a carver and gilder, who had been apprenticed to Lucy's grandfather, another carver and gilder, who was also called Charles Hugh Lowe. Lucy's grandmother had worked as a milliner. Although Lucy's father had been born at 13, Meredith Street in Hulme in 1845, (coincidentally the street where Jack's own grandparents had lived for a short time in the 1840s) his parents had lived in various different towns, presumably moving about to find work. In 1851 they were living at 28, Great Underbank, Stockport. From 1854 until 1861 or 1862 they were living in Preston. The census enumerator in 1861 found them at 59, Pleasant Street, Preston. By 1863 they were back in the Manchester area, living in George Street, Salford.[2]

Charles Hugh Lowe had married Lucy's mother, Jane Ann Carr, at Manchester Cathedral on 16th April 1870. Lucy's mother was the daughter of a joiner and had been born in Cockermouth, on the edge of the Lake District in 1843. As a young woman she had been in service, working in the hamlet of Dale, near Ainstable, between Carlisle and Penrith. She was employed there as a house servant by an elderly widow, Mrs Elizabeth Fisher, who described herself as "a landed proprietor", and her unmarried daughter, Mary Fisher. This was clearly a formative experience which she talked about to her daughters. Indeed one of the few surviving photographs of Jane shows her with her daughters outside a cottage in Ainstable sometime just after the turn of the century when she had revisited the village. Even after Lucy and Jack were married, the "folk in Ainstable" sent them a turkey each Christmas. Jane had come to Manchester during the 1860s, and on the eve of her marriage was living with one of Charles's elder sisters, Sarah Ann Topping, at 24, Chestnut Street, off Waterloo Road, in Cheetham, a little to the east of Higher Broughton.

After they were married, Lucy's parents had lived at 35, Chestnut Street, in Cheetham, with two of Charles's younger brothers, Edmund, a warehouse porter, and George, a joiner. Lucy had three elder sisters, Annie Maud who was born in 1875, Edith who was born in 1877 and Sarah Ellen who was born in 1880. Lucy was born on 28th November 1882. However Lucy's father Charles died the following year, on 26th September 1884 of an acute obstruction of the bowels and phthisis pulmonalis, or tuberculosis. He was aged thirty-eight. One of her elder sisters, Annie, died during the summer of 1889 when she was aged fourteen. Her mother then moved to 12, Waterloo Road, and took in paying guests to make ends meet.

Perhaps as a result of the family's financial circumstances, Lucy only received an elementary education. She left school the day that she was thirteen and started work with a firm of dressmakers, Madame Louisette, who had rooms at 80, Deansgate. Initially Lucy worked as something like an apprentice dressmaker, learning to measure customers and to make clothes for them. Although by 1913 there were some six hundred dressmakers listed in *Slater's Directory* in the Manchester area, Madame Louisette was one of a relatively small number of "Court" dressmakers in the Deansgate, St Ann's Square, King Street area of the city who made gowns and dresses for "society ladies". Each year they sent designers to the

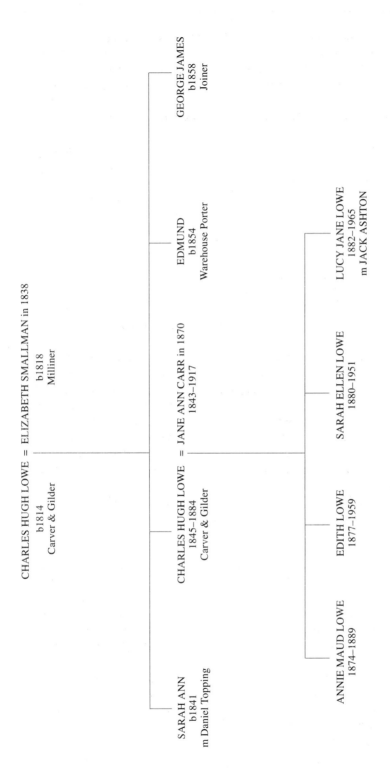

CHARLES HUGH LOWE = ELIZABETH SMALLMAN in 1838
b1814                    b1818
Carver & Gilder          Milliner

SARAH ANN
b1841
m Daniel Topping

CHARLES HUGH LOWE = JANE ANN CARR in 1870
1845–1884                 1843–1917
Carver & Gilder

EDMUND
b1854
Warehouse Porter

GEORGE JAMES
b1858
Joiner

ANNIE MAUD LOWE
1874–1889

EDITH LOWE
1877–1959

SARAH ELLEN LOWE
1880–1951

LUCY JANE LOWE
1882–1965
m JACK ASHTON

*Fig. 15 – Lucy Jane Lowe's immediate relatives.*

Paris collections where they sketched the latest clothes which were being modelled there. The dressmakers, like Lucy, measured, cut and sewed each dress individually, often based on these sketches. Sometimes Lucy went to customers' homes to make the final fittings and, occasionally, the dressmakers were allowed time off work to go to weddings where clothes which they had been made were being worn. While she worked for Madame Louisette she made friends with another dressmaker, Annie Myles who was to remain a close friend for the rest of her life.

Jack and Lucy "courted" for a long time before they were married. She pasted a pen and ink drawing of him wearing a high-buttoned jacket into her autograph book in September 1904. In February 1907, probably for Valentine's Day, he painted an intricate design of forget-me-knots in her autograph book. The central motif which they formed was a heart containing a quotation from Sir Walter Scott's poem "Lay of the Last Minstrel":

> Love rules the Court, the
> Grove, and men below and
> saints above, for love is
> Heaven and Heaven is Love.

Above he painted cherubs with quivers of arrows and to the side the initials "L" and "J", also made up of forget-me-knots. Jack also gave Lucy gifts, such as a small gold heart with diamond chippings and a silver dressing table set. Lucy gave him a silver cigarette case.

Sometimes Jack took Lucy by train for trips in the country, to Wales and to Derbyshire, and, after they were engaged, they went on holiday together. As a child Jack had been taken by his parents by train into the countryside, but because her mother had to bring up four daughters on her own, Lucy's childhood experiences had been far more limited. In later years Jack and Lucy talked in particular about a holiday in Aberystwyth and a day when they had walked half a dozen miles along the cliffs to the small village of Borth and back and had seen a man in his pyjamas coming out of a tent at Clarach Bay. They also took part in social activities such as dances organised by the Church.

Jack and Lucy were married on 30th June 1913 at St Matthew's, Crumpsall by the Reverend H E Stevens. Lucy was thirty and Jack was twenty-eight. A brief announcement of their wedding appeared in the *Manchester Evening News* the following day. Lucy gave up her job as a dressmaker just before they were married. As a wedding present Jack's mother, rather impractically, gave them a dinner service which she had bought in Stephensons, a china shop in Barton Arcade, Deansgate, which included twelve soup plates, twelve main course plates, twelve dessert plates, twelve cheese plates, sauce tureens, a soup tureen and vegetable dishes. Jack and Lucy were never to have a table which would seat a dozen people, and for the first few years of their married life had to keep the dinner service in its hamper because they did not have a cupboard large enough to store it. The couple travelled by train to Anglesey for their honeymoon.

Initially Jack and Lucy lived near to Heaton Park, renting 85, Milton Road from Benjamin Lofthouse who owned five houses in the street.[3] The gross estimated rental value for rating purposes was nineteen pounds ten shillings per annum. The house was one of many in the street which had been built on the edge of countryside not long before. Although number 85 no longer survives, the neighbouring houses are all small, built of red brick with two or three bedrooms. They have yards to the rear which would have contained outside toilets and small front gardens. Jack caught the train into town each day from nearby Heaton Park station.

Lucy soon became pregnant and gave birth to a son, Leslie Ward Ashton, on 8th April 1914. He was born in their home in Milton Road. She was a slightly built woman and had a

*Fig. 16 – Jack Ashton – self portrait (1904).*

long and difficult labour. A nurse called Mrs McLennan stayed in the house for a while after Leslie's birth to clean and provide meals for Lucy and Jack. In accordance with the normal medical practice of the time, Lucy did not get out of bed for two weeks after her confinement.

Jack and Lucy found that the house in Milton Road was too expensive. Later in 1914 or early in 1915 they moved to a cheaper house at 5, Lily Street (now Lidiard Street) in Crumpsall. They rented it unfurnished for fifteen shillings per week from Thomas Frederick Harrington, a boot dealer who had a shoe shop at 463, Cheetham Hill Road. It was a small terraced house, in a short cul-de-sac. Downstairs there were a back kitchen, a dining room and a sitting room. Upstairs there were three bedrooms, but no inside toilet. There was an outside toilet at the bottom of the small back garden. Both the inside of the house and the street were lit by gas lamps. There was a patch of grass to the rear, where Leslie and his friends piled up bonfire wood and other combustibles for Guy Fawkes night celebrations. Lucy made treacle toffee and parkin and Leslie put small bags of toffees through neighbours' letter boxes.

The routine of their day-to-day life was shattered by The Great War which was to have a devastating effect upon their generation. When war was declared in 1914, Britain, unlike the

*Love
rules the Court, the
Camp, the Grove, & men
below and saints above,
for love is Heaven, &
Heaven is
Love*

*Fig. 17 – Valentine from
Jack Ashton to Lucy
(1907).*

continental powers, did not have a conscript army. Field Marshal Lord Kitchener, the
Secretary of State for War, sought to augment the small professional army, and the voluntary
Territorial Force of partially trained citizens, who had originally enlisted for home defence,
by recruiting a new army of volunteers. He launched a forceful campaign to persuade men to
join the army. The pressure to enlist was great. Volunteering was portrayed as a patriotic
duty, and promises were made in recruiting leaflets that "You will not be sent to the Front till
you are trained and fit to take the field against the enemy". By the end of 1915 almost two
and a half million volunteers had enlisted. Among them were Jack's brothers Val, Tom and
George. All the brothers were photographed in their uniforms before travelling to the
Western Front. (Val had already travelled back to Manchester from South America. On 29th
May 1914 he had sent a postcard to Jack from Guayaquil, Ecuador, writing: "Hope to leave
here in a week or so & shall proceed to Panama. Expect to be home sometime in July.")

Val and Tom enlisted together, in November 1914. They joined the Royal Artillery and
were given regimental numbers 49534 and 49532. They arrived in France almost
simultaneously, Tom on 7th August 1915 and Val the following day. Val served in the 294th
Siege Battery.[4] He became a corporal, was then commissioned as a second lieutenant and

*Fig. 18 – Postcard from Val Ashton in Guayaquil, Ecuador, 1914. Val is standing on the right.*

later became a captain. He was wounded in 1916. Tom became a Corporal but was subsequently reduced to the ranks. He was also very badly wounded in 1916. He received shrapnel wounds to his head and injuries to his leg.

George, Jack's youngest brother, volunteered on 6th December 1914. He went to a recruiting office in Eccles and joined the 16th Battalion of the Lancashire Fusiliers, known at the time as "The Salford Pals". The MP for Salford, Mr Montague Barlow, played an important part in raising four battalions for the Lancashire Fusiliers and, in September 1914, had organised "a magnificent Recruiting Meeting"[5] at the Salford Hippodrome. George became Private 12536 in "B" company. He was aged eighteen. At first the new recruits were trained in Salford, but during the spring and early summer of 1915 they were housed in wooden huts, near Conway in North Wales. Their training was somewhat hampered by the fact that, due to shortages of weapons, they were not issued with any rifles. This was not uncommon among the volunteer regiments, and many drilled using wooden replicas. In June George and his comrades in the 16th Battalion left Conway for Catterick Bridge, and then, in late July or early August, they proceeded to Codford St Mary on Salisbury Plain for their

*Fig. 19 – Val Ashton.*

final training. The Battalion received its first Lewis Gun on 25th September and service rifles were issued on 20th October. The Battalion crossed to France barely a month later, on 22nd November 1915.

After two years of war, the English and French armies on the one side and the German army on the other side were bogged down in lines of trenches stretching from the Channel coast to the Swiss border. George spent the winter of 1915–1916 on the front near La Boisselle, in the Ancre Valley, to the north of the River Somme. The official *Roll of Honour of the Salford Brigade*, edited by Sir Montague Barlow, KBE MP, as he had become, referring to the trenches at La Boisselle, stated:

> The condition of the trenches was appalling, sometimes two or three feet deep in mud and water, and the enemy, holding the high ground surrounding, was particularly active in sniping.[6]

During the winter of 1915–1916 the British, French and Russian commanders planned a coordinated series of attacks on the German lines, all to take place on 1st July 1916. The main British assault was to take place between Maricourt and Serre, in the area to the north of the River Somme, against German positions which mainly ran along the ridges of a range of low hills. The aim was that the British infantry, after heavy bombardment of the German lines, would climb the hills and storm the trenches and other fortifications.

*Fig. 20 – George Ashton.*

The headlines of the *Manchester Evening Chronicle* on 1st July announced:

GREAT BRITISH OFFENSIVE BEGINS.
16 MILES OF TRENCHES CAPTURED.
British Drive North of the Somme.
Fighting Continues; Many Prisoners Taken.

A Press Association report referred to British troops having already occupied the first German lines and continued, "As far as can be ascertained our casualties have not been heavy." The following day the same paper referred to the British soldiers' "impetuous dash", but said that their advance was slowing down because the troops had "advanced too far" the previous day.

The reality was rather different. The allied artillery bombardment had not succeeded in destroying the enemy positions or in making holes in the German barbed wire. On many sections of the front, the lines of British infantrymen walking slowly towards the German trenches were scythed down by machine gun fire. On 1st July alone, there were almost sixty thousand British casualties. Twenty-two thousand men were killed, while thirty-five thousand other men were wounded.

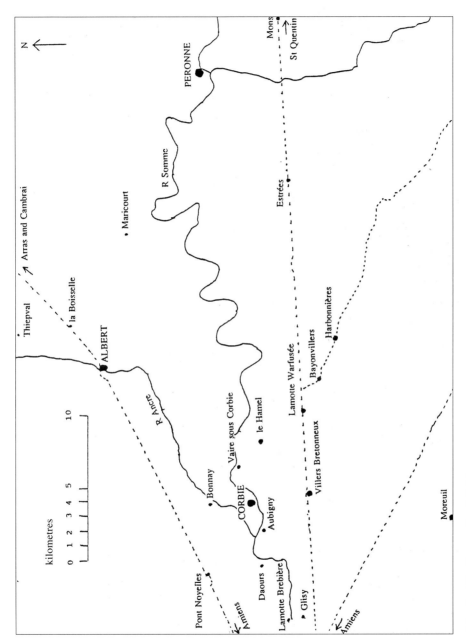

N

kilometres

0 1 2 3 4 5          10

Thiepval

Arras and Cambrai

la Boisselle

ALBERT

R Ancre

R Somme

Maricourt

PERONNE

Mons

St Quentin

Estrées

Vaire sous Corbie

le Hamel

Lamotte Warfusée

Bayonvillers

Harbonnières

Bonnay

CORBIE

Aubigny

Villers Bretonneux

Pont Noyelles

Amiens

Daours

Lamotte Brebière

Glisy

Amiens

Moreuil

*Map 8 – The Somme Battlefields.*

George was among those who were killed. Early on the morning of 1st July he was in a communications trench in the Ancre Valley, beneath strong German fortifications around the village of Thiepval, which the British troops planned to attack. At half past two a shell landed in the trench killing George instantaneously. Later, in reply to a letter from George's brother Jack, Captain T F Tweed, the officer commanding the company, wrote:

In reply to your enquiry I regret to have to inform you that your brother, Private George Ashton, was killed with several others by a shell, which burst in a communications trench as we were moving up to the point of assembly on the night of the attack. It would be about 2.30 a.m. (new time) on July 1st. It may be some measure of consolation in your great loss to know that his death was instantaneous and that he suffered no pain. He was a good soldier and I feel certain that when time has lessened your grief, you and yours will be proud to recollect that he gallantly gave his own life that England might live.

Very few of George's comrades survived July 1st. At ten to eight the same morning "B" and "D" companies set off towards the German lines, but soon disappeared into a wood. The undergrowth hid strong wire defences with machine guns which had been stored by the Germans in pits and so had remained virtually unscathed during the earlier British bombardment. The Salford Pals met with withering machine gun fire. The two companies had comprised slightly over five hundred officers and men. All were killed or injured, apart from the officer commanding them and seventeen other men. Thiepval was not to fall until 26th September, although the *Manchester Evening Chronicle* reported on 5th July that it had not only been captured by British troops, but also that a German counter-attack had been "easily repulsed".

In the weeks that followed, the *Manchester Evening Chronicle* printed announcements of the deaths of hundreds of men from Manchester and Salford. Soldiers' families scanned the columns fearfully each day, as soon as the papers appeared. The names of those who died on 1st July seem to have been released gradually by the War Office to disguise the true extent of the day's casualties. On Monday 24th July, underneath a headline "HEAVY WEEK-END LIST OF CASUALTIES. 6,105 OFFICERS AND MEN KILLED AND WOUNDED", came news of George's death:

Private George Ashton (20) was attached to the Eccles Pals, killed, lived at 192, Great Clowes Street, Broughton. Two other brothers are serving.

The next day, the family inserted their own personal announcement in the Roll of Honour in the same paper, which referred to George's death as "deeply regretted".

George's name is now recorded on the Thiepval Memorial to the Missing. This huge monument, overlooking the valley of the Ancre, lists the names of the 73,367 men of the British army who died in the Battle of the Somme and who have no known grave. His name appears on Pier 3, Face D.

The Battle of the Somme was "the glory and the graveyard" of Kitchener's new army.[7] By 18th November 1916 the Somme offensive had succeeded in gaining a stretch of land only twenty miles wide and six miles deep. There had been four hundred and twenty thousand casualties.

Unlike his brothers, Jack did not volunteer. Even after the Military Service Act of 1916 had introduced conscription, Jack was at first exempt from service because he was married, had a child and was over thirty. However in 1917, in view of the horrendous losses on the front, conscription was extended to older married men. Jack enlisted as "a gunner" in the

Garrison Royal Artillery. His regimental number was 179793. At first he was sent to Hull, and while there was among a party deployed in collecting coal from a collier which had gone down off Spurn Head. Soon though, he received the news that he would be sent to the Front. Before leaving for France he was stationed at barracks in Cosham, just north of Portsmouth. He went home on leave early in February 1918, returning to barracks on 8th February on the 11.55 a.m. train from Manchester and the 6.40 p.m. train from Waterloo.

An advance party left Cosham for France on Friday 15th March. The rest of the company stood by to depart, and apart from fatigue duties at the docks, were confined to barracks for the next two days. A farewell concert was laid on for the troops, including Jack, during the evening of Sunday 17th March.

Early in the afternoon the next day, Jack boarded the SS Huntscape. The ship, which weighed almost 3,000 tons, had been built in the German port of Bremen in 1911, but was subsequently captured and requisitioned by the British government.[8] Although the Huntscape left Portsmouth Docks during daylight, she anchored outside the port until dusk, when an escort of destroyers arrived to take the Huntscape up the Channel. When he woke the next morning Jack saw an airship and sea planes. The troop ship arrived outside Boulogne at 10 o'clock, but Jack did not disembark until 2 o'clock. Then the soldiers marched to St Martin's camp. Despite his training Jack was seemingly ill-equipped mentally and physically for what was ahead. He found the march to the camp "punishing" and noted complainingly in his diary the next day that he "had to turn out in the rain to unload a lorry". He can have had little idea of what was in store.

*Fig. 21 – Jack Ashton.*

The troops were billeted in tents at St Martin's Camp for three nights, fourteen to a tent. Whilst there they heard the sound of war for the first time – a "heavy bombardment and air raid close to". Jack had a medical examination and, on the Thursday evening, "a good hot supper" with orders for reveille at half past three the next morning.

On Friday 22nd March Jack and the other soldiers had breakfast at 4 a.m., and then started marching down to the docks at 5 a.m. They joined a motor convoy with a "destination unknown". The lorries headed south-east through countryside with hamlets which Jack thought were "very like English villages". After a lunch of bully beef and tea they passed through the strategic village of St Pol which had been bombed by German aeroplanes the previous day. They spent the Friday night at Frévent.

The convoy left Frévent at nine o'clock the next morning, with the troops believing that they were travelling to Péronne, a small town in the Somme valley. In fact they were approaching the front at the time that the English and French faced one of the gravest military crises of the war. On 21st March the Germans had broken through the Allied Lines to the east of Amiens, and during the next few days advanced up to forty miles westward, recapturing much of the countryside which they had lost during the 1916 Battle of the Somme, including Montdidier and Moreuil to the south-east of Amiens. Only hours before Jack and his comrades had left Frévent, Péronne had been abandoned and captured by the German army.

Oblivious of this, the English soldiers went on through Albert, a town on the River Ancre which fell to the Germans shortly afterwards. Jack noted in his diary that he saw the earlier Somme battlefields. Indeed he must have passed within a couple of miles of Thiepval where his brother George had died almost two years previously. He was perhaps unaware of this, and made no reference to Thiepval in his diary.

As the day wore on and they continued south-eastwards, Jack and his comrades found that "a great retreat [was] taking place." As a result, the convoy changed direction and travelled westwards through the night until they eventually arrived early the next morning at Corbie, another small town in the Somme valley, sixteen kilometres east of Amiens. The journey of about one hundred miles had taken two whole days and a night. After sleeping on the road in the bitter cold, Jack washed and shaved in a shell hole, had a good breakfast from the limited stores which had been brought in the motor convoy and mused that he had had a "narrow escape from capture", and perhaps even worse. If he had arrived a day earlier, he would almost certainly have been caught-up in the German advance. He noted that the "peasants [were] all flying."

The convoy was clearly in a state of confusion. Communication, which was largely by telephone, had broken down. Jack noted that he had seen nothing of the advance or rear parties which had left Cosham.

For a couple of days Jack was short of food. He tried unsuccessfully to get to Amiens to buy provisions, and had to content himself with coffee and wine which he bought in Corbie. Apart from this, despite the effect which the death of his brother George must have had, the early entries in Jack's diary contain few signs of the terror or the brutality of the war which the front line troops experienced. Jack was relatively lucky, not only that he had just missed the German advance of 21st March, but also that as a "gunner", he was stationed behind the front line. Although he feared air raids and shelling, he did not face the near certainty of injury or death experienced by infantrymen in the forward trenches. Instead, for the next few weeks, his diary displays the naïve interest and, at times, excitement of a man who had never previously set foot outside England. For example, when passing through Boulogne, he had been "much amused at the Chinese labour corps" unloading at the docks. The entry in his diary for 25th March, which was written the day after arriving in Corbie and while some German troops in this sector were still advancing westwards, read:

Lovely day. Bivouac in wood a few miles away. Make improvised tents. Go shell hunting on road to Amiens. Roads thick with refugees. Very pretty woods, lovely wild flowers.

From 28th March, the battery to which Jack was assigned was billeted at Vaire-sous-Corbie, a hamlet on the floor of the Somme Valley, about a mile behind the front line. At first he slept in a barn. His first few days at Vaire were relatively quiet. The German armies were exhausted and unable to sustain the advance which they began on 21st March. Jack took part in fatigue parties and there was occasional gun fire, but it does not seem that the experience was particularly unpleasant for Jack. The entries in his diary for early April were:

*Monday 1st April*
Rifle parade. Another good feed. Air fighting. Went fishing, no luck.
*Tuesday 2nd April*
Fatigues at Gun Park all day. Another good feed but resources nearly at an end. Able to buy chocolate. Received six letters from Lu[cy] & one from Joe [Walker – a friend]
*Wednesday 3rd April*
Rifle parade. Wrote long letter to Lu on bank of stream. Many troops pass through village & bands playing. Food resources at an end. Heavy firing.
*Thursday 4th April*
Very wet. Rifle parade. Wrote to Lu, Mother & Val. Bathe in river, cold but enjoyable.

He passed much of his time playing cards, reading on the banks of a stream, and writing letters. He tried fishing again, still without success. His military tasks mainly comprised guard duty, rifle parades and loading and unloading stores. One day he suffered from diarrhoea and a sore throat after being on guard duty in the rain. At times Vaire was bombarded by Germans, particularly between 8th and 11th April, but Jack's diary displays no recognition of the potentially deadly effect of the shell fire. On 9th April Jack wrote

Very exciting all day. Fritz shelled us all day on & off during previous night. Got very close, cottages smashed nearby. Wrote letter to Lu. Coffee in cottage.

Two days later, despite the German bombardment, he "spent [the] day on banks of stream reading & playing cards."

This relatively relaxed pattern was broken a week later when, after spending part of the day fishing, Jack received orders that he was to move the following day. He took part in "fatigues all day & night". After the guns had been drawn by horses to a location nearer Amiens he had two days of hard work, digging and marking out the new gun positions. On 20th April he noted that he had not washed or shaved for two days and that his hands were very sore. Once the guns had been repositioned, he erected a bivouac, and slept well, despite a hard frost on the night of 21st April.

He also began firing the artillery pieces. One of his tasks was to calculate the elevation of the guns needed to reach their targets. The Germans returned the fire and, on 24th April, he wrote:

In action all day. Occasionally shelled. Narrow escape, piece of shell falling between Alec and I. Wrote to Lu. 331 Batty came alongside, but depart.

The next day, presumably as a result of this near miss, he started building a dug-out. He worked on this task until 2nd May, when he wrote:

Completion of dug out. Action. First night in dug out. Excellent. Bathe at pump.

Two days later though, Jack was playing cards in the dug-out when rain started to come through the roof.

May and June passed by. Jack spent some days digging trenches. On other days he was on guard duty at the Brigade Command Post. At the end of May he was involved in taking down one gun and digging a new position for it. On some Sundays he went to Divine Service conducted by the Brigade Chaplain and received Holy Communion, once to the sound of shell-fire. He wrote most days to his wife Lucy, sometimes sending letters, and sometimes completing standard form printed field post cards by deleting the statements which did not apply. He wrote slightly less frequently to his mother. Occasionally he wrote to his brothers Val and Tom. In turn he received letters on most days from Lucy and sometimes parcels with food, Pear's soap, brilliantine or cigarettes. He received a few copies of the Manchester Guardian from his friend Harry Walton. Lucy's letters normally took between four and six days to arrive. On days off he was given a pass, enabling him to visit the nearby village of Daours where he had a hot bath and, on another day, Lamotte-Brebière and Bussy where he saw a German aeroplane shot down and heard a "band playing, [and] machine guns and shells bursting whilst having lunch".

In general May does not seem to have been a month when there was much action on this sector of the front. Jack's diary only refers to him being in action and firing the guns on five occasions during May, but activity intensified during June. He described several days as "very busy." He began only to note the occasions when he was in action during the night. On 9th June he noted that an officer in the Royal Engineers was killed during hostile shelling. On 18th June he saw an observation balloon brought down in flames. On 24th June Jack wrote:

Action 4.0 a.m. Fire 40 [rounds]. Battery all ill. 75 rnds ammn delivered. Only about 3 to deal with it. Hell of a day. Rcd Lu's letter of 18. Write letter to Lu.

As June ended the British troops were preparing to advance and to try to recover the land which they had lost during the March offensive. Artillery pieces were moved forward and Jack spent most of the night of 29th June working on new gun positions. They made a surprise attack on German positions at Le Hamel,[9] a couple of kilometres south-east of Vaire, during the early hours of Thursday 4th July. Jack's diary records:

*Wednesday 3rd July*
Worrying day. Receive long letter from Lu [of] 27th. Write letter to Lu. Up all night. Bombardment. Over the top. Chaos. Shooting all night.
*Thursday 4th July*
See heaps of German prisoners put in cage close by. On duty with Mr [Kirk]. Prisoners sad looking lot. No letters. Write letter to Lu. Parties from wood come down here. Shooting all night.

Although Jack had the time the following day to chat to an Australian soldier, Private Wes Gard of the 51st Battalion of the Australian Infantry Forces, and "to invite him to supper", the beginning of July marked the start of the real war for Jack. Until then, although there had been periods of hard work and shelling, there were times when he was able to relax. From early July, as the British, French, Empire and newly arrived American forces were preparing to counter-attack, there was far more shelling. Jack was no longer noticing the pretty flowers or reading by streams. Instead his diary mentions shooting on five consecutive nights. There are references to "heavy bombardment", and on Sunday 7th July he noted that some Australians and "Yanks" were killed in the woods nearby. In the middle of July five observation balloons were shot down during a period of four days. There was particularly heavy shelling around 17th and 18th July, coinciding with the Second Battle of the Marne which took place to the north, near Reims. Jack wrote in his diary "'Jerry' counter attacks and suffers . . . Good news from [the] French."

The rest of July was quieter, although the weather was wetter. On two successive days Jack's dug-out was flooded. Soon though, the Allied commanders began to prepare for a further surprise offensive to the east of Amiens, although soldiers like Jack were probably not aware of the plans until thirty-six hours before the attack commenced.[10] On Friday 2nd August, in heavy rain, Jack toiled through to the small hours of the morning dismantling a gun. He continued working on the gun during 3rd and 4th August when it was moved, presumably by a team of horses, to Aubigny, a hamlet on the south bank of the Somme. Jack spent the next three days digging dug-outs and dumping ammunition at night. It rained continuously and Jack was wet through. He was shelled for three days running, and, on 5th August Mr Kirk, an officer with whom Jack had often been on guard duty, and several men were wounded by shell fire. Jack noted in his diary that he was "tired out", that the roads were "packed" and that there was "much activity".

For Jack this was the most intensive period of activity yet, but these exertions were only the prelude to the attack of 8th August, which has been described[11] as "a famous victory, the most brilliant ever gained by British arms in the World War, and, better still, the most economic" although the "economy" was only relative. There were some twenty thousand Allied casualties between 8th and 12th August. The German commander Ludendorff called it "the black day of the German Army in the history of the war." Sixteen thousand German prisoners were taken on the first day of the attack. It was also significant because of the successful use of tanks by the Allied forces.

Jack had been working late into the previous night, and did not get to Daours where he slept until midnight. He was up at 4 o'clock the next morning. The Fourth Army's main offensives by Australians on the south bank of the Somme, and the Canadians to their right, were launched at 4.20 a.m., with the support of a heavy bombardment by British soldiers using over two thousand guns and Howitzers. The infantry gained six to eight miles over much of this part of the front on the first day. Jack wrote:

*Thursday 8th August*
Up at 4 a.m. Went over. Howitzer stunt. British made big advance. Terrible sights. See many prisoners. Cavalry go into action. Start letter but didn't finish it.

Despite their initial successes the advance soon slowed down, and on 10th August, Field Marshal Haig gave orders delaying the further attacks which had been planned. Jack spent a few days at Aubigny, before taking apart some of the Royal Artillery's guns, ready for them to be moved forward towards the new lines. After the dug-out had been dismantled he spent one night sleeping in a chateau. He was then posted to Brigade Headquarters which had moved forward to Harbonnierres. He worked hard for the three days from 15th to 17th August, digging a gun-pit and mounting the guns, under hostile shelling each day. He noted that for two days he was unable to wash or shave. On 17th and 18th August, Jack was billeted with soldiers from the 15th and 16th Lancashire Fusiliers and he was able to make some enquiries about the death of his brother George. On 19th August he worked building the detachment dug-out and despite hostile shelling nearby slept well in a dug-out with the stores.

21st August was very hot. Jack noted in his diary the "fearful stench from dead horses & men". During the night he was in action, firing towards the German lines. Probably this shelling was coordinated with attacks by other forces to the north, near Albert. Jack wrote "Big strafe Albert way". Despite their setbacks, the German troops were still returning shell fire, and on Thursday 22nd August, Jack had "a narrow escape from a dud shell". Indeed there was hostile shelling on the next five consecutive days.

By this time Jack was suffering from recurrent attacks of bad diarrhoea, a common occurrence in the light of the insanitary conditions which the troops had to endure. He was ill on 21st August. On 27th August he was "very poorly in night. Up all night with diarrhoea". The following day the Captain sent for a doctor who gave him tablets. Although he improved a little, he spent all the following day in bed. On 30th August after receiving orders to prepare to move, Jack tried to get ready for parade, but found that he could not manage it because of diarrhoea. He went to Bayonvillers where he eventually found another doctor. He spent two more days in bed, and so was out of action when the Fourth Army advanced again, with the Australians, recapturing Mont St Quentin and Péronne on 31st August.

Following the infantry's advance, the Artillery's guns were moved forward towards the new front line. On 2nd September, Jack moved eastwards to a new position near Estrées. By the following day he was feeling much better and was ready for light work on a gun before going on duty at the Brigade Command Post.

The next three weeks were a time of repeated Allied advances. They recaptured much of the ground which they had lost in March. For Jack this meant dismantling guns before they were moved forward to new positions and then reassembling them again. For example 3rd and 4th September were spent putting up guns. After "Jerry [was] reported retiring and exploding" on 5th September, Jack spent three days dismantling the same guns and moving stores. On 11th September he moved on to Mons. The next day he saw troops "moving up in char a bancs" and he himself was on the move the following day, again travelling eastwards, this time to Nobescourt Ferme – a large isolated farm with a high pitched gable roof in a sheltered valley, a couple of kilometres north of Hancourt.

Conditions during this period varied from day to day and from place to place. One day a soldier near to Jack was injured by a grenade. Hostile shelling and bombing continued. The weather often played a significant part. Sometimes there were thunderstorms and heavy rain. Occasionally he was able to light a fire and had hot water with which to shave. One night he slept in a gun pit with rats. Another night he slept in a cellar. Sometimes he slept in dug-outs which were comfortable, but on the morning of 17th September, he wrote

Terrible night. Thunder, lightning, wind and rain & Jerry shelling. We managed to keep dry. Others flooded out & some buried in.

Wednesday 18th September was similar:

Get action about 4.30 a.m. & continue until 1.30 p.m. Raining all the time. Get wet through. Manage to get a wash and shave in afternoon. Many prisoners coming down. Balloon brought down by Jerry. Receive no letters. Bombed in night. Sleep well, but in action 5 a.m. and 8 a.m.

The English and Dominion advances continued. On 24th September, after two days spent dismantling guns, Jack moved another seven kilometres north-eastwards to the village of Templeux. He worked all night "putting in" a gun while the Allied commanders began to prepare for an attack on the German fortifications along the Hindenburg Line.

The fact that the Germans were retreating did not mean that they were putting up less resistance. Indeed Jack's diary shows that his own personal experiences were getting worse and worse:

*Wednesday 25th September*
Work on gun pit & rest until evening. Wet during day. Open Mother's parcel. Hot time of it. Work all thro' night, bombed, shelled & gas. Terrible night. Not able to write letters.
*Thursday 26th September*
Break off at 7.0 a.m. & have to get up again to man wheels. Shelled badly. Receive Lu's letter of 19th. Write [field card] to Lu & letter to Mother. Up all night. Wet thro', make fire, dry clothes & continue until 7 a.m.

The hostile shelling continued during 27th September and Jack noted in his diary that there were "casualties". The next day there was heavy shelling all round Jack's dug-out. Gas shells started to explode. Since gas had first been used successfully by the Germans on the Western Front at Ypres on 22nd April 1915, it had become one of the weapons most feared by the ordinary soldiers on both sides of the front line. (The British and French were as ready to use gas as the Germans and on 12th July Jack had gone to an English "gas chamber" where gas shells were stored.) Two types of gas were used. Chemicals such as chlorine, chloropicrin and phosgene affected soldiers' lungs while nerve agents such as mustard gas brought about inflammation of the skin and temporary blindness.[12] Wilfred Owen was probably referring to the effect of chlorine when he wrote:

> Gas! GAS! Quick, boys! – An ecstasy of fumbling,
> Fitting the clumsy helmets just in time;
> But someone still was yelling out and stumbling,
> And flound'ring like a man in fire or lime...
> Dim, through the misty panes and thick green light,
> As under a green sea, I saw him drowning.
>
> In all my dreams, before my helpless sight,
> He plunges at me, guttering, choking, drowning.
>
> If in some smothering dreams you too could pace
> Behind the wagon that we flung him in,
> And watch the white eyes writhing in his face,
> His hanging face, like a devil's sick of sin;
> If you could hear, at every jolt, the blood
> Come gargling from the froth-corrupted lungs,
> Obscene as cancer, bitter as the cud
> Of vile, incurable sores on innocent tongues, –
> My friend, you would not tell with such high zest
> To children ardent for some desperate glory,
> The old lie: Dulce et decorum est
> Pro patria mori.[13]

By 1918 all English troops were supplied with gas masks. The most common type used, the "box respirator", consisted of a face mask connected by a flexible rubber tube to a large filter containing sodium permanganate-lime granules and charcoal. Jack's diary had referred to a gas inspection on 9th August. Although masks provided protection against poisonous gases such as chlorine and tear gas which affected the lungs, they gave little protection against mustard gas which affected the skin. It has been estimated that gas caused just over 1 per cent of all deaths among soldiers in the British Expeditionary Force and 3.3 per cent of all non-fatal injuries and sickness.[14]

It is not clear whether or not Jack was wearing a gas mask on 28th September. Perhaps he was slow in putting on his mask, but soon he was suffering from the effects of either Smith Onion Gas or Nightingale Gas.

At first he carried on "in action", but then reported to the Casualty Clearing Station at the rear of the Allied positions. The next day he was sent on to hospital in Rouen. His eyes, throat and chest were "terrible". On 30th September, when he saw a doctor, his eyes were feeling better, and he had managed to shave. However his relief must have been immense when he was told that he would be returning to England. He stayed in hospital in Rouen until 3rd October when he wrote "leave Rouen for Blighty on SS Essequibo", an 8,464 ton Royal Mail packet steamer which had been built in Belfast in 1914.[15] On the ship he handed over his remaining French francs to a money changer. Jack had selected an old man with a white beard, thinking that he looked honest, but was later convinced that he had been swindled.

The war was over for Jack, but its memories remained for the rest of his life. On the boat, Jack's emotions were probably similar to those of Siegfried Sassoon, who after leaving the battlefield wrote:[16]

> The rank stench of those bodies haunts me still
> And I remember things I'd best forget . . .
>
> To-night I smell the battle; miles away
> Gun-thunder leaps and thuds along the ridge;
> The spouting shells dig pits in fields of death,
> And wounded men, are moaning in the woods.
> If any friend be there whom I have loved,
> God speed him safe to England with a gash.

Jack arrived at Southampton the next day and was sent to the Bath War Hospital where he arrived late that night. He stayed in hospital for slightly over a fortnight before being transferred to Rock House Annexe in Lansdown which was run by the Red Cross. Lucy and their four year old son Leslie visited Jack on 22nd October. He convalesced there until 8th November when he was transferred to Crown Hill, Plymouth.

Armistice Day on 11th November passed by without Jack making any reference to the end of the war in his diary. By then 650,000 men in the British and Empire armies had been killed, with two million more wounded. As a visit to any French church shows, French losses were even heavier. 1,350,000 French men were killed and three times as many wounded. Only 30 per cent of the French army escaped the war unscathed. Two million German soldiers were killed and four million wounded. Most households in England, France and Germany had lost at least one relative or friend.

Jack's journey back north started on 2nd December. He caught the 7.55 p.m. train from Plymouth to Manchester and arrived in Manchester at seven o'clock the next morning. He went home and visited his mother, before setting off to Blackpool that evening to complete his convalescence. He stayed in Blackpool for a week before finally returning home.

Later Jack received two medals through the post. One, made of bronze, was like a larger version of a sovereign, with the head of King George V on one side and a depiction of Saint

George slaying the dragon on the reverse. The other medal, made of a light brassy metal, bore the words "The Great War of Civilisation." Jack never wore them. On leaving the army he also received "a gratuity" which he used to buy a pearl and diamond ring for Lucy.

The war was without doubt the most significant event of Jack's life. When he talked about it in later life, the adjective which he used most was "terrible". He was critical of the slaughter, the mismanagement and the muddled thinking among the commanders at the top and of the squalid conditions, but he was not bitter. Like most men of his generation he was proud to have served and at times he had enjoyed the comradeship of his fellow soldiers.

After returning to Manchester Jack worked again for W M Christy and Sons. The firm had pioneered the manufacture of "Turkish Towels and Bath Sheets" in the United Kingdom. The company's advertisements described themselves as:

Cotton spinners and manufacturers; the original inventors and patentees of the Royal Turkish towels in both cotton and linen, also terry cloth, bath blankets, bath gowns, bathing costumes, honeycomb and huckaback towels, also all classes of fancy towels, dusters and house cloths.

The towels were made at Christy's mill in Droylsden, but their wholesale showroom where Jack was employed was in Lower Mosley Street in central Manchester. Apart from a period during the Second World War when their offices had been bombed and Jack was based at the mill in Droylsden, he worked in Lower Mosley Street from nine till five on weekdays and from nine till midday on Saturdays until his retirement in 1953. His job was not directly affected by the widespread unemployment of the Depression in the 1930s and the family's living standards did not suffer, although his daughter Mildred can remember seeing long queues of unemployed men outside the "dole offices" in Stockport. Jack was described as "a clerk", but his job involved meeting commercial buyers who in turn sold towels to retail shops. When he talked about Christys, he referred to it as "our firm", although that did not stop him from criticising the way the firm was run, or his immediate superior. He was meticulous and scrupulously honest and seems to have been well respected. Initially he was paid weekly, but during the 1930s, became a salaried employee.

At home, Lucy did all the housework and cooking. She was the first up each morning and lit the fire in the kitchen so that it was warm when the others came down for breakfast. She had more common sense about day to day financial matters and paid all the household bills. Jack's work at home seems to have been limited to doing odd jobs, gardening, putting coal on the fire and cleaning shoes on Sunday mornings. There was a clear division of roles of the kind that was the norm for their generation. When Lucy became pregnant again in 1924, she had assistance in the house from a help called Mabel who came in on Wednesdays and who continued to work for her for the next five years.

Lucy and Jack's second child, Lucy Mildred, who was always known as Mildred, was born on 11th April 1925 at home in Lily Street.

Leslie went to Crumpsall Lane School just along Lansdowne Road until he was twelve and then, like his father, went to Manchester Central School in Whitworth Street. Leslie was bright, but often mischievous and did not apply himself well to school work. When he was fourteen and a half, he found himself "in a spot of bother" for what he described as "no more than a boyish prank". He was caned in front of the whole school assembly at morning prayers. On a later occasion Lucy was summoned to his school to hear about what he had done wrong. Jack, who was meticulous in complying to the letter with all conceivable regulations, was horrified and furious.

In January or early February 1929 Jack, Lucy and their two children moved from Lily

Street, to Cheadle Hulme, a suburb about eight miles south of Manchester. Cheadle Hulme had been no more than a small hamlet with a few houses and an isolated station until the end of the nineteenth century. However the ease of railway travel to Manchester and the desire of people to move out of the city meant that it grew rapidly in the 1920s and 1930s. By 1931, the "village" had a population of almost three and a half thousand people.

Jack bought a newly constructed house in Princess Avenue on the Grange Estate. (The names of most of the adjoining roads had "royal" connections, Queen's Road, Kings Road, Buckingham Road, Balmoral Avenue etc.) The estate, which was built by the Rough Cast Building Company Limited of 23, King Street West, Manchester was made up of similar houses which were typical of the inter-war suburban semis which were being built around most large cities. Jack and Lucy's house was built of red bricks with stucco at first floor level and a roof of red Staffordshire tiles. The top parts of the casement windows and the front door had leaded lights of red, green and blue stained glass. On the ground floor there was a kitchen and pantry, a dining room at the rear, and a front room. There were three bedrooms. The dining room, the front room and the two larger bedrooms had coal fire places, although Jack and Lucy only lit fires upstairs when someone was ill. The fireplace in the dining room was, according to the builder's particulars, surmounted by a "Jacobean Oak panelled mantel", while that in the front room had a "polished mahogany mantel with oval mirror." The house had "all mod cons". There was not only electricity and gas, but also, upstairs, a toilet with a "W.C. fitted with polished mahogany seat". Even though the house had an inside toilet which flushed, Jack and Lucy retained the habit of keeping chamber pots under the beds in case someone was ill. The bathroom, which was separate, was described as having a "Porcelain enamelled parallel bath. Taps fitted to bath, lavatory basin and sink are Nickel plated easy clean type." The house had gardens to the front and rear and space to the left hand side for a garage. Behind the back garden there were fields which sloped down to the Ladybrook, where, as she grew older, Mildred sometimes played.

The basic price of the house was £470. This was undoubtedly cheap, largely due to a Government scheme for subsidising house building, a policy which was aimed not only at increasing the number of homes available but also at reducing unemployment. The builder's particulars described the houses as the "MOST ASTOUNDING VALUE EVER OFFERED". In fact the final cost of the house was more than £470. Jack noted the following additional payments which came to a further £95 5s 1d:

| | | | |
|---|---:|---:|---:|
| Kitchen Grate | 21 | 5 | 0 |
| Lead Lights | 13 | 7 | 0 |
| Concreting Wash House & Fixing Gas Pipe | 3 | 3 | 6 |
| Concreting under Dining Room Window | 1 | 17 | 6 |
| Conveyance | 15 | 3 | 8 |
| Wash House | 6 | 2 | 6 |
| Mantels | 5 | 15 | 0 |
| Electric Cable | 4 | 2 | 8 |
| Joiner and Electrician | 8 | 3 | |
| Garden | 20 | 0 | 0 |

The builders required a deposit of £50. They offered to arrange a mortgage to cover the balance and in their sale particulars produced calculations showing that the weekly cost, including repayment to the building society, rates and chief rent totalled exactly £1. In fact Jack and Lucy did not have a mortgage. They borrowed some money from Lucy's sisters, with Jack keeping a note book in which he recorded his repayments.

# GRANGE ESTATE, CHEADLE HULME.

### GRANGE AVENUE, CHEADLE ROAD, QUEEN'S ROAD.
#### CHARMING HOUSES.
## MOST ASTOUNDING VALUE EVER OFFERED.
## NO PAVING LIABILITIES.

**The Secret of Grange Estate Success :—**

(1)  The beauty and healthiness of the Estate.  (Altitude—200 feet above sea).

(2)  Houses exclusively designed for taste and comfort.

(3)  Unique access to Manchester and Stockport by rail and bus.

(4)  Houses liberally spaced, providing ample room for garage.

(5)  Liberal advance granted by Building Society to House Purchasers exclusively on the Estate.

(6)  Amazing price of House includes Road Charges.

PRICE **£470**     DEPOSIT **£50**     MORTGAGE **£420**
CHIEF £5 PER ANNUM.

*Fig. 22 – Builders' description of houses on Grange Estate, Cheadle Hulme.*

The house was solidly built, but on several occasions after they moved in, Lucy took Mildred with her when she went to grumble about defects to a Mr Mortimer, the clerk of works, at the builder's site office in a hut at the corner of Buckingham Road and Queens Road.

Jack and Lucy were typical of the members of their generation who moved from the cities into the estates of semis which surrounded them. They were conservative, self-reliant and Christian. They led a secure and ordered life. The centre of their lives was their small nuclear family and their reasonably comfortable home. In material terms, they considered that they had what they needed, even though they lacked many of today's consumer goods and were careful with their money.

They never owned a car. Until sometime during the 1950s, all Lucy's cooking was done on the kitchen range, with its coal fire on the left hand side, an oven on right hand side and a back boiler for heating water. She boiled kettles and grilled chops and steaks on the fire, although she did have one gas ring on the hearth. The range had to be lit and cleaned out daily because it did not stay 'in' overnight. Every week it was cleaned by rubbing black lead on to it with a cloth and then brushing it off. Sometime in the 1950s they bought a gas cooker, but Lucy continued to use the range until her death. They never bought a fridge, but Lucy used the pantry which opened off the kitchen.

For cleaning, Lucy initially used a Ewbank carpet sweeper and twice a year took up carpets and beat them over the washing line in the garden. Just before the Second World War she bought a Hotpoint vacuum cleaner from the Co-op in Stockport. She never used an ironing board, but instead ironed on the kitchen table which she covered with folded blankets and a sheet. At first she used three flat irons which she heated on the fire, but she bought a Morphy Richards electric iron in the late 1930s. A telephone was installed in 1946, and their son Leslie bought them a television in the late 1950s.

Lucy made the curtains, most of her clothes and all of Mildred's clothes using a Singer sewing machine which was operated by a foot treadle and which she had owned since before she was married. She did not have a washing machine until she took over her daughter Mildred's Hoover washing machine in 1961. Until then she washed clothes in a galvanised zinc tub in the wash house using a dolly peg with three legs to stir clothes which she had soaked, a wash board made of corrugated glass to rub the clothes and a mangle to squeeze out the water.

There was no really effective means of keeping fresh food for any length of time and so Lucy shopped almost every day, mainly at the shops on Cheadle Road and Buckingham Road which had been built at the same time as the estate. They were about five or ten minutes' walk away. Most days she bought a large white loaf of bread from the Co-op, which was also her source for tea and sugar. She bought groceries such as bacon and ham from John Williams, the nearest grocer's shop. Every day she bought half a pound of butter, which the grocer cut from a block, patted, wrapped in greaseproof paper and then tied up in brown paper with string. Normally she bought meat from McClintons or Pimlotts, butchers on Station Road. Fish normally came from Broadbents, the fishmongers who had a wooden hut in a cul-de-sac nearby, although sometimes she bought fish from the fish market in Manchester. The other shops nearby on Cheadle Road and Buckingham Road included Hayes, the chemist and optician, Edwards, the ironmongers where Jack bought seeds for the garden, an off licence and Shutts the newsagents who sold tobacco and sweets. Lucy went to Stockport market most Fridays by train to buy vegetables, fruit, cheese, eggs and, sometimes, a chicken.

Initially milk was delivered twice a day to Jack and Lucy's house by Mrs Farnell, a farmer's wife who had a farm between Cheadle and Cheadle Hulme. She drove a pony and trap with milk churns and wore a black leather coat. She poured milk from the churns into customers' jugs.

Jack and Lucy's doctors were a father and son who were in partnership together, both called Doctor Craig. Their fees for visiting the house were normally seven shillings and six pence. One Sunday, after Jack and Lucy had taken up the carpet and removed the furniture, both doctors operated on Mildred, who was laid out on the dining room table under an anaesthetic, to remove her tonsils. Although, like many men of his generation, Jack smoked heavily, both he and Lucy were very healthy. He had the occasional cold or stomach upset, but never had to stay in bed and their daughter Mildred can only recall Lucy ever being ill in bed on one occasion when she had 'flu and cystitis. Although colds did tend to "go to her chest", she always "worked them off".

Lucy and Jack lived mainly in their dining room which had a settee against the wall facing the window and Jack's chair near the fire place. They rarely used the front room. Jack spent most evenings reading the newspaper and listening to the wireless while he smoked. He had a keen interest in current affairs and read the *Daily Mail* every day. Lucy normally sewed or read the *Manchester Evening News* or the *Church Times*. On Saturday evenings they usually listened to "Saturday Night Theatre" on the wireless, but did not go out to the pictures. Lucy did not really approve of them, although Jack took Mildred to see the films "Victoria Regina" and "Fire Over England" at the Elysian Picture House in Cheadle Hulme.

Every Sunday they both went to All Saints Anglican Church, often attending both eight o'clock communion in the morning and Evensong. They took an active interest in Church affairs, both locally and nationally. Jack was a sidesman and a member of the Parochial Church Council for many years. Lucy made sandwiches for the Parochial Church Tea once a year and helped to organise whist drives to raise money for Church funds. In religious matters, as with most other things, Jack held firm, if rather narrow, views. He was strongly critical of both Low Church Anglicans and Catholics. He was concerned that things were done properly and on more than occasion wrote to the bishop about matters which particularly concerned him. They were both outraged when they heard that the vicar had been seen one evening kissing a parishioner under the lych gate by the church. Jack and Lucy's friend who had spotted them reportedly confined himself to a loud "Good Night Vicar!" Mildred attended Sunday school, and, when she was older, taught there. Lucy felt strongly about what should and should not be done on Sundays and believed that it was wrong to knit, sew or put out washing on Sundays.

They had a relatively small circle of friends. Their closest friends were the Ashwells. Mr Ashwell had worked in a bank, but had been very badly injured during the First World War. As a result he had lost a leg and an arm and was only partially sighted. Jack and Lucy had coffee with them on Sundays after evensong. They played whist with them fairly regularly. They also saw their next door neighbours, the Dupoys regularly. Mr Dupoy had been in the Indian Army, but after the First World War worked as the manager of The Fifty Shilling Tailors in Manchester. For years they came round to Jack and Lucy's house on Saturday evenings for supper. Between the wars they had a Morris car and one Saturday took Jack, Lucy and Mildred on an overnight journey to London and drove back with them the following night. Jack and Lucy were also friendly with the Davidsons, a retired couple. Mr Davidson had worked as a journalist on a Manchester newspaper, but they moved away from Manchester to Surbiton. Most days Lucy visited her sisters, Edith and Nellie, who had moved from a bungalow at Cleveleys, a little to the north of Blackpool, to Cheadle Hulme in 1930 or 1931. Lucy's closest friend was Annie Myles, whom she had known since the days when they both worked as dressmakers. She did not marry and lived in Eccles. She came to see Lucy at Princess Avenue after work every couple of months.

Otherwise Jack and Lucy took part in few social activities. Although they were both members of the local Conservative Association, they were not very active. Jack went canvassing for the M.P. during one election. Lucy once went with the Womens' Branch of the Conservative Association to see the Grand National.

Jack had two weeks holiday every year. Until the outbreak of the Second World War curtailed holidays, the family always went away for a fortnight to the sea-side by train. Over the years they stayed in apartments in Prestatyn on the North Wales coast, Port Erin on the

Isle of Man, Shanklin on the Isle of White, Morfa Nefyn on the Lleyn Peninsula and Rhoscolyn on Anglesey. Other excursions before the Second World War included one night spent camping with the Dupoys in a tent in Derbyshire and one Easter they travelled by charabanc to Colwyn Bay for a holiday. Apart from Jack's service during the First World War, neither Lucy nor Jack ever went abroad.

After the outbreak of the Second World War, Jack continued to travel daily to work in Manchester by train, returning home for 5.40 p.m. on weekdays and 12.40 p.m. on Saturdays, even after Christy's office in Lower Mosley Street was bombed. However, as a result of a cut back in business, his salary was reduced by 15 to 20 per cent during the war years. He also had to take part in fire-watching duty at their offices, with a stirrup pump to put out any fires caused by German incendiary bombs. On one occasion he discovered from serial numbers on towels that one of the customers was supplying towels to Germany.

Cheadle Hulme suffered little from bomb damage during the war, although on many nights Jack, Lucy and Mildred could see the sky to the north lit up from the back of the house as Manchester was bombed. Even so, Jack and Billy Dupoy dug an air raid shelter. One night Jack and Billy Dupoy thought that they saw someone across the fields to the rear of the house signalling with lights to enemy aircraft.

Another important consequence of the war was food rationing, which was first introduced in January 1940. Quantities allowed varied from time to time, but basic items remained subject to rationing until well after the end of the war. Among the items which were rationed were meat (limited, in the summer of 1942, to one shilling and tuppence worth per week per person[17]), cheese (limited to four ounces), butter (two ounces), bacon (four ounces), tea (two ounces) and sugar (eight ounces). For some items, such as meat and butter, customers had to be registered with a particular shop – Lucy was registered with the Co-op and John Williams – but for other groceries which were covered by a points system, it was possible to take ration books to any shop. Some items, such as sausages and offal, were not rationed but were in extremely short supply, and butchers normally only sold these to their own registered customers. Clothes and material were also rationed. Jack, Lucy, Leslie and Mildred never went hungry, although Leslie had insisted that Lucy buy up a large stock of tinned food before rationing started, and Jack, when carving, always cut the thinnest possible slices of meat.

Lucy had always been close to her sisters, Edith and Nellie. They were known within the family as Eshie and Atten, after the way in which Leslie had tried to pronounce their names when he was young. After the war, when Leslie and Mildred had left home, they moved into 23, Princess Avenue. They both slept in the double bed in the larger back bedroom. Nellie died on 22nd January 1951. Edith died on 21st June 1959.

After Jack's retirement in 1953, Jack and Lucy continued to live in Princess Avenue. Both were physically active and able to look after themselves without help until Lucy died suddenly in her sleep in February 1965. She was eighty-two and had a stroke. Jack, who had just turned eighty, did not want to carry on living in the house on his own, even if he had been able to do so. He moved into a residential retirement home in Bramhall. He remained active, both physically and mentally, taking walks into the village before breakfast, until 1974. Then, as a result of failing health, he moved to a nursing home in Hull, a short drive away from his daughter Mildred's home. He died on 17th July 1975 after having a stroke. He was aged ninety.

## Notes

1. For Fawcett's account of this area, see *Exploration Fawcett*, pp 150–2. In a letter dated 18th June 1953, Val described Fawcett's account of the district as "exaggerated".
2. Baptism of their daughters, Lucy Mary and Elizabeth, at Holy Trinity, Salford on 27th December 1863.

3.  Bury RO, Valuation List for Prestwich, 1910. The terrace opposite has a plaque indicating that it was built in 1909. cf *Slater's Directory*, 1914 which refers to a John Ashton living at nearby 29, Merton Road.
4.  In the 98th Brigade.
5.  The account and quotations which follow are from *The Lancashire Fusiliers, The Roll of Honour of the Salford Brigade*, edited by Sir Montague Barlow KBE MP, 1919. See too Major General J C Latter CBE MC, *The History of the Lancashire Fusiliers 1914–18.*
6.  Montague Barlow, p 66.
7.  B H Liddell Hart, *History of the First World War*, p 231.
8.  *Lloyds Register of Shipping*, 1918–19.
9.  B H Liddell Hart, *History of the First World War*, p 426.
10.  Liddell Hart, p 427.
11.  Liddell Hart, p 423–31.
12.  Dr L F Haber, *Gas Warfare 1914–45, The Legend and the Facts* and William Moore, *Gas Attack, Chemical Warfare 1915–18.*
13.  "Dulce et Decorum Est", *The Penguin Book of First World War Poetry*, p 182.
14.  Haber, p 10. See too Moore, Appendix D.
15.  *Lloyd's Register.*
16.  "The rank stench of those bodies haunts me still", *The Penguin Book of First World War Poetry*, p 124.
17.  All quantities given here are for the summer of 1942.

# 10

Jack and Lucy were my grandparents. Their daughter Mildred is my mother. Their son Leslie was my uncle.

The latter years of Jack and Lucy's lives and the details which I can recall about them are the hardest to describe. It seems artificial for me to continue the story in an objective style when I have my own personal impressions of the people concerned and the way in which they lived. It was tempting to end the account of the Ashtons at a neat historical watershed, such as the end of the Second World War, but for me one of the important things about this kind of history is the relationship between the past and the present, and how the way in which our ancestors lived their lives ties in with the way in which we live our lives today. We are all the products of the past in general and of our families in particular. So, I want to bring the narrative up to date with my own personal, subjective, description of Jack and Lucy and with details of what became of the next generation, the children of Violet, Val, Tom and Jack.

My earliest memories of my grandparents are probably no different from those of any other young child. The first time I can remember being with them was a picnic among some trees in a park on a sunny day. There was my first visit, by double-decker bus, to the sea-side at Blackpool on a cold grey day, when Jack held my hand on the promenade, and I am supposed to have said, while looking at the sea, "Isn't it angry?". Several times he took me to Cheadle Hulme station to look at the steam trains and to write down engine numbers in a blue note-book which he had bought for me. He used to post pictures of steam engines and their carriages which he drew for me on brown wrapping paper and to tell me stories which he made up about talking parrots. I can remember him taking me to the post office on Cheadle Road to buy a book about animals for my younger brother and to buy a clock to help me to learn to tell the time. He made a road and a painted garage from wood for my cars which I played with on the lawn in their back garden.

My memories of the house in Cheadle Hulme are of a warm dining room where we all sat with a fire blazing. At lunch-time Jack carved the joint and in the afternoon we ate teas which Lucy made with sandwiches and Dundee cake and, once a year, simnel cake which she had cooked. In contrast there was a cold front room which was never used and which had far more furniture. Upstairs there was the smell of Pears soap in the bathroom, the patterns of coloured light from the small pieces of stained glass in the windows and the vaguely frightening figure of Lucy's grey haired sister Eshie who was lying ill in bed.

Later there were family holidays at the seaside in Wales. The sun shone and Jack suffered from sun stroke. Even though Jack and Lucy were well into their seventies, we all played cricket on the sand. On one occasion he apologised when I was trying to make my first century and he bowled me when my score was in the eighties. On other days it was cold and windy and they sat on chairs on the beach muffled with heavy coats. Then there were rides in our first car, an Austin Somerset, through the Shropshire countryside on bright and showery April days, just before Lucy had an operation to remove cataracts from her eyes. They were probably ideal grandparents, warm and kind, secure and solid, and devoted to their grandchildren. Jack had the wisdom which, in the eyes of young children, age seems to bestow.

This period ended when Lucy died suddenly in her sleep. After fifty years of marriage, Jack was devastated. For what seemed like days, he sat in a chair, smoking and saying he did not know what to do. The house was cleared and sold and Jack moved into a residential home. He remained active, and talked of cricket and current affairs, asked about school and gave us money, but somehow the intimacy of our relationship had gone. Although he was well looked after and was obviously liked and respected by the other old people and staff in the home, when he sat in the shared lounge, or even in his own room, there was something missing. As I became a teenager, we seemed more remote. The apparent equality of the relationship between the seven year old and the seventy-five year old had gone and instead he had become someone to be respected, someone concerned about appearances and with whom I had to sit up straight, talk loudly and be careful about what I said. Despite this, he was still my favourite grandparent and I enjoyed visiting him.

He retained his dignity until he had a stroke and had to be moved to a dark room in a nursing home in Hull. Nine months later, as a student, I was spending the summer travelling in Asia, when I received a letter at the Poste Restante in Kabul to say that he had suffered another stroke and died. I felt terribly guilty. I should have been at his funeral.

Jack had survived his younger brother Val by over ten years. Val had some of the same characteristics as Jack. He was well ordered, meticulous, strong minded, and, in his business dealings, honest and ethical. However whereas Jack was conservative and conventional, Val was a maverick with a strong sense of independence and adventure. He was well over six feet tall and cut an impressive figure. His height and a corruption of his Christian name gave rise to the nick-name Tiny. Like his namesakes, who were born seventy-five and a hundred and fifty years before him, in financial terms he was the most successful among his immediate family. He had a sharp business mind, and would have a go at anything. He could work out what people wanted and then find ways of providing it. However he was a headstrong man, with a fierce temper. He also drank heavily.

After the First World War, whilst in Liverpool, Val met Isabel Grace Michell, whom he had first known as a young girl in Arequipa, Peru. Bessie, as she was known, had been born in 1896 in the Tarapaca Province of northern Chile, not far from Iquique, a port used to export nitrates mined in the Atacama Desert. Her father, a mining and civil engineer from Truro, had been murdered in Chile. Her mother, who had American and Scottish ancestry, had died in Puno on the shores of Lake Titicaca when Bessie was nine years old. Bessie had three sisters, Faith, Hope and Charity.

Val and Bessie were married on 17th July 1920, at Wandsworth Registry Office. He was the first of his family to be married in a registry office ceremony.[1] Soon after their wedding, they returned to Arequipa. Val was again employed by the British Consul, Reggie Stafford. Bessie gave birth to two daughters, Kathleen Diana who was born on 5th October 1921 and Bessie Joan who was born on 13th December 1922. Another daughter, Dolores who was born in Paignton in 1926, died shortly after her birth. Val's attitudes to his wife and daughters were rather Victorian and he saw little of Kathleen and Joan when they were children. When they were seven and six they were sent away to be educated at a girls' boarding school in Huyton, near Liverpool. They did not see either parent for several years.

Meanwhile Val enjoyed the freedom and independence which came with living in South America. He led an interesting life, part merchant, part insurance agent and part explorer. He spoke Spanish fluently and picked up some of the Quechua and Aymara Indian dialects. For a while Val and Bessie lived in Cuzco in Peru. From Cuzco, Val went to La Paz where he came into contact with a merchant called Thompson who owned El Condor, a department store in the centre of the city. Later Val went into partnership with a German emigré called Schultz, and bought El Condor from Thompson. Although the shop was small by British standards it was the largest in La Paz. Val and Schultz bought and sold all kinds of merchandise including mining machinery and alkalis, used in the dyeing of wool. Val was particularly involved in selling goods to mining concessionaires and men running cantinas in the mining communities. Val also became an agent for Lloyd's of London and joined the New York Board of Underwriters.

Val was clearly good company, with a strong sense of humour and the ability to spin a good yarn. It is hard though to separate the reality of his life from the myth. He told how he went into the Amazon basin looking for aeroplanes which, although contracted to be sold to the Bolivian government during the Chaco Wars, had in fact been diverted to the Paraguayan Government, and that when he found the fuselage of one of the planes, he was awarded the Order of "El Condor de las Andes" by the Bolivian government. He also talked about his involvement in looking for Fawcett after he finally disappeared in the Matto Grosso in 1925.

Val came to Europe for an extended visit in 1937 or 1938, partly to conduct business and partly to see his daughters. He took Bessie, Kathleen and Joan to Hamburg. Whilst there he became rather drunk in a beer hall and caused havoc by putting a cork moustache on his upper lip and raising his right arm in imitation of Hitler. He was arrested and imprisoned for a day or so, before being released and escorted onto a boat for Hull.

It was during this stay in Europe that Val made his last visit to see Jack and Lucy. He stayed at the best hotel in Manchester, but turned up in Cheadle Hulme one Sunday morning wearing his slippers. There had been some mix up involving his shoes, but Lucy was convinced that he had been drunk the night before. To Mildred he appeared very sophisticated.

Back in Bolivia, Val ran into problems when the Americans and, in time, the Bolivians, entered the Second World War, because his partner was German. The department store, El Condor, was either confiscated or went into voluntary liquidation, and Val lost a huge amount of money.

For some years Val was separated from Bessie and lived on his own in a bungalow in La Paz. Her health was not good and the altitude of La Paz was clearly a problem. However in 1954 he retired to Arequipa, partly because it had a perfect climate and partly because this was where he and Bessie had spent their happiest years. He built a large house in the affluent suburb of Yanahuara.

Val died on 3rd April 1963 in Arequipa, aged seventy-six. He thought that he had been suffering from a duodenal ulcer and, not long before his death, had returned to England for an operation. The cause of his death was in fact lung cancer. Like Jack and Tom he had been a heavy smoker. His wife Bessie died on Maundy Thursday 1971, aged seventy-five. Both are buried in the municipal cemetery in Arequipa, alongside the body of Bessie's mother which was later brought from Peru. Their graves, overlooked by the 18,000 foot volcano El Misti, are in a small section at the rear of the cemetery, close to those of other protestants and Jews and convicts who are excluded from the main Catholic part of the graveyard. The plain dark grey granite headstones of the Ashton family contrast sharply with the lavish and ornate vaults in much of the rest of the cemetery.

The course of Tom's life was far closer to that of Jack's than Val's. He lived in Manchester all his life and became the departmental manager of the Whites Department at Jaffe and Son. Relatives have described him as being good company, kind, charming and jovial. He was a good billiards player and met his wife Gertie because her father, who was called Denton, was the manager of a group of temperance billiard saloons. She had married a

*Fig. 23 – Tom and Gertie Ashton's wedding (1924). Back row: ?, Gertie's brother, Jack Ashton, Eric Hale, ?, Bernard Hale, Gertie's father (G F Denton), ?. Front row: Lucy Ashton, Sarah Ellen Ashton, Tom, Gertie, Gertie's sister, Gertie's mother. Seated at front: Winifred Hale, Leslie Ashton.*

pilot called Richardson during the First World War, but he had been called back to the front and killed very soon after their honeymoon. After she had given birth to a boy who was still born at Church Road, Tom and Gertie moved to Lyndhurst Avenue, Davyhulme. Gertie gave birth to three more children, Tom, Alan and June. For a time, after the death of Sarah Ellen, Tom and Gertie were joined in Lyndhurst Avenue by Tom's aunt, Lizzie. Gertie died in 1977. Tom died on 9th January 1986 aged ninety-seven.

Just as there were great contrasts between the lives led by Jack and Tom and Val, the differences between the members of the next generation (John and Sarah Ellen's grandchildren) are enormous. Although John and Sarah Ellen had eleven children, their sons and daughters only produced twelve children of whom ten survived to adulthood.

After Violet's death in 1909, her children were brought up by Sarah Ellen. Her eldest son Eric became a merchant seaman and, at one stage in the 1930s, was based in Calcutta as the second officer on the SS Garada, a 400 foot schooner which had been built at Sunderland in 1918 and which was owned by the British India Steam Navigation Company.[2] Later he lived in Glasgow, although during the war he worked for the Bahrain Petroleum Company at Awali in the Persian Gulf. His sister Winifred was converted to Catholicism during the 1930s and became a nun. At various times she lived in convents in Notting Hill, Tavistock and

Newcastle, before leaving the order and living for a while with her father. She died at 66, New Lane, Winton, near Eccles[3] in 1981, aged seventy-two. Violet's youngest child, Bernard, won scholarships to Manchester Grammar School and Oxford, where he read Greats. During the war he served as a pilot officer in the R.A.F. Afterwards he taught Latin. Although he married, his wife Margery did not have any children. Bernard was always a caring person. As a young man he spent much of his time cycling round visiting elderly relatives and in his retirement he worked as a volunteer in the Citizen's Advice Bureau in Chorley, Lancashire. He died in 1990.

Val's eldest daughter Kathleen went into the Forestry Commission after leaving school and, towards the end of the War, worked as a rehabilitation officer with soldiers in the Far East. Later she returned to South America where she worked as a teacher. There she married a lecturer employed by the British Council and had three children. After living in Lima for a number of years, she moved to Jamaica where she became the honorary Peruvian Consul. Although she still feels a strong affinity towards South America she now lives in County Durham. Joan, Val's other surviving daughter, trained as a state registered nurse at Bart's during the war. She worked there until 1947. She married Stephen, an architect. They have four children and now live in the country near Salisbury.

Tom and Gertie's children, like their cousins, settled in different parts of the country. Their eldest son, Tom stayed at home and devoted himself to caring for his parents as they grew older. After their deaths his main interest was gardening. He died in August 1994 in the house in Lyndhurst Avenue where he had lived throughout his life. Tom and Gertie's daughter June married Syd, an environmental health officer. After having three children she worked as an adult literacy teacher until she retired. June and Syd moved to Newbury in Berkshire in 1954 and still live there. Alan, Tom and Gertie's other son, attended agricultural college and held several posts as a farm manager before setting up his own business as a fruit and vegetable supplier. He married Rene and has one daughter.

After leaving school Jack and Lucy's son Leslie worked as a pathological assistant in a hospital laboratory in Crumpsall. Later he was in charge of the pathology laboratory at Altrincham Hospital. Outside working hours he organised dances, both before and during the Second World War. Just before marrying in 1945 he and his wife Margaret bought a ladies' dress shop in Bramhall. As the business became more profitable Leslie gave up work in the hospital and concentrated on the business side of the shop. He also worked as a salesman and at one time ran an investment company. He was a keen golfer and drove large American cars. He was the most enterprising, in commercial terms, of his generation of Ashtons. He died in December 1990.

Jack and Lucy's daughter Mildred attended Manchester High School and then, after a year's student teaching in a Montessori School, went to teacher training college in Ripon. In 1950 she married my father Ken, who was also a teacher. They had first met on holiday in Wales in 1939. They lived in Loughborough, Leicestershire and Cannock, Staffordshire before moving to a village in North Humberside when Ken went to teach at a school in Hull. Mildred had a varied career, teaching in an approved school, an infants' school and several junior and secondary schools, but found most fulfilment in a large comprehensive in North Humberside where she was responsible for organising all "remedial" teaching for children with special needs.

## Notes

1. They went through a religious blessing in Arequipa in the 1950s with a few close friends present.
2. *Lloyd's List.* Gross tonnage of 5,333 tons.
3. Her grandfather's uncle, Valentine Ashton, had died in the same street in 1898.

# Appendix

I have written this book in the hope that it will be read not only by people who already have some knowledge of social, economic and family history, but also by people who have no prior experience in these fields. I have written this chapter for those who know nothing about family history, but who wish to start to find out something about their own family roots. It is no more than the most basic introduction, and anyone who wishes to pursue their own research would be well advised to buy or borrow one of the books which have been written on the subject. There can be nothing more annoying for the hard-pressed staff in record offices than to have to answer basic questions from people who have not taken the trouble to find out about the first steps themselves.

## BOOKS

The books which I personally found to be the most helpful with the basic "family tree" stage were Arthur Willis's *Genealogy for Beginners* and Don Steel's *Discovering Your Family History*. Colin Roger's *The Family Tree Detective* is also helpful. W B Stephen's *Sources for English Local History* is invaluable for those who leave the main roads of basic family tree discovery to explore the winding lanes of local social and economic history. David Hey's *Family History and Local History in England* and W G Hoskin's *Fieldwork in Local History* are also important reading.

## RELATIVES

The next step is to talk to relatives and to find out as much information as possible from them. The obvious details which are needed to enable you to work backwards from known relations are the names, dates and places of birth, marriage and death, addresses and occupations of as many people as possible. It is important though to treat what relatives say with some caution, since it may be inaccurate. Memories may be faulty, or people, often in earlier generations, may either have wanted to gild the lily ("we're related to Lord So and So") or to conceal less desirable facts (eg illegitimacy). The information obtained from relatives is a crucial starting point, but should always be checked against documentary evidence to ensure its accuracy. Sometimes this can be done from documentation which relatives have themselves (such as birth certificates, family bibles, photograph albums, address books, correspondence, etc). Sometimes it is necessary to use the documentary sources listed in the rest of this chapter.

It is important not only to ask about these "vital statistics", but also to find out as much as possible about people themselves and their way of life. Although we do not have any equivalent to the West African griots (men who can recount generations of family history, whom Alex Haley described in Roots as "walking archives of oral history"), our society has changed so rapidly that valuable information about times gone by and the way in which ordinary people lived out their lives, is lost whenever elderly relatives die without being "de-briefed".

## St Catherine's House

The next stage for most family historians is St Catherine's House on the corner of Aldwych and Kingsway in London. This is where details of all births, marriages and deaths in England and Wales since 1st July 1837 are kept, although in the early years some births and deaths escaped registration. The shelves at St Catherine's House contain large bound indexes. There are separate volumes for births, marriages and deaths, kept in chronological order, with one book for each quarter. Names in each volume are in alphabetical order with the registration district and the reference needed to order a certificate.

The entries themselves cannot be viewed, but copies costing £5.50 (February 1995) can be ordered. They can either be collected (normally forty-eight hours later) or posted (which usually takes longer). Birth certificates contain the date and place of birth, parents' names and the father's occupation. Marriage certificates contain the names, addresses and occupations of both parties and their fathers' names and occupations. Death certificates contain the name, age, address and occupation of the deceased together with the cause of death.

The normal method of working is to follow families backwards from the information obtained from relatives, using birth and marriage certificates. For example the names of someone's father and mother revealed on a birth certificate will mean that a search can be made for the parents' marriage certificate. The details on their marriage certificate will in turn give the information which is needed to make a search for their birth certificates. At the same time, the addresses obtained can be used to look at census returns (see below).

While at St Catherine's House it is worth visiting nearby Somerset House (on the Strand) to look at wills kept at the Principal Probate Registry there. They keep copies of all wills proved in England and Wales since 1858. Again there are chronological indexes. Here though, there is one volume for each year. The indexes contain details of the occupation and address of the testator, the names of executors and the value of the estate. Volumes containing copies of the wills are produced quickly and it is possible to order photocopies of the wills themselves. Sometimes, if it is thought that someone died leaving a will, it is quicker to search for the will at Somerset House, than to look for a death certificate at St Catherine's House.

## Censuses

The first national census was compiled in 1801. Since then censuses have been taken every ten years, except for 1941. However the only enumerators' schedules which are normally used by family historians are those for 1841, 1851, 1861, 1871, 1881 and 1891. They can be examined on microfilm in the basement of the Public Record Office, Chancery Lane, London WC2, although many local record offices and local history libraries now have copies. The enumerators' schedules for the years before 1841 do not survive. Census returns within the last 100 years are only produced by special request.

The enumerators' schedules contain the following information for each house:

address;
names of all people staying there on the night of the census;
their relationship to the head of the household;

their age (rounded down to the nearest five years for adults in 1841);

their occupation; and

their place of birth (except in 1841 when the only information is whether they were born in the same or a different county).

The normal way for family historians to use the censuses has been to find out an address (eg from a birth certificate) and then to search for that address in the census returns, in order to find more information, such as someone's place of birth. Alternatively in villages or small towns, it is possible to search the whole of the place, but that is extremely time consuming for somewhere like Manchester. Now however some of the census returns have been indexed by surname so that, if a surname is unusual, it may not be necessary to know someone's address before making a search. It should also be noted that the Church of Jesus Christ of Latter Day Saints is currently in the process of preparing an index for the whole of the 1881 census.

The census returns are particularly useful for finding out where people who moved to the new industrial cities in the nineteenth century came from. For example, if I had not already known that Robert Ashton had been born in Darley, by looking at any of the census returns between 1851 and 1881, I would easily have been able to establish where he was born.

Although many family historians only use the census returns as a stepping stone to earlier years, it is important to remember that they contain huge amounts of information about demographic and social conditions which should not be overlooked.

## PARISH REGISTERS AND THE INTERNATIONAL GENEALOGICAL INDEX

The national registration of births, marriages and deaths only started in 1837. For births, marriages and deaths before then, the basic tools for family historians are parish registers. Thomas Cromwell first ordered that parish registers should record every baptism, wedding and burial in 1538, but there are many parishes where the surviving registers start much later – eg in the Derbyshire Peak District, although there are exceptions, many now only survive from the mid-seventeenth century. Even those which do survive vary greatly. Many have missing years, particularly around the time of the Civil War and the Commonwealth. Many contain parts which are illegible. It is also likely that many events, particularly marriages in the early years, were not recorded at all. Although parish registers were originally kept in the particular parish, copies should have been sent to the cathedral city of the diocese, and these bishops' transcripts, although often containing transcription errors, may be used where there are gaps or illegible passages in the originals.

The information given in parish registers varies greatly, generally improving as the years go by. Early baptismal entries often omit the name of the mother. Later entries often have the date of birth as well as the date of baptism, the name of the mother and details of the father's occupation and address. Early marriage certificates often only record the names of the parties and the date of their wedding. Later entries have places of residence, occupations, names of witnesses etc. Early registers omit the age of the person buried, although this is normally recorded in later entries. Often, when children were buried, the name of the father was given.

Parish registers are now generally in the custody of local record offices. Often they have been microfilmed, which means that although they may be harder to read, they have been copied and so are available to be consulted in local public libraries or local history libraries.

Searching parish registers can be a time-consuming and eye-straining business, especially when a family moved from parish to parish and there are no clues as to which of the, hopefully, neighbouring parishes, the family came from. This task has however been made considerably easier by the compilation of the International Genealogical Index by the Church of Jesus Christ of Latter Day Saints. They have transcribed baptismal and marriage entries, computerised them and placed them in alphabetical order by surname on microfiches for each county. These microfiches can be searched, free of charge, at the Church's Family History Centres in various parts of the country. (Addresses can be obtained by telephoning the Hyde Park Family History Centre on 0171 589 8561). In addition many local record offices and local history libraries have copies of the microfiches. They are particularly helpful in finding where families have moved from. If you are interested in a surname which is not particularly common, the easiest way of working is to pay for a photocopy of the relevant sheets of microfiche of the IGI. This saves further visits and enables you to study, highlight and re-check the entries at leisure at home as further discoveries are made.

Although the IGI is extremely useful in helping to find references to baptisms and marriages in parish registers, it is no substitute for the original records. There are a number of reasons why IGI references should always be checked in the registers themselves. Firstly there are frequent transcription errors in the IGI, which mean that the entries are not necessarily reliable. Both the dates and the names of people can be incorrect. Secondly they lack some of the information which may be available in the original parish registers – eg the date of birth, as opposed to date of baptism, the parties' occupations or localities where people live. Thirdly, they do not contain any burial entries at all.

## WILLS

Copies of all wills proved in England and Wales after 1858 are kept at Somerset House (see above). Before 1858 wills or copies of wills are kept locally, normally in the record office which contains documents from the relevant diocese – eg wills for Derbyshire are to be found at the Joint Record Office in Lichfield because until 1884 Derbyshire was in the diocese of Lichfield.

A significant proportion of the population did not have sufficient property to warrant making a will, but for those who did, wills are a very important source of information. In leaving bequests to relatives, testators often provided important details about family relationships. Sometimes these can be used to "jump" gaps in parish registers. For example, I have not been able to find details of the baptisms of most of John and Mary Ashton's children in the third quarter of the seventeenth century. Also it was some time before I found the baptism of Henry Ashton in 1761. The problems caused by this were solved by the wills of Mary Ashton and Thomas Ashton. The will of Thomas Ashton, by referring to "my cottage house at Rowland" also gave the clue as to where Thomas had been born.

Wills also provide fascinating details about the lives of ordinary people, particularly through the inventories of possessions which are attached to many of the earlier wills, although there are generally few inventories after the middle of the eighteenth century.

## TAXATION RECORDS

Both national and local taxation records can be of assistance. The main categories are:

### *Land tax*

Although the land tax was first introduced in 1693, it is rare to find returns before the 1770s (cf the assessment for Rowland referred to at pages 28–9). However, from the 1770s until

1832 annual lists of people liable to pay the tax exist for many areas. They generally reveal not only details of the owners of land but also of tenants and the amount of tax paid. Sometimes the returns indicate which particular property was farmed. Sometimes though they are merely lists of owners, occupiers and amounts of payment. From a narrow genealogical point of view they can be used to date, fairly precisely, when families moved from one place to another. From a wider family history point of view they can be used to study changes in the patterns of land ownership and to compare, roughly, the relative sizes of different farmers' holdings. Land tax returns can be consulted in local record offices.

## Hearth tax

Lists of people liable to pay hearth tax (and in some cases, those exonerated from making payment) are kept at the Public Record Office in Chancery Lane, London WC2, under classification E179. Often returns, compiled by county, exist for three or four years between 1662 and 1689. They provide useful lists of heads of household, but often omit any reference to the poor.

## Other assessments

Other assessments, for example for poll tax or lay subsidies, exist for the sixteenth and seventeenth centuries. Like the hearth tax returns they are kept at the Public Record Office in Chancery Lane. The number of heads of household recorded varies form year to year and from county to county.

## Local taxation

The amount and the quality of information contained in poor rate assessments, other rates books, churchwardens' accounts etc vary from parish to parish and from period to period, but they can provide useful information about where people lived, their comparative wealth, and more generally, the way in which local government functioned.

## OTHER SOURCES

There are numerous other sources of information which can be used by family historians. Most are referred to in passing in the main part of this book and in more detail in the other books listed at the beginning of this chapter. They include nineteenth-century directories, enclosure awards, tithe commutation records, marriage licences, manorial records (such as minutes of manorial courts), militia muster rolls, poll books, constables' accounts, apprenticeship deeds, quarter sessions records, settlement certificates etc.

   Before calling at a record office it is always wise to telephone first, partly to check that they have the particular documents which you wish to consult, but also because it may be necessary to book a seat or a microfilm reader in advance.

# Glossary

**Amercie** – to fine.

**Barmaster** – representative of lord or owner of mining liberty, responsible for ensuring compliance with mining law and for measuring ore.

**Barmoot Court** – court with jurisdiction over lead miners and lead mining, with jury of miners.

**Berewick** – a demesne farm – i.e land retained for the lord of the manor and not let out to tenants.

**Cope** – duty paid to lord of a mining liberty by ore purchasers.

**Cordwainer** – a shoemaker or worker in leather.

**Costermonger** – someone selling fruit or vegetables from a barrow.

**Court Baron** – a manorial court which dealt with land transfers, enforced regulations and heard minor civil claims.

**Court Leet** – a manorial court which dealt with minor infractions of the criminal law.

**Galena** – lead sulphide, the most common form of lead ore.

**Grove** or **Groove** – a mine.

**Headborough** – strictly speaking, a deputy constable, but in Rowland, it was the name given to the constable.

**Heriot** – duty paid to lord of the manor on the death of a tenant, normally in the form of the tenant's best beast.

**Indenture** – a deed or sealed agreement.

**Jake** – toilet.

**Journeyman** – a craftsman or artisan, originally paid on a daily basis.

**Liberty** – an area, comprising several manors, where the lord held certain privileges given by the Crown.

**Lot** – duty paid by miners to the lord or owner of a mining liberty.

**Male Primogeniture** – the custom whereby the eldest son inherited all of his father's estate.

**Meer** – a measure of length along a vein of lead, between twenty-seven and thirty-two yards in length.

**Midden** – a pile of refuse or dung hill.

**Mountebank** – someone selling quack medicines in a public place.

**Perch** – a measure of 16½ feet.

**Pinder** – parish or manorial officer responsible for keeping the pinfold.

**Pinfold** – the pound where animals which strayed were kept until their owners had redeemed them by paying the customary fine.

**Rake** – a vertical fissure of lead ore, running in a straight line across the countryside.

**Recusant** – literally someone who refused to take Holy Communion in an Anglican Church. Used especially as a term for Catholics.

**Rood** – a measure of forty square rods or perches – i.e. a quarter of an acre.

**Sough** – a drain.

**Thirdborough** – strictly speaking a deputy constable, but in Rowland, another name for the constable.

**View of Frankpledge** – see Court Leet.

**Whitesmith** – either a tinsmith or someone who polished and finished metal goods, as opposed to someone who forged them.

# Bibliography

ADSHEAD *Joseph: Distress in Manchester – Evidence of the State of the Labouring Masses in 1840–1842* (1842)

ADSHEAD Joseph: *State of Education in Manchester* (1852)

ANDREWS C Bruyn and Fanny: *The Torrington Diaries* (1954)

ASHTON T S: *Economic History of England*

AULT Warren O: *Open Field Farming in Medieval England* (1965)

BACON F: *The Office of Constable* (1618) in SPEDDIN, *Works of Bacon*, vol VII (1857–9)

BAGSHAW Samuel: *History Gazetteer and Directory of Derbyshire* (1846)

BAKER Shirley: *Photographs of Manchester and Salford* (1988/9)

BARLOW Montague: *The Lancashire Fusiliers: Roll of Honour of Salford Brigade* (1919)

BERGIN Tom: *Salford, A City and Its Past* (1975)

BERRY B M and SCHOFIELD R S: Age of Baptism in Pre-Industrial England in *Population Studies*, Vol 25 (1971) pp 453–63

BEST H: *Rural Economy in Yorkshire, being the farming and account books of Henry Best* (1641), Surtees Society, Vol 33, 1857

BLACKSTONE William: *Commentaries on the Laws of England* (1765–9)

BOSSY J: *The English Catholic Community 1570–1850* (1975)

BRAY William: "A Tour Through some Midland Counties and Journal of a Three Week Tour in 1797 Through Derbyshire" in MAVOR: *British Tourists* (1798)

BRIGGS Asa: *A Social History of England* (1983)

BRIGGS Asa: *Victorian Cities* (1968)

BROWN R J: *The English Country Cottage*

BROWN T: *General View of the Agriculture of the County of Derbyshire* (1794)

BURNETT J: *Plenty and Want: A Social History of Diet in England from 1815 to the Present Day.* (1989)

CAMDEN W: *Brittania* (1637)

CAMERON Kenneth: *English Place Names* (1961)

CAMERON Kenneth: *Place Names of Derbyshire* (1959)

CAMPBELL Mildred: *The English Yeoman under Elizabeth and the Early Stuarts* (1942, Yale)

CANNAN Edwin: *History of Local Rates in England* (1912)

CHAMBERS J D and MINGAY G E: *The Agricultural Revolution 1750–1880* (1966)

CHENEY: *Handbook of Dates*

CLARK Alice: *The Working Life of Women in the Seventeenth Century* (1919)

CLARK Richard: *The Derbyshire Papist Returns of 1705–6* (1983 Derb Rec Soc)

CLARK Richard: *Derbyshire Pedigrees* (1984)

COLE G D H and POSTGATE Raymond: *The Common People 1746–1946* (1961)

COX J Charles: *Derbyshire* (1915)

COX J Charles: *Notes on the Churches of Derbyshire* (4 vols) (1875–9)

COX J Charles: *Three Centuries of Derbyshire Annals* (1890)

DAVIES E: "The Small Landowner", *Economic History Review*, Vol 1 No 1 (1927)

DEFOE Daniel: *A Tour Through the Whole Island of Great Britain* (1724)

DERBYSHIRE ARCHEOLOGICAL AND NATURAL HISTORY SOCIETY JOURNAL: "List of Recusants in the Peak of Derbyshire 1616–"(1894 vol 16 pp·140–151). See too Vols 22 and 23 for part of Baslow Court Rolls

DERBYSHIRE MISCELLANY: Vol V, part I p 38 (Darley roads)

DOWELL S: *History of Taxation and Taxes in England* (1884)

DRAKE Michael (ed): *Population Studies from Parish Registers* (1982)

DRUMMOND J C and WILBRAHIM A: *The Englishman's Food: A History of Five Centuries of Diet* (1939)

EDEN F M: *The State of the Poor* (1797)

EDWARDS David G: *Derbyshire Hearth Tax Assessments 1662–70* (1982 Derb Rec Soc)

ENGELS F: *Condition of the Working Class in England*

ERNLE: *English Farming, Past and Present* (1961)

FAREY J: *A General View of Agriculture in Derbyshire* (1811)

FARINGTON Joseph: *The Farington Diary* (1922)

FAUCHER Leon: *Etudes sur L'Angleterre* (1845)

FIENNES Celia: *The Journeys of Celia Fiennes* (1949)

FIRTH C H: "Marston Moor" (including transcript of The Journal of Prince Rupert's Marches and De Gomme's plan), *Transactions of Royal Historical Society*, New Series, Vol XII pp 17–79 (1898)

FISHER F J: *Essays in Economic and Social History of Tudor and Stuart England* (1961) – JOAN THIRSK: "Industries in the Countryside"

FITTON R S and WADSWORTH A P: *Strutts and Arkwrights*

FITZHERBERT A or J: "The Book of Husbandry" (1534) in *English Dialect Society 13*, (1882) edited by W M Skeats

FLETCHER A J: "Petitioning at the Outbreak of the Civil War in Derby", *Derbyshire Archeological Journal* (1973) XCIII 33–44

FOLEY H: *Records of the English Province of the Society of Jesus* (1877), 7 vols

FORD Trevor D and RIEUWERTS J H: *Lead Mining in the Peak District* (1983)

FOWKES D V and POTTER G R: *William Senior's Survey of the Estates of the First and Second Earls of Devonshire c*1600–28 (1988 Derb Rec Soc)

FURNESS Peter: *The Family of Eyre of Hassop* (The Reliquary (1870), Vol 10, pp 232-6)

GARDINER S R: *The History of the Great Civil War, 1642–9* (1893)

GASKELL Elizabeth: *Mary Barton* (1848)

GLOVER Stephen: *History of the County of Derby* (1829)

GLOVER Stephen: *The Peak Guide* (1830)

GLOVER Catherine and RIDEN Philip: *William Woolley's History of Derbyshire* (1981 Derb Rec Soc)

GOUGH Richard: *The History of Myddle* (Penguin Edition, 1981)

HABER Dr L F: *Gas Warfare 1914–45, The Legend and the Facts* (1976)

HAIR P E H: *Bridal Pregnancy in Rural England in Population Studies,* Vol 20 (1966)

HALL Dr Spencer: *The Peak and the Plain – Scenes in Woodland, Field and Mountain* (1853)

HAMMOND J L and Barbara: *The Village Labourer 1760–1832* (1919)

HAMMOND J L and Barbara: *The Skilled Labourer 1760–1832* (1919)

HARRISON HARROD: *Directory of Derbyshire* (1860)

HAYES Louis M: *Reminiscences of Manchester* (1905)

HEAD Sir George: *A Home Tour Through the Manufacturing Districts of England in the Summer of 1835*

HENRIQUES V R O: "Bastardy and the New Poor Law" (1967), Vol 37 *Past and Present*, p 103

HEY David: *Family History and Local History in England* (1987)

HOBBES Thomas: *De Mirabilis Pecci* (1683)

HONE Nathaniel J: *The Manor and Manorial Records* (1906)

HORN Pamela: *Life and Labour in Rural England 1760–1850* (1987)

HOSKINS W G: *Fieldwork in Local History* (1982)

HOSKINS W G: *Local History in England* (1972)

HOSKINS W G: *The Making of the English Landscape* (1955)

HOSKINS W G: *The Midland Peasant* (1957)

HOUGHTON J: *A Collection of Letters for the Improvement of Husbandry and Trade* (1681) – 3 vols

HOULBROOKE Ralph A: *Church Courts and the People During the English Reformation* (1979)

HOULBROOKE Ralph A: *The English Family 1450–1700* (1984)

HOWE G M: *Man, Environment and Disease in Britain: A Medical Geography of Britain through the Ages* (1972)

HUNTER Joseph: *Hallamshire* (1875)

HUTCHINSON John: *Hutchinson's Tour through the High Peak of Derbyshire 1809*

JEFFERYS James B: *Retail Trading in Britain, 1850–1950* (1954)

JOHNSON Marion: *Derbyshire Village Schools in the Nineteenth Century* (1970)

KAY Dr P: *Moral and Physical Condition of the Working Classes* (1832)

KENNEDY W: *English Taxation 1649–1789*

KIERNAN David T: *The Derbyshire Lead Industry in the Sixteenth Century* (1989)

KIRKHAM N: "Longstone Edge Mines and Soughs" (*Cave Science*, Vols 5 and 6, Nos 39 and 40, pp 354–368, 440–469) (1966)

KITCHEN Fred: *Brother to the Ox* (1981)

LASLETT Peter: *The World We Have Lost* (1965)

LASLETT Peter and WALL R: *Household and Family in Past Time* (1972)

LATTER Major Gen J C: *History of the Lancashire Fusiliers 1914–1918* (1949)

LESTER C E: *The Condition and Fate of England* (1843)

LEVETT E: *Studies in Manorial History* (1938)

LEVINE David: *Reproducing Families* (1987)

LIDDELL HART B H: *History of the First World War* (1970)

LOVE B: *Handbook of Manchester* (1842)

LOWE J: "The Town of Bakewell in Derbyshire Described" (*Royal Magazine* – 1765 pp 234–237)

LYSON D and S: *Magna Britannica* (Vol 5) (1817)

MacDONALD Lyn: *Somme* (1983)

McFARLANE Alan: *The Family Life of Josselin* (1970)

de MAUSE L: *The History of Childhood* (1976)

MEREDITH Rosamond: "A Derbyshire Family in the Seventeenth Century: The Eyres of Hassop and their forfeited estates" (*Recusant History*, Vol 8, No 1)

MEREDITH Rosamond: "The Eyres of Hassop and some of their connections from the Test Act to Emancipation" (*Recusant History*, Vol 9 1967 pp 5–52 and 267–287)

MEREDITH Rosamond: "The Eyres to 1640", *Derbyshire Archeological Journal* (1964) XXXIV

MIDDLEBROOK Martin: *The First Day on the Somme* (1971)

MILWARD Rosemary: *A Glossary of Household, Farming and Trade Terms from Sixteenth Century Probate Inventories* (3rd ed., 1986 Derb Rec Soc)

MITCHELL B R AND DEANE Phyllis: *Abstract of British Historical Statistics*

MOLL H: *A New Description of England* (1724) (2nd edn)

MOORE William: *Gas Attack, Chemical Warfare 1915–18* (1987)

NEF J V: *Rise of the British Coal Industry* (1966)

NEWMAN Peter R: *The Battle of Marston Moor* (1981)

NEWMAN Peter R: *Marston Moor 2 July 1644: The Sources and the Site* (1978)

PARTRIDGE M: *Farm Tools Through the Ages* (1973)

PAULSON Ernest: "William Ulithorn Wray", *Derbyshire Miscellany*

PEACOCK M G W: "National List of Delinquents", *Index Society* (1879)

PIGOT: *Directory of Derbyshire* (1835)

PILKINGTON J: *View of the Present State of Derbyshire* (1789)

PINCHBECK Ivy: "Social Attitudes to the Problems of Illegitimacy" (1954), *British Journal of Sociology* p 309

PINCHBECK Ivy and HEWITT M: *Children in English Society* (1969)

POCOCKE: *Travels Through England* (1751)

POLLARD S and HOLMES C: *The Process of Industrialisation 1750–1870* (1968)

PRENTICE A: *Historical Sketches and Personal Recollections of Manchester* (1851)

REDFORD Arthur: *History of Local Government in Manchester* (1939)

REPORT OF THE COMMISSIONERS OF INQUIRY CONCERNING CHARITIES AND EDUCATION, DERBYSHIRE (1815–39)

RIEUWERTS J H: *History and Gazetteer of Lead Mine Soughs in Derbyshire* (1987)

ROBERTS M: "Sickles and Scythes, Womens' Work and Men's Work at Harvest Time", *History Workshop Journal* – 1979 Vol 7, pp 3–28

ROGERS Colin and SMITH John: *Local Family History in England* (1991)

ROSE Michael E: *The English Poor Law 1780–1930* (1971)

SAINTSBURY G E B : *Manchester* (1887)

SAVAGE J: *Baslow Shepherd's Book* (1777–1779)

SHAW W A: *Manchester Old and New* (1896)

SHELDON Robert: *A Short History of Baslow and Bubnel* (1986)

SIMPSON H B: "The Office of Constable", *English Historical Review* (October 1895, Vol 10, XL, p 625)

SLACK Peter: *Poverty and Policy in Tudor and Stuart England* (1988)

SLATER Isaac: *Pigot and Slater's General and Classified Directory of Manchester and Salford* (1841–1915)

SLEIGH J: *Old Peak Families* "1879"

SLUGG J T: *Reminiscences of Manchester* (1861)

SMITH E: "On the Food of the Poorer Labouring Classes in England" – Appendix 6 to the *Sixth Report of the Medical Officer of the Privy Council* (1863)

STEPHENS W B: *Sources for English Local History* (1981)

STERNDALE Mary: *Vignettes of Derbyshire* (1824)

STOKES A H: *Lead and Lead Mining in Derbyshire* (1964)

STONE Lawrence: *The Family, Sex and Marriage in England 1500–1800* (1977)

SWINDELLS T: *Manchester Streets and Manchester Men* (1906)

TANNAHILL Reay: *Food in History* (1988)

TATE W E: *The Parish Chest* (1983)

THORNHILL Robert: *Further Longstone Records* (1937)

TILLEY J: *Old Halls, Manors and Families of Derbyshire* (Vol 1) (1892)

TURNER Michael: *Enclosures in Britain 1750–1830* (1984)

VICTORIA COUNTY HISTORY, *Derbyshire*, Vol 2 (1907)

WARD W R: *The English Land Tax in the Eighteenth Century* (1953)

WEBB Sidney and Beatrice: *English Local Government*, Vols 1, 2, 3, 7, 8 and 9

WHELLAN W: *New Directory of Manchester etc* (1853)

WHITE Francis: *History, Gazetteer and Directory of Derbyshire* (1857)

WILSON C A: *Food and Drink in Britain from the Stone Age to Recent Times* (1973)

WRIGHT George Thomas: *Longstone Records* (1906)

WRIGLEY E A AND SCHOFIELD R S: *The Population History of England 1541–1871* (1981)

YEATMAN Pym: *Feudal History of the County of Derby* (1886)

YOUNG Sir Arthur: *A Six Months' Tour Through the North of England* (1770)

# Index

Aberystwyth, Wales 117
Accountants 94
Act of Uniformity 1559 21
Aeroplanes 128
Agents 94
Agricultural prices 72
Ainstable, Cumberland 115
Air raids 126, 138
Albert, France 126, 130
Aldwark, Derbyshire 2
Ale 26
Allen, Rev John 71
Altrincham, Cheshire 144
Ambergate, Derbyshire 79
American Civil War 98
Amiens, France 126, 127, 129
Ammunition 129
Ancre, River, France 121, 124, 126
Apprenticeship 74, 99, 115, 149
Arequipa, Peru 114, 141–144
Artillery 11, 127–131
Arkwright, George 79
Arkwright, Richard 55
Armistice Day 132
Articles, leadmining 21
Ashbourne, Derbyshire 9
Ashbourne, Joseph 63, 69, 72, 73
Ashburie, Robert 6
Ashburner, Charles 99
Ashburner, Elizabeth 99
Ashford, Derbyshire 1, 2, 6, 17, 20, 36, 38–40
Ashton, Alan 144
Ashton, Alex (of Whiteley Wood) 23
Ashton, Alice (niece of Samuel) 23
Ashton, Alice (b 1725) 36
Ashton, Ann (1772–1800) 58, 64, 66
Ashton, Ann (b 1803) 80
Ashton, Ann (b 1804) 85
Ashton, Ann (wife of Valentine) 99
Ashton, Anne (b 1720/1) 36
Ashton, Anne (b 1854, m Carpenter) 88, 99, 110
Ashton, Annie (b 1891) 102, 111
Ashton, Benjamin (of Hathersage) 24, 66
Ashton, Benjamin (of Baslow) 51, 59
Ashton, Bernard (b 1879) 102, 111
Ashton, Bertram (b 1883) 102, 111
Ashton, Bessie Joan 141–142
Ashton, Charity (b 1728) 36, 74
Ashton, Charles (b 1768) 58, 59, 64, 69, 84, 85
Ashton, Charles (b 1818) 85, 90, 91
Ashton, Debora (b 1728) 47
Ashton, Dolores 141

Ashton, Dorothy (niece of Samuel) 23
Ashton, Elizabeth (b 1718) 36, 43
Ashton, Elizabeth (b 1701/2) 36
Ashton, Elizabeth (b 1810) 80
Ashton, Elizabeth (née Ashburner) 99
Ashton, Ellen (wife of John) 36
Ashton, Ellen (b 1820) 85
Ashton, Ellen (née Steel) 87–96, 98, 110
Ashton, Ellen (1894–96) 102, 111
Ashton, Ellena (b 1710) 36
Ashton, Francis 16, 17, 28, 29, 31, 37, 41, 42
Ashton, George (b 1796) 80
Ashton, George (1896–1916) 108, 111, 119–124, 126
Ashton, Gertie (née Denton) 110, 142–144
Ashton, Hannah (née Froggatt) 46–51, 59, 63
Ashton, Hannah (daughter of Ellen) 79
Ashton, Hannah (b 1824) 85
Ashton, Harriet (b 1815) 79
Ashton, Harriet (b 1799) 80
Ashton, Henry (1702–65) 36, 46–51, 54, 64
Ashton, Henry (b 1740/1) 47, 64
Ashton, Henry (1761–1850) 51, 56, 69–80, 84
Ashton, Henry (1803–1860) 70, 80, 85
Ashton, Henry (b 1839) 95, 98
Ashton, Henry Ashburner (b 1871) 100
Ashton, Isabel Grace (née Michell) 141–144
Ashton, Jack (1885–1975) 106, 110, 112, 114–138, 140–144
Ashton, Jane (wife of Francis) 22
Ashton, Jane (b 1808) 71, 85
Ashton, Jane (1843–1926) 90, 96, 98, 110
Ashton, Joane (c1610–c1660) 1–13, 16, 29, 47, 74
Ashton, John (1638–1690) 16–31, 76
Ashton, John (d 1664/5) 18
Ashton, John (d 1753) 18, 26, 28, 31, 35–37, 41–43, 47, 74
Ashton, John (b 1699) 36
Ashton, John (b 1711) 36, 47
Ashton, John (b 1807) 80
Ashton, John (1841–1916) 88, 99–112, 114, 142
Ashton, June 144
Ashton, Kathleen Diana 141–142, 144
Ashton, Lizzie (1877–1953) 108, 110–112, 142
Ashton, Leslie Ward 110, 111, 117, 118, 133, 138, 140, 144
Ashton, Lucy Jane (née Lowe) 103, 111, 115–138, 140–144
Ashton, Margaret (b 1848, m Turner) 88, 110
Ashton, Margaret (née Bardsley) 144
Ashton, Martha (b 1738) 55
Ashton, Mary (d 1702/3) 18–31, 35, 43, 76
Ashton, Mary (1715–1716/7) 36
Ashton, Mary (m Knisson) 18, 29, 31

Ashton, Mary (née Marple) 51, 69–80, 84
Ashton, Mary (wife of Thomas) 79, 80
Ashton, Mary (1837–1931, m Blears) 87, 98, 110
Ashton, Mildred 110, 111, 133–138, 140, 142, 144
Ashton, Nicholaus (d 1682/3) 22
Ashton, Rachel (niece of Samuel) 23
Ashton, Rebecca (niece of Samuel) 23
Ashton, Robert, of Bradway 23
Ashton, Robert, of Stony Middleton 2, 18, 22, 23, 66
Ashton, Robert (nephew of Samuel) 23
Ashton, Robert (son of John and Mary) 18, 28, 29, 31,
    35–44, 46, 47, 69
Ashton, Robert (b 1712) 36, 38–40
Ashton, Robert (b 1715) 36
Ashton, Robert (1807–1886) 71, 84–96, 98
Ashton, Robert (1845–1900) 90, 96, 99, 102
Ashton, Robert (1892–1896) 102, 111
Ashton, Samuel (d 1761) 18, 26, 28, 29, 31, 35, 36, 47
Ashton, Samuel (b 1707/8) 36, 39, 40
Ashton, Samuel (b 1713) 36
Ashton, Samuel (of Stony Middleton) 10, 23–25
Ashton, Samuel (b 1808) 80
Ashton, Sarah (m Hodgkinson) 18, 28, 29, 31, 35, 36
Ashton, Sarah (b 1718) 36
Ashton, Sarah (née Taylor) 51, 54–67, 69, 73
Ashton, Sarah (1827–1847) 70, 79
Ashton, Sarah Ellen (née Ward) 95, 101–112, 114, 142
Ashton, Sarah (b 1852, m Parkinson) 96, 101, 110
Ashton, Thomas (c1610 – c1644) 1–13, 16, 20, 29, 47, 74
Ashton, Thomas (1731–88) 50, 51, 54–67, 69, 73
Ashton, Thomas (1764–1845) 57, 64, 69, 72, 78, 79
Ashton, Thomas (of London) 66
Ashton, Tom (b 1850) 99, 106, 110, 140
Ashton, Tom (1888–1986) 110, 112, 114, 119, 120, 128,
    142–144
Ashton, Tom (1929–1994) 144
Ashton, Valentine (1737/8–1820) 69, 71, 74, 76
Ashton, Valentine (1809–1810) 71
Ashton, Valentine (1811–1898) 71, 74, 85, 87, 88,
    90–91, 94, 99
Ashton, Valentine (1886–1963) 106, 112, 114, 119, 120,
    127, 128, 140–144
Ashton, Violet (m Hale) 94, 106, 110, 140, 143
Ashton, Violetta (1857–1858) 94
Ashton, William (b 1736) 74
Ashton's Vein 37
Ashwell family 137
Assizes 22
Atacama Desert, Chile 141
Aubigny, France 129
Australian Infantry Forces 128–130
Awali, Bahrain 144

Baby farmers 102
Bacon 94, 136, 138
Bacon, Joshua 64
Bagshawe, Francis, 6, 16, 17
Bagshaw, James 29
Bagshaw's Directory 79
Bahrain Petroleum Company 144
Bakewell, Derbyshire 2, 5, 6, 21, 23, 27, 28, 35, 43, 47,
    51, 54–56, 58, 59, 69, 73, 78, 79, 84, 94
Balguy, John 74
Balloons 128–130
Banks 85, 94
Barker, John 63

Barker, Mary 69
Barker, Percy H 112
Barlow, Sir Montague, MP 120, 121
Barlow, Thomas 101
Barmasters 38–40
Barmoot courts 20–21, 37–40, 42
Barratt, Isaac 55
Barrel makers 95
Barrow-in-Furness, Lancashire 99
Barton, Anthony 35, 36, 43
Baslow, Derbyshire 2, 47–51, 55, 56, 69, 73, 74
Bath War Hospital 132
Baths 106
Bayonvillers, France 130
Beans 58
Beck, Rebeckah 43
Becks, Robert 41
Beef 24, 89
Beer 12, 88, 100–101, 104
Beer houses 100–101
Beer retailers 88, 101
Bell ringers 51
Beni, River, Bolivia 114
Berg, Nathan 109
Bill of Rights 27
Billiards 98–99, 106, 142
Birkenhead, Cheshire 101
Blackpool, Lancashire 132, 140
Blacksmiths 27, 76, 94, 98
Bland family 27
Bland, John 29, 31, 41, 43
Blande, Richard 6, 43
Blande, Rowland 6, 16, 17, 43
Bland, Widow 17
Blears, James 98
Board of Guardians 109
Boatbuilders 88
Boddingtons (brewers) 101
Bolton, Lancashire 10
Bombing 138
Bookies 99
Book keepers 94
Booth, John 42
Borth, Wales 117
Boulogne, France 125–126
Bowe, Thomas 6
Bower, Alles 20
Bowers, Christopher 59
Boylestone, Derbyshire 9
Box respirator 131
Brailsford, Samuel 60
Bramhall, Cheshire 138, 144
Brampton, Derbyshire 48
Bramwell, Jane 69
Bramwell, Stephen 70
Brassington, Derbyshire 54
Brass finishers 95
Bray, William 54
Bread 12, 26
Breast feeding 47, 70
Breda, Declaration of 16
Brewers 94, 101
Brewster Sessions 101
Brick layers 95
Bright, Elizabeth 23
Brightmore family 21

Brightmore, Francis 17, 28
British Council 144
British Expeditionary Force 132
British India Steam Navigation Company 143
Brockenhurst, Betty 99
Broncho-pneumonia 102
Broughton, Lancashire 85, 91–109 passim, 115, 124
Broughton Bridge Paper Mills 93
Broughton Copper Works 93
Broughton Overseers 109
Buckland, Mr 86
Builders 94, 98, 100
Building work 50
Building societies 85
Burial 13, 29, 51, 63, 66, 108, 148
Burlers 99
Bussy, France 128
Butchers 76, 89, 101
Butter 26, 58, 136, 138
Buxton, Derbyshire 23, 79, 84
Buxton, Mark 39
Buxton, Thomas 39, 40
Bye-laws 91

Cabs 90–91
Calcutta, India 144
Calver, Derbyshire 2, 6, 8, 19, 20, 25, 38, 39, 41, 46,
    47, 55
Canals 55
Cancer 142
Cannock, Staffordshire 144
Cap makers 94
Cardiac dilatation 95
Cardiac muscle failure 111
Carlisle, Cumberland 102
Carpenter, Eric Ashton 99, 110
Carpenter, Howard 99
Carpenter, Richard 99
Carpenters 27, 76
Carr, Jane Ann 115
Cars 136
Carts 1, 58
Carvers and guilders 115
Castleton, Derbyshire 1
Casualties 7, 12, 122, 124, 129, 131, 132
Catholicism 2, 6, 8, 12, 13, 18, 21, 22, 27, 137, 142, 145
Catterick Bridge, Yorkshire 120
Cattle 5, 10, 12, 41, 42, 59, 73
Cavendish, George Henry 79
Cavendish, Lord 79
Censuses 76, 79, 95, 99, 115, 146
Cess pools 85
Channel, The 121, 125
Chapman, Humphrey 50
Charity schools – see schools
Charles I, King 5–8, 12
Charles II, King 16, 17, 27
Charwomen 94
Chatsworth, Derbyshire 1, 2, 8, 9
Cheadle, Cheshire 136
Cheadle Hulme, Cheshire 110, 134–138, 140, 142
Cheese 58, 94, 138
Cheetham, Lancashire 115
Chemists 95, 136
Chester 101
Chesterfield, Derbyshire 2, 24, 27, 47, 56

Childbearing 36, 47, 70, 88, 100, 102
Childcare 102
Child labour 50, 71
Children 23, 26, 46, 47, 50, 55, 70–71, 80, 86, 94, 98,
    102, 114
Chorley, Lancashire 99, 144
Chorlton-cum-Medlock, Lancashire 85, 88
Christianity 88
Christy, W M and Sons 115, 133, 138
Church attendance 21–22, 88, 103, 106, 137
Church of Jesus Christ of Latter Day Saints 148
Church Times 137
Churchwardens 35, 43, 50–51, 69
Churchwardens' accounts 50–51, 149
Citizen's Advice Bureau 144
Civil Wars (1642–9) 6–12, 27
Clarach Bay, Wales 117
Clark, Emma 102
Clarke, Rowland 6
Clarke, Thomas 87
Clerks 94, 106, 114, 115, 133
Cleveleys, Lancashire 137
Cleyton, Bryan 6
Clitheroe, Lancashire 10
Cloth agents 106
Clothing 29
Clowes family 92, 101, 105
Coachmen 90–91, 95
Coal 24, 64, 98, 110
Cockermouth, Cumberland 115
Cocks, William 20
Codford St Mary, Wiltshire 120
Cohen, John 104
Collector of Taxes 105
Columbell family 58
Commission agents 99
Condor de las Andes, Order of El 142
Congestion of the lungs 96
Conscription 119, 124
Conservative Association 137
Constables 17, 28, 41, 149
Conway, Wales 120
Cooking 24, 72, 136
Coombs Dale, Derbyshire 38
Cope 29, 38
Corbett, Matthew 88–90
Corbie, France 126
Cordwainers 27, 76, 99
Corn 25
Corn laws 72–73
Cosham, Hampshire 125, 126
Costermongers 95
Cottages (construction) 1–2, 4, 18, 48, 72
Cottages (contents) 24–26, 58
Cotton 55, 85, 88, 91, 98, 99, 101, 114
Court Baron 19, 40
Court Leet 19
Court Rolls 2
Courts – see Assizes, barmoot courts, magistrates
    courts, manorial courts, View of Frankpledge etc
Coventry and Lichfield, Diocese of 21
Cows 26, 29, 48, 58, 77
Craftsmen 95
Craig, Dr 136
Cromford, Derbyshire 55
Cromwell, Oliver 12

Crumpsall, Lancashire 117, 118, 133
Cuckold's Venture (mine) 38, 40
Cuffaud, Ignatius 22
Culloden, Battle of 50
Cuzco, Peru 141

*Daily Mail* 137
Dakin, William 40
Dale, Cumberland 115
Damme, Alexander 48, 50, 55, 56
Daours, France 129
Darley Dale, Derbyshire 55–80 passim, 90
Darley Enclosure Act 60
Daud, Ellen 23, 25
Davidon family 137
Davyhulme, Lancashire 110, 143
Death, Causes of 95, 96, 102, 108, 111, 113, 115, 138, 142
Defoe, Daniel 23, 38, 50, 54
Denman, Thomas 74
Denton, Yorkshire 10
Depression 73, 84, 89, 112, 133
Derby 6, 10, 48, 50, 54, 84
Derby Journal 54
Derbyshire, Elizabeth 79, 80
Derbyshire, Hannah 80
Derbyshire, John 79, 80
Derbyshire Sequestration Committee 12
Derwent, River 47, 48, 51, 56, 58, 62, 63, 77, 79, 84
Devonshire, Duke of 39, 58, 79
Devonshire, Earl of 1, 2, 6, 8, 20, 28
Diet 24, 94
Directories 149
*Dispatch*, The 112
Disraeli, Benjamin 85
Doctors 80, 95, 96, 100, 108, 110, 130, 136
Domesday Book 2, 20
Dowries 31, 58, 66
Drapers 106
Dressmakers 94, 115–117
Droylsden, Lancashire 133
Druggists 106
Drunkenness 101
Dug-outs 127–128, 130
Dupoy family 137–139
Dupoy, Billy 139
Dye works 94
Dyers 102

Eccles, Lancashire 95, 98, 124, 137, 144
Eden F M 58
Edensor, Derbyshire 2, 31
Edgehill, Battle of 7
Edinburgh, Scotland 48
Education 21, 50, 58, 71, 98, 109, 114, 115
Education Act 1870 114
Education Act 1876 114
Education Act 1891 114
Edward VI, King 56
Elections 78–79, 94
Electricity 110, 134
El Misti, Peru 142
Elton family 94
Elton, Ann 94
Elton Jos 94
Emigration 85
Enclosure 60–61, 74, 150

Enclosure Acts 60
Engels, Friedrich 90, 92, 94
Engineering 85, 94
Engineers 106
Engine drivers 95
Essequibo, France 132
Estate agents 95, 106
Estrées, France 130
Evans, William 79
Eyam, Derbyshire 18, 48
Eyre family 18, 22, 25, 36, 40, 46, 48, 64
Eyre, Rowland 2, 8–10, 12, 13, 16, 19, 23, 28, 29, 36, 37
Eyre, Thomas (d 1637) 2, 5
Eyre, Thomas (d 1749) 47

Factories 55, 84, 89, 99
Factory Act 1844 114
Factory workers 85
Fairfax, Sir Thomas 11
Fairs 73, 76
Fancy box makers 94
Farming 12, 19, 23, 25–26, 28, 29, 35–37, 40, 42–43, 48, 59–60, 62, 69, 72–74, 76, 77, 80, 86
Farming implements 26
Farnell, Mrs 136
Farrell and Brownhill 100
Faucher, Leon 85, 92, 106
Fawcett, Colonel 114, 142
Fields, medieval strip 60
Fiennes, Celia 23
Fifty Shilling Tailors 137
Fildes, Ann 94
Fine Cotton Spinners and Doublers' Association 106
Fines 20–22, 41, 42, 47, 91
Fire brigade 85
Fire services 109
First World War 106, 118–133, 138, 141, 144
Fish 136
Fisher, Elizabeth 115
Fisher, Mary 115
Flax 25, 76
Flooding 93–95
Forestry Commission 144
Foundries 93
Fowler, Samuel 72
Freeholders 78
Freehold land 58, 61–63, 72, 84
French polishers 95
Frescheville, John (of Staveley) 10
Frévent, France 126
Froggatt, Alexander 48
Froggatt, Elizabeth 56
Froggatt family 46
Froggatt, Hannah – see Ashton, Hannah
Froggatt, Henry 56
Froggatt, Robert 48, 51
Froggatt, Thomas (various) 46
Froggot, William 20
Funeral 108–109
Furniture 24–6, 29, 58, 59, 64, 109

Garada, SS 144
Gard, Private Wes 128
Gas (household) 85, 134, 136
Gas (in war) 131–132
Gaskel, Mrs 84, 100

Gell, Sir John 8–10
Gibbon, Elizabeth 59, 69
Gibbon, Joshua 59
Gibbons, Ann (née Taylor) 59, 61
Gibbons family 59, 69
Gibbons, John 64, 70
Gibbons, Matthew 59, 61, 63, 64, 69
Girls 55, 70
Gisborne, Thomas 78
Glasgow, Scotland 143
Glead Rake 40
Glenfinnan, Scotland 48
Glorious Revolution 27
Glover, Stephen 76
Goldman, Jacob 104
Gooddey, John 29, 43
Goring, General 10–12
Gorsebank Farm, Baslow 47–51, 55, 56
Grafton, Mary (née Ashton) 74
Grafton, Valentine 76
Grafton, William 74
Grand National 137
Gravediggers 66
Graves 51, 63, 80, 111, 124
Great Reform Act 1832 78, 94
Great War, The 106, 118–133, 138, 141
Greene, William 20
Greenheys, Lancashire 90
Gregg Brothers 111
Gregory, Anthony 20, 42
Gregory family 59
Gregory, Mr (schoolmaster) 71
Grey, Lord 78
Grocers 88–89, 98, 100, 110, 136, 138
Gryme, William 6
Guayaquil, Ecuador 119
Gun pits 130, 131

Hamburg, Germany 142
Hackney carriages 90, 98, 99
Haig, Field Marshal 129
Hairdressers 88
Hale, Bernard 101, 106, 111, 112, 144
Hale, George Ernest 106
Hale, Eric 106, 112, 143
Hale, Margery 144
Hale, Phyllis 106
Hale, Winifred 106, 112, 143–144
Hall, Dr Spencer 67
Hancourt, France 130
Hankison, Edward E 109, 111
Hankison, Richard 110
Harbonnierres, France 129
Hardie family 17, 21
Hardie, John 6
Hardwicke's Marriage Act 1753 18
Hardy, John 43
Hartley, H 112
Hassop, Derbyshire 1,2, 8, 9, 19–22, 36, 38, 39, 41, 43
Hassop Hall 2, 8, 16, 18, 21, 22, 41
Hathersage, Derbyshire 6, 21, 31, 35, 36, 47, 48, 66
Hawley, John 79
Hay 25, 58, 60
Hayes, Louis 92
Headborough 41
Health 86, 89, 94, 137

Hearth tax 16–17, 28, 149
Heathcote, Arthur 71, 72
Heaton, Henry 22
Heaton Norris, Cheshire 107
Heaton Park, Lancashire 117
Heriots 16, 36
Heyward, George 39
Hibbert, Peter 73
Higes, George 62
Highways 42
Hilton and Sons 111
Hindenburg Line 130
Hobbes, Thomas 1
Hodgkinson, Francis 20, 31
Holidays 90, 117, 137, 142
Holland, Mary (née Taylor) 59
Holland, Thomas 59, 64
Holmes, Abel 72
Holmes family 59
Holmesfield, Derbyshire 74
Holmes, Mr (deputy town clerk) 104
Hoovers 136
Hope, Derbyshire 48
Horse hair 51
Horses 26, 58
Hospitals 85, 107, 132, 144
Household goods 29, 51, 58, 59, 64
Houses (construction) 1–2, 4, 18, 48, 72, 134
Housing conditions 86, 90, 92–95, 105
Howe, Christopher 39–40
Howitzers 129
Hudson, Thomas 16, 29, 43
Hull 125, 138, 141, 142
Hulley, George 43
Hulme, Lancashire 90, 102, 115
Humble Petition of Twentie Thousand Myners 20
Hungry Forties 89
Hunt, Thomas 39
Hunting 36
Huntscape, SS 125
Husbandmen 27
Huyton, Lancashire 141

Illegitimacy 43, 70, 79, 87
Importers 94
Industrialisation 73, 76, 85
Industrial Revolution 27, 54–55, 80, 88
Infant mortality 18, 36, 47, 70, 86, 87, 94, 100, 102
Inflation 106
Inheritance 56, 63, 84
Inland Revenue 105
International Genealogical Index 148
Inventories 21, 24–27, 31, 58, 59
Iquique, Chile 141
Irish 87, 94, 102
Iron 27
Iron turners 95
Irwell, River 87, 91, 92, 94–95, 100, 104, 105
Isle of Man 94

Jacobs, Hyman 109
Jackson, James 43
Jackson, John (attorney) 8
Jackson, Mr (school master) 106
Jaffe and Son 114, 142
Jamaica 144

Jebson, William 90
Jepson, Adam 28
Jepson, Richard 6, 17
Jesuits 16, 18, 22
Jewish immigration 104–105
Jews 104–105, 106, 142
Johnson, Dr M 102, 108
Joiners 76, 88, 94, 115
Juries 19–21, 37, 40, 41, 44, 47
Justices of the Peace 22, 74, 101, 104

Kabul, Afghanistan 141
Keeling, William 87
Kinship networks 48, 59, 69, 90
Kirk Mr 128, 129
Kirkham, James 108–109
Kitchener, Field Marshal Lord 119, 124
Knisson, Ellen 28, 31
Knisson, George 28

La Boisselle, France 121
Labourers 25, 95
Lamotte-Brebière, France 128
Lancashire Fusiliers 111, 120–122, 129
Lancashire Raw Cotton Dyeing Company 100
Land ownership 58, 61–63, 72, 73, 77–78
Land tax 28–29, 43, 61, 63, 69, 72, 148–9
Lansdown, Somerset 132
La Paz 142
Lawrence, Rev Benjamin 71, 77
Lead mining 1, 20–21, 37–40, 42, 76
Leases 19
Leece, Lancashire 99
Legge, James 6
Le Hamel, France 128
Lent, Richard 28
Lewis Gun 121
Licences (for sale of alcohol) 100–101
Licences (hackney carriage) 90–91
Lichfield, Staffordshire 12, 80
Life assurance 109
Life expectancy 85
Lima, Peru 144
Literacy 20, 50, 56, 64, 70, 74, 87, 99, 102, 114
Liverpool 10, 141
Livestock 58
Lloyd's of London 142
Local government 21, 50, 109
Lodgers 88, 100
Lodging houses 88
Lofthouse, Benjamin 117
London 54, 66, 84 , 137
Longsight, Lancashire 87
Longstone Edge 1–2, 20, 24, 37–38, 40, 48
Longstone, Great, Derbyshire 1, 2, 6, 12, 13, 16, 18,
　　20–22, 27–29, 36, 38, 47, 74
Longstone, Little, Derbyshire 74
Lot 29, 38
Loughborough, Leicestershire 145
Louisette, Madame 115–117
Lowe, Annie Maud 115
Lowe, Charles Hugh (senior) 115
Lowe, Charles Hugh (junior) 115
Lowe, Edith 115, 137, 138
Lowe, Edmund 115
Lowe family, of Rowland 2

Lowe, George 115
Lowe, John 54
Lowe, Lucy Jane – see Ashton, Lucy Jane
Lowe, Sarah Ellen (Nellie) 115, 137, 138
Lowe, Thomas 17
Lowe, William 6
Lucas, Bernard 60
Ludendorff, General 129

Macclesfield, Cheshire 48, 99, 106, 110
Machine guns 122, 124
Machinists 104
Madge, Ken 144
Magistrates 22, 74, 101, 104
Makinson, Mr (magistrate) 104
Male primogeniture 31, 36, 37
Manchester 48, 59, 69, 76, 79, 84–118 passim,
　　132–138, 142
Manchester and Salford Water Works Company 85
Manchester Bedding and Clothing Fund 89
Manchester Borough Council 86, 94
Manchester Building and Sanitary Relations Committee 94
Manchester, Buxton, Matlock and Midland Junction
　　Railway 79
Manchester Central School 114, 133
Manchester Chamber of Commerce 111
Manchester, Earl of 11
Manchester Evening Chronicle 109, 122, 124
Manchester Evening News 112, 117, 137
Manchester Grammar School 144
Manchester Guardian 112, 128
Manchester High School 144
Manchester Paving and Soughing Committee 86
Manchester Ship Canal 106
Manchester Watch and Hackney Coach Committee
　　90–91
Manchester Weekly Times 94
Manorial courts 18, 19, 36, 38, 40–43, 47, 149
Manufacturing 54, 85, 98
Maricourt, France 121
Markets 23, 54, 73, 84
Marne, Battle of 129
Marple, Mary – see Ashton, Mary
Marple, Robert 51, 69
Marple, Thomas 69
Marriages 18, 36, 46, 55–56, 59, 69, 70, 87, 88,
　　99–101, 116, 117, 145–48
Marston Moor, Battle of 10–12
Marte, Peru 114
Mary Barton 84, 100
Mary, Queen 27
Masden, William 40
Mason family 69
Mason, John 56, 59, 61
Mason, Mary (née Taylor) 56, 59, 61–63
Mason, Mary 73
Mason, Robert 73
Mass 22
Matlock, Derbyshire 54, 57, 58, 73, 77, 79
McClintons, Cheadle Hulme 136
McGriffie, William 88
McLennan, Mrs 118
McPherson, PC 104
Meat 21, 60, 94, 110, 136, 138
Mechanics 94
Mechanisation 73

Medals 132–133
Meers 38
Meningitis 102
Merchants 88, 106
Mersey Docks and Harbour Board 106
Michell, Isabel Grace – see Ashton, Isabel Grace
Michell, Charity 141
Michell, Faith 141
Michell, Hope 141
Migration 76, 84, 87
Military Service Act 1916 124
Milk 136
Millers Dale, Derbyshire 79
Milliners 115
Mills 25, 58, 85, 89, 93, 99
Millward, John (of Snitterton) 10
Minniglow, Derbyshire 2
Moidart, Scotland 48
Money 76
Mons, France 130
Monsal Dale, Derbyshire 2
Montdidier, France 126
Montefiore family 99
Mont St Quentin, France 130
Mortimer, Mr (clerk of works) 135
Moreuil, France 126
Morfa Nefyn, Wales 138
Mortality 86
Moses, Jacob 104
Mosley, Anthony 20, 29, 42
Mossley, Thomas 43
Musical instrument makers 102
Muster Roll 6–7, 46, 150
Myles, Annie 117, 137

National Society for Promoting the Education of the
    Poor 71
Needham, John 54
Neighbour disputes 42
Nelson, James 94
Newbury, Berkshire 144
Newcastle, Earl of 8
Newcastle Upon Tyne 144
Newspapers 85
Newton, Robert 59
New York Board of Underwriters 142
Nichols, Rev Joseph 50
Nicholson, William 19
Night soil 86, 93
Nine Years War 28
Nobescourt Ferme, France 130
Northern Counties Hospital for Incurables 107
Northwood, Derbyshire 55–80 passim, 84
Northwood Carr 56
Nottingham 7, 54, 84
Notting hill, London 144
Numeracy 114
Nurses 108, 117
Nuttall, Goerge 77

Oats 12, 26, 48, 58–60
Occupations 76
Opiates 102
Orchards 48, 84
Organ builders 88
Oswestry, Shropshire 101

Overseers of the poor 35, 46, 74, 88, 89, 109
Oxen 25
Owen, Wilfred 131

Paignton, Devon 141
Parish registers 13, 16, 18, 36, 44, 51, 55–56, 69, 71,
    88, 96, 147–148
Paris 117
Parkes, Benjamin 64
Parkinson, John 99
Parkinson, Rev R 85
Parks, Thomas 61
Parliament 27, 28, 60, 78
Parliamentary Commissioners 71
Parochial Church Council 137
Patricroft, Lancashire 94, 107
Pawnbrokers 106
Pearce, Amelia 102
Pearson, Mary 104
Peas 58
Peel, Lydia 106
Peel, Sir Robert, MP 89
Pendleton, Lancashire 88
Pentrich, Derbyshire 57
Péronne, France 126, 130
Petit bourgeois 106
Pewter 24
Photographs 103
Pickford and Co 88
Pigs 26
Pilkington 59
Pilkington family 59
Pilsley, Derbyshire 2
Pimlotts, Cheadle Hulme 136
Pinder 19, 20, 41
Pinder, Dr G H 95, 102, 108
Plague 18
Plasterers 95
Plompton family 58
Ploughs 25, 73
Plymouth, Devon 132
Pneumonia 94
Police 86, 100, 104, 109
Police Courts 100, 104
Poll books 149
Poll tax 6
Poor law 1598 35
Poor law Amendment Act 1834 78
Poor law unions 78
Poor rate 35, 43, 78, 88, 89, 94, 109, 149
Poor relief 43, 74, 78, 94, 109
Population 6, 54–55, 70–71, 76, 85, 90–92, 98, 101
Port Erin, Wales 137
Portions 31
Portsmouth 125
Post 76
Potter, Thomas Stanley 72
Poultry 26
Poundbreach 20
Poverty 85–87
Prestatyn, Wales 137
Preston, John 79
Preston, Lancashire 115
Principal Probate Registry 147
Print works 94
Privies 18, 86, 93, 94

Property tax 105
Prostitutes 90, 106–107
Protestant Non-Conformists 21
Provision dealers 101
Public buildings 85
Public houses 76
Public Record Office 146–149
Pulmonary congestion 95, 102
Puno, Peru 141

Quayle, A 110
Quarter Sessions Records 149

Race, Dr W 96
Railways 79, 99, 117, 125, 134, 136, 137, 140
Rates 35, 43, 78, 88, 89, 94, 109, 114, 117, 149
Rationing 138
Reform Act 1832 78, 94
Reform Act 1867 94
Refuge Assurance Company 109
Registrar General 87
Registrar of Births etc 80, 102
Reims, France 129
Rent 5, 12–13, 36, 47, 74, 88–90, 94, 105, 118
Rhoscolyn, Wales 138
Rifles 120, 121
Rivers 92–93
Rowland, Derbyshire 1–48 passim, 50, 63, 64, 74
Roads 23, 55
Rouen, France 132
Rowsley, Little 76, 79
Royal Artillery 119–133
Royal Engineers 128
Rupert, Prince 10, 11
Rubella 102
Rutland, Duke of 48, 50, 61
Rye 60

St Catherine's House 146
St Pol, France 126
Saintsbury 98
Salary 138
Salford 85–110 passim, 115
Salford and Broughton Funeral Establishment 108
Salford County Borough 109
Salford County Telephone 104
Salford Hippodrome 120
Salford Pals 120
Salford Police Court 100, 104
*Salford Reporter* 104
Salford town hall 100
Salisbury, Wiltshire 144
San Carlos, Peru 114
Sanitation 18, 86, 93, 94, 118, 130, 134
Sassoon, Siegfried 132
Saunders, Major 9, 10
Sausages 138
School masters 50–51, 71, 106
Schools 50, 51, 58, 71–72, 98, 106, 110, 114
Scots 87
Scott, Sir Walter 117
Second World War 133, 136–138, 140, 142
Seedlow Rake (mine) 39, 40
Sellars, John 27, 29, 36
Senectus 96
Senior, Richard 56

Serre, France 121
Servants 69–70, 79, 87, 88, 90, 99, 102, 103
Service 25, 69–70
Settlement 35, 74, 88, 149
Sexual relations 70, 87
Sewers 86
Sewing machines 136
Shanklin, Isle of White 138
Shares 106, 112
Sheard, Jenny 67
Sheep 5, 12, 24, 26, 42, 48, 58, 59, 62, 73, 77
Sheffield, Yorkshire 48, 59, 76, 84
Sheldon family 21
Sheldon, Nicholas 16, 17, 20
Sheldon, Widow 94
Shells 124, 126, 129–131
Shepheard, John 84
Ship money 8, 17
Shipping merchants 114
Shoemakers 95
Shopkeepers 85, 89, 98, 101, 105
Shops 76, 85, 88, 89, 100–102, 136
Shuttleworth, Major James 66
Sidesmen 103–104
Silverstone, Myer 104
Simonson, Moses 104
Sitwell, Sir George 78
Skipton, Yorkshire 10
*Slater's Directory* 115
Slinne, Sarah 36
Slumps 72, 89
Smith, Thomas (of Rowland) 6
Smith, Thomas (stagecoach proprietor) 54
Smithfield Market, Manchester 84
Snitterton, Derbyshire 76
Society for the Propagation of Christian Knowledge 50, 71
Solicitors 109, 110, 112
Somerset House 148
Somme, Battle of 108, 121–124, 126
Somme, River, France 121–124, 126, 127, 129
Southern, Thomas 60
Spinning 24–27, 55, 58, 59, 76, 84, 88
Spurn Head 125
Stafford and Company 114
Stafford family of Eyam 2
Stafford, Reggie 114, 141
Stafford, Robert 50
Stage coaches 54, 84
Stanley, William 42
Stanton Ford School, Baslow 50, 51
Station masters 99
Statute of Distributions 1670 27
Steam 85, 98
Steel, Dr 108
Steel, Ellen – see Ashton, Ellen
Stockport, Cheshire 10, 84, 115, 133, 136
Stocks 41
Stonemasons 76
Stony Middleton, Derbyshire 1, 23, 48
Strangeways Prison, Manchester 95
Street, John 29
Streets 85
Strokes 108, 138
Stuart, Charles Edward 48, 50
Sugar 101, 138

Surbiton, Surrey 137
Surveyors 105
Swift, John 56
Syncope 96
Syphilis 106–107

Taddington, Derbyshire 84
Tailors 74, 94, 104, 137
Tambopata, River, Peru 114
Tanneries 93
Tarapaca, Chile 141
Taxation 6, 16–17, 20, 28, 105, 148–149
Taverns 102
Tavistock, Devon 143
Taylor, Ann (mother of Sarah) 55
Taylor, Benjamin 59
Taylor family 56, 69, 76
Taylor, Henry (father of Sarah) 55, 61, 63
Taylor, Henry (grandfather of Sarah) 58, 60, 61
Taylor, Henry (great-grandfather of Sarah) 56
Taylor, Henry (great-great-great-grandfather of Sarah) 56
Taylor, John 58
Taylor, Jos 58
Taylor, Joshua 62
Taylor, Mary 69
Taylor, Samuel 72
Taylor, Sarah – see Ashton, Sarah
Taylor, William 59
Tea 101, 138
Telephones 136
Televisions 136
Temperance movement 101, 142
Templeux 130
Textiles 76, 85, 98
Thiepval, France 108, 111, 124, 126
Thirdborow 19, 20
Thomson, William 94
Thornhill, Bache 74
Tideswell, Derbyshire 21, 74
Times, The 114
Tithes 77–78, 149
Tithe Commissioners 77
Tithe Commutation Act 77, 149
Titicaca, Lake, Peru 141
Toilets 118, 134
Tolls 94
Tonsils 136
Toothill, Dr 111
Topping, Sarah Ann 115
Torrington, Viscount 55
Trains 79, 99, 117, 125, 134, 136, 137, 140
Transport 54, 55, 89, 101
Trenches 121
Trent, River 23
Truro, Cornwall 141
Tuberculosis 115
Tucker, Rev WHB 101
Turner, John 55
Turner, William 99, 110
Tweed, Captain T F 124
Twigge, Messrs 72

Unemployment 72, 89
United States of America 85
Urmston, Lancashire 110–112

Vaire-sous-Corbie, France 127, 128
Valentine's Day 74, 117
Vallance, Edward 20, 25
Vegetables 25, 84
Vickary, Elizabeth 55
Victoria, Queen 86, 87
View of Frankpledge 19, 40
Vine Tavern, Lower Broughton 100, 104

Waddinton, Thomas 16
Wages 51, 84, 89, 91, 94
Waggoners 76
Waitresses 99
Wall family 59
Wall, George 69
Walton, Cheshire 99
Walton, Harry 128
Wandsworth Registry Office 141
War 28, 72, 84, 106, 118–133, 136–138, 140–144
War Office 124
Ward, Daniel 101
Ward, Eliza 101
Ward, Sarah Ellen – see Ashton, Sarah Ellen
Wardlow, Derbyshire 20, 39
Warehouseman and Clerk's School 110
Warehousemen 94, 115
War stock 106
Washing machines 136
Watch committees 90
Water closets 86, 134
Waterhouse, Sarah J 102
Watermen 101
Water rates 109
Water supply 42, 48, 85
Weaving 24–27, 59, 84, 85, 94
Weedon, John 22
Wensley, Derbyshire 76
Wet nurses 70, 102
Wheat 25, 48, 58, 59, 72, 77
Wheelwrights 76, 79
Wheldon, Mary 62
Wheston, Derbyshire 50
White, Thomas 23–24
Whitesmiths 76
Whooping cough 94, 102
Wichnor, Staffordshire 80
Wigan, Lancashire 10
Wildgoose family 59
Wildgoose, John 66
Wildman, Major John 13
William of Orange 27
Williams, John 136, 138
Wills 20, 23, 27, 29, 31, 64, 74, 80, 96, 107, 109–111, 148
Wilson, William 20
Winton, Lancashire 107, 144
Wirksworth, Derbyshire 39
Wolley, William 56
Women 26, 36, 56, 61, 72, 76, 100, 102, 133
Wood, John 18
Woods, Aaron 106
Woods, Hannah 106
Woolley, Thomas Smith 77
Worsted 93
Wragg, Alice 36
Wray, Rev William Ulithorn 59, 61, 69, 70, 77
Wright family 47

Wright, Rev F B 99
Wye Valley 1, 2, 84

Yanahuara, Peru 142
Yeardley, Samuel 100
Yeomen 27, 48, 58, 64, 74

York 7, 10–12
Youlgreave, Derbyshire 6
Young, William 105
Ypres, France 130

Zoological gardens 85